Sound the Trumpet

Sound the Trumpet

The United States and Human Rights Promotion

Lawrence J. Haas

ROWMAN & LITTLEFIELD PUBLISHERS, INC.
Lanham • Boulder • New York • Toronto • Plymouth, UK

Published by Rowman & Littlefield Publishers, Inc.
A wholly owned subsidiary of The Rowman & Littlefield Publishing Group, Inc.
4501 Forbes Boulevard, Suite 200, Lanham, Maryland 20706
www.rowman.com

10 Thornbury Road, Plymouth PL6 7PP, United Kingdom

British Library Cataloguing in Publication Information Available

Library of Congress Cataloging-in-Publication Data

Haas, Lawrence J.
Sound the trumpet : the United States and human rights promotion / Lawrence J. Haas.
p. cm.
Includes bibliographical references and index.
ISBN 978-1-4422-1658-7 (cloth : alk. paper) -- ISBN 978-1-4422-1660-0 (electronic)
1. United States--Foreign relations--1945-1989. 2. United States--Foreign relations--1989- 3. Human rights advocacy--United States--History. I. Title.
E744.H24 2012
327.730090'49--dc23
2012007718

Printed in the United States of America

To Marjie:

"You're the Best Thing That Ever Happened to Me"

Jim Weatherly, 1973

To Samantha:

"Thank Heaven for Little Girls"

Alan Jay Lerner, 1958

Contents

Acknowledgments   ix

Introduction: The Advance of Human Rights   1

1   America the Essential   21
2   Laying the Groundwork: From Truman to LBJ   47
3   The Perfect Storm: From Nixon to Ford   75
4   Cold War Victory and Beyond: From Carter to Clinton   103
5   Terror and Its Aftermath: From Bush to Obama   129

Epilogue: Of Challenges and Opportunities   157

Bibliography   165

Index   171

About the Author   183

Acknowledgments

Book writing is often described as a solitary pursuit, but *Sound the Trumpet* was a true team effort.

The American Foreign Policy Council, a leading Washington think tank, was central to it from the start. Its president, Herman Pirchner Jr., and vice president, Ilan Berman, welcomed me to AFPC, where I hold the title of senior fellow for U.S. foreign policy, and they encouraged me to pursue this book when I broached the idea. Richard Harrison, a research fellow and program officer, lightened my work load considerably by providing me with the assistance of five wonderful research interns. My first three interns— Amanda Lamb, Adam Shusterman, and Anushya Ramaswamy—cheerfully fulfilled my requests for information by finding and outlining scholarly articles, scouring online archives for primary source material, and pursuing other research paths. I could not have completed the book in a timely fashion without their help. My fourth—Sarah McKeever—read the manuscript from start to finish, caught numerous errors, and offered useful comments that improved the draft. My fifth—Gianluca La Manno—gathered the materials that enabled me to update chapters to account for recent events as the book moved toward publication.

As my work progressed, Berman introduced me to Jon Sisk, senior executive editor at Rowman & Littlefield, who, along with Darcy Evans, enthusiastically embraced the project. Gail Ross, my long-time agent and friend, provided her usual wise counsel and timely assistance at contract time.

John Peterson, a retired journalist and now a media consultant with whom I have worked for years, helped me to crystallize my thinking about foreign policy in general, and U.S. human rights promotion in particular, by soliciting, shaping, and placing my op-eds with the McClatchy-Tribune News Service. So, too, did Alan Mendoza and his colleagues at the Henry Jackson

Society, for which I have written "Letters from Washington," delivered speeches, and participated in conferences. Before the Henry Jackson Society began to distribute my "Letters," they were published in a wonderful quarterly online journal, *Democratiya*. Many other friends and colleagues gave me plenty to think about as they told me why my latest op-ed or "Letter" was either brilliantly reasoned or, alas, woefully misguided.

Other than my AFPC colleagues, only two people knew that I was at work on a book—my wife, Marjie, and my daughter, Samantha. They respected my somewhat unorthodox request to keep it a secret until a contract came through. They also were unceasingly patient with my requests for weekend time to research and write. If my colleagues nourished the intellectual seeds of this book, Marjie and Samantha provided the emotional support that grew increasingly important as my deadline loomed.

Of course, Marjie and Samantha are not just *a* reason why I could write this book. They are *the* reason why I do . . . everything.

Introduction

The Advance of Human Rights

Muhammad Al Bouazizi was an unlikely historical figure. A poor man of twenty-six with "black curls, deep brown eyes, and a wry smile,"[1] he lived in Sidi Bouzid, in the central part of Tunisia, the smallest nation in North Africa. He could not find a regular job, but that wasn't unusual in a country where, in some places, half of the college graduates were unemployed. Bouazizi refused to join Tunisia's "army of unemployed youth," however. Determined to provide for his family, he sold fruit on the street for about $10 a day.

One morning in late December 2010, a female city official stopped at Bouazizi's fruit cart, discovered he had no license, and took his scale. The two argued, and she may have slapped him as well. When he went to government buildings to complain, officials wouldn't see him. Angry and desperate, he went to a nearby gas station and filled a canister with gas. He then returned to the front of the local governor's office, stood in the middle of traffic, doused himself, screamed the words "how do you expect me to make a living," and set himself on fire, suffering severe burns over his entire body. Lying in a hospital bed, wrapped head to toe in bandages, he died from his wounds a few weeks later.

At the time, Tunisia had been ruled for twenty-four years by Zine Ben Ali, a corrupt dictator who lived with his family in breath-taking extravagance. His jet-setting second wife "would dispatch government airplanes to Saint-Tropez for shopping trips" while her daughter and son-in-law, who had a huge mansion on the Mediterranean with a pet tiger, "[o]n at least one occasion . . . sent a government aircraft to Europe to fetch their favorite frozen yogurt." The family seized land and businesses at will and often forced companies that sought to locate in Tunisia to give them a cut of their returns.[2] Nor did the dictator brook any dissent. Tunisians knew that a disparaging remark about Ben Ali would land them in prison.

Something about Bouazizi's story, however, tapped their deep-seated frustration. Ignoring their fears, they gathered by the hundreds in Sidi Bouzid to protest, and the protests spread to other cities where people gathered by the thousands. They had suffered enough. "Degage," they shouted at Ben Ali. "Get out." The police fired on them, leaving hundreds dead, but still they would not disperse. On January 14, with tens of thousands gathered in Tunis, the nation's capital, Ben Ali fled with his family to Saudi Arabia. Though Bouazizi would not live to see Ben Ali's departure, the fruit seller had lit a match that inspired the people of a backward land to rid themselves of a ruthless tyrant.[3]

Bouazizi's match, in turn, lit a flame that spread across the region. In the ensuing weeks, protests brought Egypt to a stand-still, forcing its long-time strongman, Hosni Mubarak, to step down. The revolutions in Tunisia and Egypt, in turn, prompted uprisings in Libya, Syria, Jordan, Saudi Arabia, Algeria, Morocco, Bahrain, Yemen, and elsewhere. Some of the ruling autocrats offered political reforms to defuse the protests, while others responded with brute force. When Libya's Muammar Gaddafi turned the military on his people, NATO launched air strikes to protect the protestors, enabling rebels to topple Gaddafi. Syria's Bashar al-Assad responded with similar brutality, gunning down thousands in Damascus and other cities and, as of this writing, maintaining his grip on power.

No one knew where this "Arab Spring" would go in years to come, but it had already proved historic. By early 2012, it had claimed four tyrants and shaken the foundations of autocratic rule across the Middle East and North Africa, a region that had largely resisted the political and economic liberalization that had swept the world in earlier decades. Indeed, the Arab Spring marked another chapter in the historic advance of "human rights"—which generally refers to one's right to live in freedom and dignity, speak one's mind, worship as one wishes, choose one's leaders, and pursue one's dreams.

The Arab Spring also raised a series of tough questions for the United States: What should President Obama say? Whom should America support? How much, and what kind of, foreign aid should it provide? Who should get it? Where should America use military power to assist democratic forces? How could it promote human rights without jeopardizing its other interests in the region? How should America view the uprising in, say, Libya compared to that in Syria or Bahrain?

These kinds of questions have been central to U.S. human rights promotion for decades. That's because the United States has been the world's leading promoter of human rights over the course of modern history.

When we refer to "human rights promotion," however, let's be clear about what we mean. The United States advances human rights around the world in two basic ways.

First, ever since the colonists launched their "American Experiment" in 1776, the United States has served as a beacon for would-be democrats.

By sheer example, by the freedoms it offers and the democracy it practices, America has inspired dissidents and activists, rebels and revolutionaries, in far-off lands to work for change within their societies, to reform or topple authoritarian governments, and to create free and democratic systems. Those so inspired include France's Jacobins in 1789, Vietnam's Ho Chi Minh after World War II, the political prisoners of the Soviet Union during the Cold War, the free peoples of Eastern Europe after the Soviet crack-up, the students of Tiananmen Square in 1989, and the students of Tehran in 2009.

In World War II, for instance, Ho Chi Minh had successfully sought the help of agents from the U.S. Office of Strategic Services (forerunner of today's CIA) to free his Vietnamese homeland from Japanese control. On the very day that Japan surrendered, ending the war, Ho read the "Vietnam Declaration of Independence" that he had drafted to a hopeful crowd of four hundred thousand in Hanoi. "All men are created equal," it began. "They are endowed by their Creator with certain inalienable Rights, [that] among these are Life, Liberty and the pursuit of Happiness. This immortal statement was made in the Declaration of Independence of the United States of America in 1776."[4]

Then, in 1989, Chinese students gathered in Beijing's Tiananmen Square to demand a more open government. The students built and displayed a "Goddess of Democracy" that bore a striking resistance to America's Statue of Liberty.[5] After seven weeks of demonstrations, however, the communist regime forcefully crushed the uprising—before too many other Chinese caught the democratic fever.

Second, the United States practices "human rights promotion," an affirmative effort to pressure authoritarian regimes and support democratic activists in order to advance freedom and democracy around the world.

U.S. human rights promotion—the subject of this book—is the affirmative effort by America's leaders and its people, its government and private institutions, to use the force of our ideals, the strength of our economy, the power of our military, and the influence of our culture to advance the spread of human rights far beyond our shores.

To be sure, other free nations, and sometimes the international community, speak out for human rights. Nevertheless, human rights promotion remains a quintessentially American enterprise because, unlike any other nation, the United States can make the difference. That's because, in the words of former Secretary of State Madeleine Albright, "we are the indispensable nation."[6] The world looks to America for leadership, and America retains enormous power to improve the lives of millions of people.

This book is about U.S. human rights promotion since World War II—the period during which this task became a central feature of U.S. foreign policy—and it rests on several premises about the United States and the world:

- America should promote human rights around the world for both moral and selfish reasons.
- By promoting human rights, America lives up to the best of its ideals and helps build the foundation for a more peaceful, more prosperous world.
- America maintains enormous power to shape history and make the world a better place: from the power of a president's words to inspire protestors and embarrass dictators; to the power of U.S. aid to support democratic friends and influence authoritarian adversaries; to the power of U.S. leadership to build global coalitions for action; to the power of the U.S. military to halt brutality.
- America has promoted human rights at key moments since World War II, and its notable successes include the Marshall Plan of the late 1940s that strengthened Western Europe's democracies and averted the spread of communism, U.S. pressure over several decades that helped destroy the Soviet empire and end the Cold War, and U.S. intervention in the Balkans in the mid-1990s that halted genocide.
- Americans understand that U.S. leadership brings responsibility; many of them want America to do what it can to build a better world, and many regret the times when America failed to stop an unfolding horror.
- People around the world see America as a beacon of hope, a guidepost to follow, and an example to emulate.
- Political dissidents, labor leaders, journalists, and students who are working to bring human rights to their countries—many of whom face the constant threat of jail, torture, and murder—often seek America's help, and America and the world would both benefit greatly from their success.

Though generally buoyant about the possibilities of U.S. human rights promotion, this book also discusses its difficulties. Though the United States can help shape history and improve the world, it lacks the power to unilaterally impose its will, to respond to every instance of brutality, or to help every fledgling democracy. It lacks the resources to be everywhere and do everything. Moreover, not every official of a fledgling democracy or every person in a remote village welcomes America's help in every situation.[7]

Human rights, of course, are not uniquely American. Developed over thousands of years, they emerged from their roots in religion, philosophy, and political theory and were nourished by the contributions of cultures that span the globe. They have moved to center stage gradually over the last three or four centuries with the creation of the nation-state, the rise of capitalism, the arrival of the Enlightenment, and the birth of representative democracy. Nevertheless, because the United States has been so central to those developments, and because it retains enormous power to influence the course of history, the advance of human rights in modern times has been an especially American story.

FROM WHENCE THEY CAME

What are human rights? We have no single definition. In the West, the term suggests a set of basic political and civil liberties—to speak and worship freely, to create a government and hold it accountable, and so on. Human rights are considered "natural" rights; they accrue to a person not through the generosity of government, but by virtue of one's birth. They are, in the words of our Declaration of Independence, "inalienable."[8]

The Western concept of human rights is rooted in both secular and religious thought that dates back thousands of years. It is the product of much deliberation over such concepts as freedom and dignity, tolerance and justice.[9]

For the secular roots, historians often point to the Code of Hammurabi, drafted by Babylonia's King Hammurabi nearly four thousand years ago. It provided 282 rules to govern society, marking the first known set of laws that would have more authority over a society and its people than a king himself. Centuries later, the Greek philosophers Socrates, Plato, and Aristotle pondered notions of justice, virtue, and human rights and considered the models of government that would best promote them. The Roman philosopher Cicero developed the concept of natural law, while former Greek slave and leading Stoic philosopher Epictectus advanced the idea of "universal brotherhood." The Greeks and Romans grappled with basic issues of rights and responsibilities and with the question of how people can live virtuous lives while living with others in a society.

For the religious roots, scholars point to the monotheistic religions of Judaism, Christianity, and Islam—specifically, to the Ten Commandments and its prohibitions against harmful actions against others (e.g., murder, theft, false witness), to Christ's Sermon on the Mount and other biblical teachings about how to live a virtuous life, and to Koranic passages that preach justice and tolerance. Also important were contributions from the East. Confucius counseled that leaders should serve as moral examples to their followers, inspiring the Indian writer Kautilya to advance this stream of thought through his *The Arthashastra*. Buddhism, which spread from India to

China, offered a code of conduct for virtuous living through the teachings of Siddhartha Gautama—the Buddha—as did Hinduism through its code known as Dharma.

The advance of human rights gradually became a more fundamentally Western phenomenon, with the Enlightenment of the seventeenth and eighteenth centuries serving as what scholar Micheline R. Ishay called "the formative age of our modern conception of human rights."[10] The British poet John Milton fought for freedom of the press, British political theorist John Locke pushed for freedom of religion, and the French philosopher Voltaire advanced both notions. In *Leviathan*, Thomas Hobbes argued for a "social contract" through which people would leave the state of nature and form societies and governments that would protect their right to life. Jean-Jacques Rousseau also argued that people enter social contracts with government— contracts they can break when governments act against their interests. Locke argued for rights to life and property, presaging Thomas Jefferson's call less than a century later for government to protect the rights to "Life, Liberty and the pursuit of Happiness."

Driving these notions of rights was not just philosophical progress but also ground-breaking political and economic advances in the West. The Treaty of Westphalia of 1648, ending more than a century of religious war that was sparked by the Protestant Reformation, marked the onset of the modern nation-state through which governments would rule within established borders. The advance of capitalism created a Western middle class that sought political rights to accompany its rising living standards. Over time, governments succumbed to the pressure. The English Bill of Rights in 1689 protected free speech and free elections and subjected the king's power to make law, to tax, and to take certain other steps to the consent of Parliament. All of that, in turn, set the stage for the historic changes to come with the American Revolution (and then the French Revolution) of the late eighteenth century.

The American Revolution marked a quantum leap forward in human rights. It was "one of the greatest revolutions the world has known," historian Gordon Wood has written, "a momentous upheaval that not only fundamentally altered the character of American society but decisively affected the course of subsequent history."[11] The colonists created a new kind of government, a new kind of relationship between the people and their leaders. "The Revolution," Wood continued, "did not just eliminate monarchy and create republics; it actually reconstituted what Americans meant by public or state power and brought about an entirely new kind of popular politics and a new kind of democratic officeholder."[12] That explains why governments of the Old World disparaged it, predicting its speedy demise.

To be sure, the American Revolution did not bring the struggle for human rights to an end. Far from it. In fact, the revolution raised almost as many questions as it answered. The nation's founders did not free the slaves—that took a civil war in the middle of the next century that left more than six hundred thousand dead. Nor, despite Abigail Adams's playful request to John that he "remember the ladies," did the founders extend the vote to women—that took a suffragette movement that could not declare victory until the Nineteenth Amendment was ratified in 1920. Nor did legal extensions of human rights to blacks and women sweep away the social bigotry and discrimination that they would continue to face.

In the nineteenth century, economic and social forces around the world gave human rights a further boost. Industrialization and urbanization put a spotlight on severe working conditions, child labor, and widespread poverty and starvation. Workers organized into labor unions that sought higher wages, better working conditions, and the right to strike, while women marched for the right to vote. In the early twentieth century, national liberation movements began to take shape in the Third World, eventually freeing peoples from the burdens of colonialism. [13]

By the middle of the twentieth century, the horrors of war and genocide put human rights more squarely on the international agenda. In the charter of the new United Nations, which Franklin Roosevelt had envisioned as a world body that would preserve peace and protect rights, participating nations came together in 1945 to "reaffirm faith in fundamental human rights, in the dignity and worth of the human person, in the equal rights of men and women and of nations large and small." Three years later, in an effort spearheaded by FDR's widow, Eleanor, the UN's Commission on Human Rights crafted the landmark Universal Declaration of Human Rights (UDHR). Stating that "recognition of the inherent dignity and of the equal and inalienable rights of all members of the human family is the foundation of freedom, justice and peace in the world," it calls on "every individual and every organ of society" to "promote respect for these rights and freedoms" and "secure their universal recognition and observance" among all people ruled by UN member states.

Approved unanimously by the UN's General Assembly (with six Soviet-bloc nations and two others abstaining), the declaration lacks the force of law. But, like America's Declaration of Independence and its Constitution, and like the French Declaration of the Rights of Man and Citizen, the UDHR has inspired human rights activists the world over. It also has served as the basis for more than twenty UN treaties that have spelled out both human rights for women, children, refugees, and others as well as protections against genocide, torture, racial discrimination, and other forms of inhumanity. [14]

Fortunately, progress has come not just in landmark documents but also in the lives of billions of people.

MORE FREEDOM, MORE DEMOCRACY

Human rights have spread to the far corners of our planet. Whereas freedom and democracy were the exceptions not that long ago, today they are far more the rule. "In 1750," the political scientist Samuel P. Huntington has written, "no democratic institutions at the national level existed in the Western world. In 1900 such institutions existed in many countries. By the late twentieth century many more countries possessed democratic institutions."[15]

The nonprofit Freedom House has published an annual survey, *Freedom in the World*, since 1972 to measure "global political rights and civil liberties" in nations and disputed territories. It ranks nations and territories as free ("where there is open political competition, a climate of respect for civil liberties, significant independent civic life, and independent media"), partly free ("in which there is limited respect for political rights and civil liberties"), and not free ("where basic political rights are absent, and basic civil liberties are widely and systematically denied"). Its findings highlight the expansion of human rights in recent decades. From 1972 to 2006, the percentage of countries and territories listed as free rose from 29 to 47, while the percentage of those listed as partly free rose from 25 to 30. From 1989 to 2006, the percentage of countries listed as electoral democracies rose from 41 to 64.

The march of human rights, however, has not been a steady one. It has advanced in fits and starts, in bursts of progress and retreat. Over the course of centuries, the forces of freedom have fought a long-running battle with various forms of repression—emperorship and monarchy, Nazism and fascism, communism and socialism. Freedom spreads for a period of time, repression regains some (but not all) of its lost territory, and freedom then begins its next march.

Huntington identified three global "waves of democratization" over the last two centuries (with some countries riding their own particular waves from democracy to repression and back to democracy):

- The first, from the early nineteenth to early twentieth centuries, brought greater democracy to the United States and elements of democracy to more than thirty countries, including Great Britain, France, Switzerland, Italy, Argentina, Ireland, Iceland, Spain, and Chile.

- The second, from World War II to the early 1960s, brought or returned democratic practices to West Germany, Italy, Austria, Japan, South Korea, Turkey, Greece, Uruguay, Brazil, Costa Rica, Argentina, Colombia, Peru, Venezuela, Malaysia, Indonesia, India, Sri Lanka, Israel, Nigeria, and the Philippines.
- The third, from the early 1970s to the early 1990s, brought democracy or its trappings to thirty more countries, including Portugal, Greece, Spain, Ecuador, Peru, Bolivia, Argentina, Uruguay, Brazil, Honduras, El Salvador, Guatemala, India, Turkey, the Philippines, South Korea, Taiwan, Pakistan, Mexico, Chile, Grenada, Panama, Nicaragua, Namibia, and—with the fall of the Soviet empire—the Eastern European nations of Hungary, Poland, East Germany, Czechoslovakia, Romania, and Bulgaria.[16]

The advance of human rights, though, should not blind us to a basic reality: the twentieth century also has been a humanitarian horror show.

Two world wars, each launched by authoritarian forces, left scores of millions dead and societies devastated. Nor did peace bring humanitarian tranquility. Over the course of decades, the Soviet Union's Josef Stalin killed tens of millions of his people through murder and famine, and he and his successors controlled an empire of repression across Eastern Europe; China's Mao Zedong killed tens of millions of his people through political crackdown and economic disaster; Cambodia's Pol Pot and his Khmer Rouge killed 1.7 million of his people, a fifth of the population, through forced labor and political murder; Serbia's Slobodan Milosevic and his henchmen committed genocide against Bosnian Muslims; North Korea remains a political and economic nightmare; and brutality continues to plague vast stretches of Africa, Asia, Latin America, and the Middle East.

The world of today highlights the continuing ebb and flow between freedom and repression.

On one hand, progress on human rights has stalled since 2006. In an essay for the 2012 edition of *Freedom in the World*, Freedom House's director of research, Arch Puddington, wrote, "[S]lightly more countries registered declines than exhibited gains over the course of 2011," marking "the sixth consecutive year in which countries with declines outnumbered those with improvements"—the longest such period since the organization began publishing its report.[17] The number of free countries and electoral democracies fell while repressive regimes in China, Russia, Belarus, Venezuela, and Iran cracked down harder on human rights. China was determined to raise living standards without expanding political rights, creating a model of authoritarian capitalism that challenged longstanding Western assumptions that economic progress will invariably force political liberalization.

On the other hand . . . the Arab Spring. It ignited as if from nowhere. It spread across the Middle East and North Africa like a brushfire. It marked a serious challenge to archaic monarchies, clerical theocracies, and secular dictatorships. It toppled four iron-fisted strongmen and spurred protests across the region, putting other autocrats on the ropes. It brought hope to politically stultified, economically backward societies. It nourished a storm of social unrest whose ultimate outcome may not be known for years.

AMERICA'S CHALLENGE

America's birth on the foundation of high ideals catapulted the nation into the lead role of advancing human rights around the world. As outlined in the next chapter, Americans from their earliest days in the "New World" have assumed a special responsibility for shaping the course of history. They would show the world of kings and subjects, of lords and serfs, a better way—a path of freedom and tolerance and a government through which, for the first time, "we the people" would rule.

Human rights promotion is no simple task, however. The United States is powerful but not omnipotent. It can influence the course of events, but not dictate them. Moreover, not every challenge is the same. Some governments and populations welcome America's leadership and pine for its ideals more than others. The United States has more leverage over some nations than others; it's more dependent on some nations than others. Presidents push hard in some cases, less so in others; they advocate publicly in some cases, cajole privately in others; they offer economic carrots in some cases, threaten force in others. No president can take the same approach to human rights promotion in every situation.

What will work—and when? Frankly, no one can predict with certainty. Nor can anyone foresee when an uprising will succeed and when it won't. No one can know beforehand when a long-time dictator like Ferdinand Marcos will lose his grip on power in the Philippines, as he did in 1986 after three years of demonstrations during the "Yellow Revolution"; or when the people of Romania will find the courage to boo an iron-fisted dictator like Nicolai Ceausescu off the stage at an outdoor event and then capture, try, and execute him, as they did in December 1989; or when a Soviet leader like Mikhail Gorbachev will try to reform his communist system from within and lose control of events, leading to the Soviet crack-up in 1991; or when a poor young man in a tiny country in North Africa will set himself on fire to protest his plight, igniting a chain reaction of uprisings across the region whose ultimate resting point may not be known for years.

Furthermore, human rights promotion raises difficult questions:

- What human rights should the United States promote? That is, should the United States continue to focus on basic political and civil liberties (the freedoms to speak, to worship, to choose one's leaders, and so on) or should it go further and also advance the more modern, and far more expansive, notions of reproductive, gay, labor, children's, and other rights?
- Where do human rights end and cultural sensitivities begin? That is, to what extent should the United States respect cultural practices in other lands that, for instance, allow or even encourage female genital mutilation or that leave women with far fewer rights than men?
- When do the abuses of human rights in foreign lands justify U.S. intervention, whether alone or in conjunction with other nations? That is, must abuse reach the point of genocide, or do other abuses warrant military action? And to what extent should the United States respect the sovereign rights of governments to preside over their people without outside interference?[18]
- Must the United States act consistently when it comes to using force? That is, should the United States worry about charges of hypocrisy when it intervenes in one place but not in others, or should it maintain that any successful intervention to protect human rights is better than inaction?[19]

With each event, be it a popular uprising or a government crackdown, Washington weighs not just considerations of human rights but also broader considerations of national security, regional and global stability, U.S. access to oil and other natural resources, and other factors. Human rights promotion may be a key feature of U.S. foreign policy, but it's not the only one. It rises and falls in importance based on a president's strategic goals and contemporary challenges. Each president brings a new vision to U.S. national security and, with it, a new approach to human rights.

Sometimes, human rights promotion walks hand-in-hand with other U.S. foreign policy priorities; advancing the former helps to advance the latter. For instance, with its Marshall Plan to rescue the Western European democracies after World War II, the United States protected human rights for tens of millions of people and *also* prevented the Soviet Union from exploiting economic suffering on the continent and expanding its influence westward. Then, with its support for the democracy movement in Poland in the 1980s, the United States promoted human rights in Eastern Europe and *also* strengthened its own national security by destabilizing the Soviet empire.

Just as often, however, America's long-term goal of expanding freedom and democracy conflicts with its shorter-term goals of national security. Over the long run, the United States believes the advancement of human rights will create a more peaceful and prosperous world. In the short run, however, the United States works with, for instance, the autocracy of Russia on arms control, the authoritarian kingdom of Saudi Arabia to protect the free flow of Middle East oil, and the monarchy of Jordan, which has made peace with Israel and is part of a U.S.-led regional alliance that is seeking to blunt the hegemonic ambitions of Iran.

For the United States, the question is how to meet both its long- and short-term goals—how to promote human rights over the long term without threatening U.S. national security in the short term. How, for instance, should America advance human rights across the Middle East without destabilizing friendly regimes, only to see them replaced by other authoritarian regimes that will be less friendly to the United States, less willing to share their oil, and less helpful in controlling terrorists within their borders? The question vexes policymakers on a daily basis. As former State Department official Sandy Vogelgesang put it,

> Promotion of human rights requires the dexterity of a juggler, the verbal sensitivity of a poet, and the patience of a saint. Concentration on consistency misses the point. There can and should be consistent determination to take human rights into serious account for U.S. foreign policy. Yet, stress on human rights must at all times be weighed against other factors. A rigid rubric for human rights can obscure the importance of other goals, some of which may have overarching global significance. For example, nuclear proliferation and military strength bear on that most fundamental human right—survival.[20]

For more than half a century, since human rights promotion first became an integral feature of U.S. foreign policy, our presidents have ranged from dreamy idealists to cold-blooded realists. They have disagreed over how much America can improve the human condition in far-flung lands, how much it should try, and what it should do. Some, like Harry Truman, John Kennedy, and Ronald Reagan, have promoted human rights with a strong public voice while others, like Richard Nixon, Gerald Ford, George H. W. Bush, and Barack Obama, have sought to change the behavior of authoritarian regimes more by "engaging" with them privately. Some have offered economic enticements, while others have threatened or used military force.

In recent years, however, the very idea of U.S. human rights promotion has been tarnished for at least three reasons.

First, we live in cynical times.

In 1963, President Kennedy visited the Berlin Wall, which the Soviets had built two years earlier to stem the exodus from East Germany to West Berlin. In stirring fashion, he said, "So let me ask you, as I close, to lift your eyes beyond the dangers of today to the hopes of tomorrow, beyond the freedom merely of this city of Berlin, or your country of Germany, to the advance of freedom everywhere, beyond the wall to the day of peace with justice, beyond yourselves and ourselves to all mankind."[21] Kennedy was widely praised for the strength and poetry of his words.

In 2005, President George W. Bush took the presidential oath a second time and said, "We are led, by events and common sense, to one conclusion: The survival of liberty in our land increasingly depends on the success of liberty in other lands. The best hope for peace in our world is the expansion of freedom in all the world. . . . So it is the policy of the United States to seek and support the growth of democratic movements and institutions in every nation and culture, with the ultimate goal of ending tyranny in our world."[22] Bush was widely mocked for the breadth of his aspirations.

Second, we live in nonjudgmental times.

Unlike our predecessors, we are less willing to compare our governmental system with that of others. In 1947, as the Cold War took shape, Harry Truman proclaimed:

> At the present moment in world history, nearly every nation must choose between alternative ways of life. . . . One way of life is based upon the will of the majority, and is distinguished by free institutions, representative government, free elections, guarantees of individual liberty, freedom of speech and religion, and freedom from political oppression. The second way of life is based upon the will of a minority forcibly imposed upon the majority. It relies upon terror and oppression, a controlled press and radio, fixed elections, and the suppression of personal freedoms.[23]

That is not the standard language of today's America. Less willing to compare systems, less confident that we have something better to offer, we are more reluctant to promote the blessings of our system around the world.

Third, we have recently witnessed the risks inherent in human rights promotion.

The U.S.-led invasion of Iraq in 2003 toppled a brutal dictator, but its aftermath left the country in chaos, jeopardized our military victory, and forced Bush to send more troops to cement the gains and restore order. U.S. enthusiasm for Palestinian elections in 2006 paved the way for Hamas, a terrorist group that lacks any enthusiasm for real freedom and democracy, to gain control of the Palestinian parliament.[24] In Lebanon, the terrorist group Hezbollah also participated in the electoral process and, by 2011, it had gained effective control of the nation's government, giving it greater leverage to wage its war with Israel across Lebanon's southern border.

But if the idea of human rights promotion is tarnished, the case for it remains strong—as I hope this book makes clear.

THE PAGES THAT FOLLOW

This book will explore what presidents and Congresses, often assisted by private groups at home and abroad, have done since World War II to promote human rights. It will discuss why America's leaders have acted in some cases but not in others. It will analyze the tools they have used, the results they have achieved, and the obstacles that have stood in their way. It will highlight successes and failures.

This book stakes no claim to comprehensiveness. It does not discuss every presidential action, track every federal dollar, or evaluate every program of human rights promotion. Instead, it explores human rights promotion through a series of key events and activities over the course of more than six decades. Through that prism, it draws lessons about the possibilities and limits of human rights promotion.

In chapter 1, we examine the roots of America's essential role in the advance of human rights. Through the inspiring words of its founding documents and the power of its example, the United States has long served as a beacon of hope for people around the world. "The American Experiment" marked a radical break with human history, a bold effort by ordinary people to rule themselves rather than remain subservient to the whims of emperors and monarchs. Americans are justifiably proud of their heritage. Lincoln called the United States the "last best hope of earth" and presidents have long cited the words of Governor John Winthrop, who told his shipmates aboard the *Arabella* as it headed to the New World in 1630 that "we shall be as a city upon a hill," with "the eyes of all people . . . upon us."

America's leaders and its people have long viewed human rights promotion in moral terms, believing they have a responsibility to share the blessings of freedom and democracy with the rest of mankind. They consider it a practical necessity as well, for the spread of freedom and democracy will make the world a more peaceful and prosperous place. Presidents and Congresses use a wide assortment of tools to promote human rights. Presidents exploit the power of their "bully pulpit" to embarrass authoritarian regimes and inspire would-be democrats, hold high-profile meetings with dissidents from around the world to highlight their plight, and pressure regimes privately to protect human rights. Policymakers provide foreign aid to help fledgling democracies grow, and they deny aid to rights-abusing governments. They ensure the security of democratic allies, and they use military force to end genocide and repression. Policymakers balance human rights promotion against the other priorities of foreign policy. In promoting human rights, the United States succeeds beyond expectations in some cases, fails miserably in others.

In chapter 2, we explore the initial post–World War II period of human rights promotion, stretching from Presidents Harry S. Truman to Lyndon Johnson. Immediately after the war, the United States organized its foreign policy around the challenge of fighting a Cold War against its former ally, the Soviet Union. Human rights promotion became an important part of that effort. Truman enunciated the Truman Doctrine to help people who were trying to free themselves from authoritarianism, and he launched the Marshall Plan to help Western European democracies recover from the devastation of war and prevent communist takeovers. Beyond the Marshall Plan, the nation began to allocate foreign aid as a central tool of foreign policy, assisting our allies and seeking to expand our circle of friends. John F. Kennedy built on that foundation, issuing landmark calls for human rights while expanding foreign aid and focusing it more squarely on economic and democratic progress.

Illustrating the limits of human rights promotion, Washington did little to stop Moscow from suppressing popular uprisings in East Germany in 1953, Hungary in 1956, and Czechoslovakia in 1968 for fear of inciting a military confrontation with its Cold War adversary. In Hungary, the United States also learned a tough lesson about over-promising on human rights; when, during the uprising, Voice of America reports suggested that Washington would provide military assistance to the protestors, the protestors redoubled their efforts, Moscow stepped in with overwhelming force, and Washington hung back—leaving the protestors exposed and Hungarians embittered about the United States for years to come. Also in this period, the nation suffered serious wounds to its international image during its domestic struggle over civil rights, with Third World nations responding angrily to discrimination against African Americans and noting the hypocrisy of a nation that promoted its values overseas but refused to uphold them at home. The Soviet Union exploited America's domestic troubles in its quest for greater influence throughout the Third World.

In chapter 3, we explore the transformation of human rights promotion in the mid-1970s from a somewhat dreamy aspiration of earlier leaders to a far more tangible, far more operational goal. With new laws and new institutions in and out of government to promote human rights, push progress, and monitor results, human rights became a more central element of foreign policy—whether any president wanted it to be or not. As never before, presidents were judged in the court of U.S. public opinion based on how much, and how well, they promoted human rights around the world.

The transformation resulted from a perfect storm of events. Most prominent was a backlash against the foreign policy "realism" of Presidents Richard Nixon and Gerald Ford (as practiced by Henry Kissinger) through which the United States would seek nothing grander than its own security and, in doing so, consort with dastardly regimes of any kind. Other contributors to the storm included the war in Vietnam, where U.S. troop misdeeds displayed the gap between America's ideals and its behavior; crackdowns on human rights by dictators and military rulers across Latin America; humanitarian horrors in Cambodia, Vietnam, and elsewhere; and the 1973 publication of Aleksandr Solzhenitsyn's *The Gulag Archipelago*, which raised public consciousness about suffering across the Soviet empire. Also during this period, organized labor publicized human rights violations around the world and helped labor activists in authoritarian lands; the Helsinki Accords put the human rights policies of Moscow and its Eastern European puppets more squarely on the international agenda; and numerous nongovernmental organizations (NGOs) arose to monitor human rights around the world and pressure the United States to shape its policies accordingly.

In chapter 4, we explore how presidents from Jimmy Carter to Bill Clinton exploited the new tools, and sought to meet the new expectations, of human rights promotion. With Americans smarting over Nixon-Ford "realism," Carter promised to make human rights the centerpiece of his foreign policy. Though he worked to advance human rights in myriad ways in his early months, he was forced to sacrifice the goal to broader national security concerns in a host of places around the world, exposing him to charges of hypocrisy. Ronald Reagan came next, and he brought a new sense of foreign policy in general, and human rights in particular, to the job. Rather than merely "contain" the Soviet Union, as all of his post–World War II predecessors had done, he sought to win the Cold War by weakening the Soviet Union over time. That, he believed, would most effectively advance human rights around the world because, in his eyes, Moscow was the world's most serious human rights abuser.

After the Soviet collapse, George H. W. Bush and Bill Clinton each sought a new U.S. vision for the post–Cold War world. Bush, a prototypical "realist," envisioned a "New World Order" in which the United States would call the shots but cooperate with other leading powers to enforce the rule of law and keep the peace; he viewed the coalition of nations that he built to reverse Iraq's 1990 invasion of Kuwait as the first concrete example. Clinton enunciated a doctrine of "democratic enlargement," under which the United States would grow the global economy and expand the community of free-market democracies, making for a safer and more prosperous world from which Americans could benefit; he viewed NATO's addition of Poland, Hungary, and the Czech Republic, along with multiple global, regional, and bilateral trade agreements, as concrete examples. Despite their divergent outlooks on foreign policy, Bush and Clinton both used military force to promote human rights—Bush to help with famine relief in Somalia, Clinton to halt Serbian atrocities in the Balkans—reflecting heightened public expectations that Washington would alleviate horror when it clearly could do so.

In chapter 5, we explore how Presidents George W. Bush and then Barack Obama adapted human rights promotion to the post–September 11 world. Bush, who had promised a "humble" foreign policy when he ran for president, responded to the terrorist attacks of that day by launching what promised to be a decades-long "war on terror." He enunciated not only a "Bush Doctrine" to use military force preemptively to prevent terrorism, but also a "freedom agenda" to promote human rights for the people of authoritarian lands as an appealing alternative to extremist ideology and terrorism. Bush's words inspired activists and put autocrats on the defensive, generating some modest advances for democracy in the Middle East and elsewhere. But by promoting human rights "on the cheap"—that is, by pushing for elections even in places that lacked a broader architecture of freedom and democracy—Bush helped to empower some profoundly anti-democratic forces in places like Lebanon and Gaza.

In the backlash against Bush's bluster, his perceived unilateralism, and his controversial invasion of Iraq in 2003, Obama promised a different approach to the world. After praising the "realism" of Bush's father during his run for president, Obama reached out to U.S. allies and enemies alike. Seeking to nurture smoother U.S. relations around the world, he was reluctant to criticize human rights abusers, whether in Beijing, Moscow, Tehran, or elsewhere. Rather than confront U.S. adversaries, he would "engage" with them—most prominently, with the hegemony-seeking, terror-sponsoring, nuclear weapons–pursuing regime in Tehran. Committed to better government-to-government relations, he reacted tentatively when Iranians erupted in mass protest against a fraudulent presidential election in June 2009, offering little support for the protestors and condemning Tehran's subsequent crackdown only after European leaders had done so. Though the protests raised prospects of a democratic revolution in Iran, which would have dramatically improved the region and alleviated a host of U.S. concerns, Obama chose to stick with his engagement strategy with the autocrats rather than align the United States with the people on the streets.

In the epilogue, we review where we have been and outline a strategy for future U.S. action. The nearly seven decades since the end of World War II have witnessed a dramatic spread of freedom and democracy across Europe, Asia, Africa, and Latin America and, as you read these words, their possible advance in the Middle East and North Africa. The United States has had its share of success and failure along the way. On the upside, it has inspired others to challenge their repressive governments, and it has provided moral, financial, and military aid to democratic forces at key moments. On the downside, it has missed some chances to curtail humanitarian horror, and it hinted at tangible U.S. assistance for popular uprisings that never came, leaving thousands of activists exposed when their governments took revenge. Despite America's missteps, however, the world is a better place for the efforts it has made and the successes it has achieved.

Looking ahead, the challenge of U.S. human rights promotion is likely to grow only more complicated. In recent years, the advance of freedom and democracy has stalled. Authoritarian regimes in Beijing, Moscow, and else- where have found ways to raise living standards and loosen political con- straints just enough to maintain power and prevent mass uprisings. Mean- while, the Arab Spring presents the United States with a wide range of opportunities and challenges. A young, restive population across the Middle East and North Africa is demanding more freedom and opportunity, and it could well push governments across the region to finally provide the human rights that so many others around the world now enjoy. But an all-too-fast push for elections could backfire, putting power in the hands of Islamic forces (such as the Muslim Brotherhood) that would further restrict human rights while turning once-friendly governments in Cairo, Riyadh, and Am- man against the United States. The stakes for the United States could hardly be higher.

NOTES

1. Robin Wright, *Rock the Casbah: Rage and Rebellion across the Islamic World* (New York: Simon & Schuster, 2011), 15.

2. Jeffrey Goldberg, "Danger: Falling Tyrants," *Atlantic Monthly*, June 2011. See also David Gauthier-Villars, "How 'The Family' Controlled Tunisia," *Wall Street Journal*, June 20, 2011.

3. CNN Arabic Staff, "How a Fruit Seller Caused a Revolution in Tunisia," January 16, 2011, http://articles.cnn.com/2011-01-16/world/tunisia.fruit.seller.bouazizi_1_tunisian-history-street-vendor-police-officer?_s=PM:WORLD; CBS News, "How a Slap Sparked Tunisia's Revolution," February 20, 2011, www.cbsnews.com/stories/2011/02/20/60minutes/main20033404.shtml; and Wright, *Rock the Casbah*, 15–21.

4. Ted Widmer, *Ark of the Liberties: America and the World* (New York: Hill and Wang, 2008), 240–41.

5. Widmer, *Ark*, 302.

6. Secretary of State Madeleine Albright, interview with Matt Lauer, "The Today Show," February 19, 1998.

7. After Egyptian strongman Hosni Mubarak's downfall in early 2011, U.S. officials sought to assist what they hoped would be a transition to democracy by seeking grant proposals in Egypt "on a $100 million program to support 'job creation, economic development and poverty alleviation' and a $65 million program for 'democratic development,' including elec- tions, civic activism and human rights." Officials of the new government, however, warned nongovernmental organizations that "taking U.S. funding would damage the country's secur- ity," and they chastised U.S. officials for "bypassing the government to solicit proposals direct- ly from the public." Yaroslav Trofimov, "Egypt Opposes U.S.'s Democracy Funding," *Wall Street Journal*, June 14, 2011.

8. Indeed, historian Arthur M. Schlesinger Jr. looked to the Declaration of Independence in his efforts to define human rights, saying the concept connotes "roughly the idea that all individuals everywhere are entitled to life, liberty and the pursuit of happiness on this earth." Arthur M. Schlesinger Jr., "Human Rights and the American Tradition," *Foreign Affairs*, vol. 57, no. 3 (1978): 1.

9. The most useful guide to the historical development of human rights may be Micheline R. Ishay, ed., *The Human Rights Reader*, second edition (New York: Routledge, 2007), on which I relied heavily.

10. Ishay, *Human Rights Reader*, 93.

11. Gordon Wood, *The Radicalism of the American Revolution* (New York: Vintage Books, 1991), 5.

12. Wood, *Radicalism*, 8.

13. John Lewis Gaddis, *The Cold War: A New History* (New York: Penguin Press, 2005), 121–24.

14. The origin and nature of human rights was a longstanding point of contention between the free and communist worlds throughout the Cold War. The West asserted that human rights were essentially political and civil, that they derived from the individual, and that they served as a check on government. The Soviet-led communist bloc asserted that human rights were essentially economic and social, that they derived from the state, and that government bestowed human rights on the individual. The Universal Declaration of Human Rights (UDHR) transcended this point of contention, urging nations to promote a host of political, civil, economic, and social rights. The UDHR, in turn, spurred the development of both an International Covenant on Civil and Political Rights and an International Covenant on Economic, Social and Cultural Rights, which were completed in 1966. Taken together, the UDHR and the two covenants are known as the International Bill of Human Rights. Though the West has focused on political and civil rights, U.S. presidents have sometimes blurred the line between those rights and economic and social rights. FDR's call for "four freedoms" included freedoms of speech and of worship (both political rights) as well as freedoms from want and from fear (the former of which was clearly an economic right). President Carter's concept of human rights included, as Secretary of State Cyrus Vance explained in early 1977, three sets of "complementary and mutually reinforcing" rights that transcended the line between these separate categories of rights: "the right to be free from governmental violation of the integrity of the person . . . the right to the fulfillment of such vital needs as food, shelter, health care, and education . . . [and] the right to enjoy civil and political liberties." Sandy Vogelgesang, "Diplomacy of Human Rights," *International Studies Quarterly*, vol. 23, no. 2 (June 1979): 218.

15. Samuel P. Huntington, *The Third Wave: Democratization in the Late Twentieth Century* (Norman: University of Oklahoma Press, 1991), 13–15. To be sure, democracy and human rights are not one and the same. But they are closely linked, for it is a democracy—electable and accountable—that will most likely nurture and protect political and civil liberties. History has known few human rights–minded dictators.

16. Also useful is Ted Robert Gurr, Keith Jaggers, and Will H. Moore, "The Transformation of the Western State: The Growth of Democracy, Autocracy, and State Power Since 1800," *Studies in Comparative International Development*, vol. 25, no. 1 (Spring 1990): 73–108.

17. Arch Puddington, "Full Report Essay: The Arab Uprisings and Their Global Repercussions," from Freedom House, *Freedom in the World 2012*, www.freedomhouse.org/report/freedom-world/freedom-world-2012.

18. Such questions drive the longstanding debate over "just war," which has been the subject of numerous books, including Michael Walzer, *Arguing about War* (New Haven, CT: Yale University Press, 2004), and Jean Bethke Elshtain, *Just War against Terror: The Burden of American Power in a Violent World* (New York: Basic Books, 2003).

19. When it comes to advancing freedom and democracy, U.S. inconsistency can seem downright baffling. During the Arab Spring of 2011, President Obama pushed aside long-time Egyptian autocrat Hosni Mubarak (a U.S. ally) and joined with European leaders in a military campaign to prevent Libyan strongman Muammar Gaddafi from slaughtering Libyans who were seeking to topple him. But he nevertheless continued two decades of U.S. passivity in the face of humanitarian horror in Sudan. Of Sudan's dictator, Omar Al Bashir, and his totalitarian

regime, genocide scholar Daniel Jonah Goldhagen wrote in June 2011 that they have "conducted two eliminationist campaigns—of mass murder, mass expulsion, and mass rapes—over 20 years, first in Southern Sudan and then in Darfur. This has earned him not one but two distinctive places in the annals of our time, the most murderous in human history: He has committed genocide for longer than any political leader aside from Stalin and Mao, and he has slaughtered more people than anyone except Stalin, Hitler, Mao, and the Japanese leadership before and during World War II, all of whom had continental-sized populations under their control." Of Obama's policy, Goldhagen wrote, "Going after Qaddafi and not Al Bashir is like going after Mussolini but not Hitler. Going after Mubarak and not Al Bashir is like going after Antonio de Oliveira Salazar for his autocratic rule in Portugal (from 1932 to 1968) but not Hitler." Daniel Jonah Goldhagen, "The Sudan Crisis: Obama's Hypocrisy and Culpability," *New Republic*, June 22, 2011.

20. Vogelgesang, "Diplomacy," 240.

21. John F. Kennedy, Address to the People of West Berlin, June 26, 1963.

22. George W. Bush, Second Inaugural Address, January 20, 2005.

23. Harry S. Truman, Address to a Joint Session of Congress, March 12, 1947.

24. Indeed, Hamas returned to form a year later when it took control of the Gaza Strip by toppling Fatah, the party that ruled the Palestinian Authority, in a bloody coup.

Chapter One

America the Essential

Ever since our forefathers began to settle the New World, we Americans have believed that we are a special people and that we created a special nation to which the world has looked for guidance and inspiration. With a mission driven by Providence, we have sought to extend the blessings of freedom and democracy to the far corners of the earth. Proud of our values, we have been profoundly judgmental about other systems of government that withhold freedom and democracy from their people.

The modern period of U.S. human rights promotion, which began immediately after World War II, coincides with the rise of human rights as a global concern and of America as the world's most powerful nation. The United States has promoted human rights for two main reasons—idealism and self-interest. Idealistically, we believe that we have something special to share and, by promoting our values, we can improve the lives of people far beyond our borders. Selfishly, we believe that the advance of human rights helps to create a more peaceful and prosperous world from which we benefit.

Led by our presidents, the United States promotes human rights in a host of ways. Presidents use their "bully pulpit" and other means of public communication to pressure autocrats and support dissidents, and they work privately to convince rights-abusing regimes to change their behavior. They offer economic assistance and apply economic pressure to entice better human rights behavior by other nations, and they threaten or use military force to protect democracies and end humanitarian horrors. They provide money and other assistance to help construct the building blocks of democracy in nondemocratic lands, including opposition parties and a free press.

Skeptics of U.S. human rights promotion worry that it not only complicates U.S. diplomacy but also sets back the cause that it seeks to advance. Neither complaint, however, withstands scrutiny. Though human rights promotion can ruffle the feathers of autocrats, history shows that the United States can criticize authoritarian regimes while working with them to make progress in other areas. Though Washington must promote human rights carefully, with a sensitivity to the particulars of individual situations, history shows that U.S. human rights promotion helps to advance freedom and democracy over the long run. The dissidents themselves, who are on the front lines of battle to reform authoritarian nations, generally encourage the United States to more forcefully support their efforts.

AMERICA'S GIFT

"What then is the American, this new man?" J. Hector St. John de Crevecoeur asked in his *Letters from an American Farmer* in 1793.

> *He* is an American, who, leaving behind him all his ancient prejudices and manners, receives new ones from the new mode of life he has embraced, the new government he obeys, and the new rank he holds. . . . Here individuals of all nations are melted into a new race of men, whose labours and posterity will one day cause real changes in the world. Americans are the western pilgrims, who are carrying along with them that great mass of arts, sciences, vigour, and industry which began long since in the east; they will finish the great circle . . . here the rewards of his industry follow with equal steps the progress of his labour; his labour is founded on the basis of nature, *self-interest*; can it want a stronger allurement? Wives and children, who before in vain demanded of him a morsel of bread, now, fat and frolicsome, gladly help their father to clear those fields whence exuberant crops are to arise to feed and to clothe them all; without any part being claimed, either by a despotic prince, a rich abbot, or a mighty lord.[1]

U.S. human rights promotion is predicated on a simple premise: the United States of America is special. Stretching across a once-barren continent, with bustling cities and vast farms that feed its 300 million people, America is rooted in landmark values about human rights and the role of government.

Our sense of "specialness" (a.k.a. "American exceptionalism") drives our human rights promotion activities. We believe that we have values to cherish and a system to emulate, that we are a tool of Providence with a mission to fulfill, that we can inspire others around the world and change the course of history, and that our system of government is simply better than the alternatives.

Writing less than twenty years after the colonists declared independence, just four years after they adopted a constitution, and just two years after they added a bill of rights, de Crevecoeur touched on key features of our revolutionary new-ness: Here, the people rule; here, the people enjoy the fruits of their labor.

From our earliest days, we Americans have defined ourselves, and others have defined us, not by where we live, but rather by what we believe. To be French is to be born in France. So, too, to be German, Polish, Italian, or Greek. By contrast, the United States is a "melting pot" of others—French and Germans, Poles and Italians, Greeks and Turks, Chinese and Japanese, African Americans and Hispanics. They *become* American not when they arrive at the nation's shores, but when they embrace our values.

"The American," de Crevecoeur noted, "is a new man, who acts upon new principles; he must therefore entertain new ideas, and form new opinions."[2] In 2011, historian Gordon Wood restated de Crevecoeur's keen insight: "To be an American is not to be someone, but to believe in something."[3]

From the vantage point of the early twenty-first century, we sometimes take our freedom and democracy, our tolerance and opportunity, for granted. But make no mistake of what our leading historians continually remind us: coming when it did, the "American Experiment" in self-government was revolutionary to the core. As Wood writes, "In the eighteenth century, monarchy was still the standard for most people. . . . Monarchy had history on its side; the kings of Europe had spent centuries consolidating their authority over unruly nobles and disparate peoples. The Bible endorsed kingship. Had not the ancient Israelites proclaimed that 'we will have a king over us; that we . . . may be like all the nations'?"[4]

The people of this new United States understood—indeed, boasted—that they were creating something historic. They recognized the revolutionary nature of their venture, the ground-breaking idea that "we the people" would decide for ourselves what our government would do, how much power it would have, and how to control it through a system of "checks and balances" so that it never grew too powerful. Consider the words of Thomas Paine from *Common Sense*, his revolutionary tract from the revolutionary year of 1776: "A situation, similar to the present, hath not happened since the days of Noah until now. The birthday of a new world is at hand, and a race of men, perhaps as numerous as all Europe contains, are to receive their portion of freedom from the events of a few months."[5]

The colonists also knew from their earliest days that their venture would attract notice and drive history. "For we must consider that we shall be as a city upon a hill," Governor John Winthrop told his shipmates aboard the

Arabella in 1630 as it crossed the choppy Atlantic. "The eyes of all people are upon us."[6] This "city on the hill" imagery would prove irresistible to presidents over the years as they sought to renew the American spirit.

"I have been guided by the standard John Winthrop set before his ship-mates on the *Arabella* three hundred and thirty-one years ago, as they, too, faced the task of building a new government on a perilous frontier," John F. Kennedy told the people of his home state of Massachusetts, nine days before he assumed the presidency in early 1961.

> Today the eyes of all people are truly upon us—and our governments, in every branch, at every level, national, state and local, must be as a city upon a hill—constructed and inhabited by men aware of their great trust and their great responsibilities. For we are setting out upon a voyage in 1961 no less hazard-ous than that undertaken by the *Arabella* in 1630. We are committing our-selves to tasks of statecraft no less awesome than that of governing the Massa-chusetts Bay Colony, beset as it was then by terror without and disorder within.[7]

Leaving the presidency almost three decades later, Ronald Reagan described the nation as a "shining" city upon a hill,

> a tall proud city built on rocks stronger than oceans, wind-swept, God-blessed, and teeming with people of all kinds living in harmony and peace, a city with free ports that hummed with commerce and creativity, and if there had to be city walls, the walls had doors and the doors were open to anyone with the will and the heart to get here.[8]

This "city on a hill" was so different that not even its founders were sure it would last. As the Constitutional Convention of 1787 proceeded in secrecy in Philadelphia, people gathered outside Independence Hall. One of them, a Mrs. Powel, asked Benjamin Franklin one day, "Well, Doctor, what have we got, a republic or a monarchy?" Franklin replied, "A republic, if you can keep it."[9]

If you can keep it! Upon assuming the presidency in 1801, Thomas Jeffer-son felt compelled to address the lingering uncertainty about America's stay-ing power and make the case for the republic:

> I know indeed that some honest men fear that a republican government cannot be strong; that this government is not strong enough. But would the honest patriot, in the full tide of successful experiment, abandon a government which has so far kept us free and firm, on the theoretic and visionary fear, that this government, the world's best hope, may, by possibility, want energy to pre-serve itself?[10]

Three score years later, uncertainty reigned as North and South engaged in a brutal civil war that divided both regions and families. It would test, as Lincoln put it, whether "a new nation, conceived in liberty and dedicated to the proposition that all men are created equal . . . can long endure."[11]

It would endure, apparently because Providence had seen to it. Our leaders have long proclaimed that America's role in shaping history was no mere accident. It was part of a larger plan, a product of divine inspiration. "I always consider the settlement of America with reverence," John Adams wrote a decade before the colonists declared their independence, "as the opening of a grand scene and design in Providence for the illumination of the ignorant and the emancipation of the slavish part of mankind all over the earth."[12] Departing the presidency in 1837, Andrew Jackson told his fellow Americans, "Providence has showered on this favored land blessings without number, and has chosen you as the guardians of freedom, to preserve it for the benefit of the human race."[13]

"I believe that God presided over the inception of this nation," Woodrow Wilson said when running for president in 1912.

I believe that God planted in us the vision of liberty; I believe that men are emancipated in proportion as they lift themselves to the conception of Providence and of divine destiny, and therefore, I cannot be deprived of the hope that is in me—in the hope not only that concerns myself, but the confident hope that concerns the nation—that we are chosen, and prominently chosen, to show the way to the nations of the world how they shall walk in the paths of liberty.[14]

Reagan believed much the same, asserting that "there was some divine providence that placed this great land here between the two great oceans, to be found by a special kind of people from every corner of the world, who had a special love for freedom."[15] Even Barack Obama, later criticized for dismissing the notion of "American exceptionalism," sought to rally the nation in the midst of economic crisis with "the knowledge that God calls on us to shape an uncertain destiny . . . with eyes fixed on the horizon and God's grace upon us."[16]

De Crevecoeur had promised that this "new race of men . . . will one day cause great changes in the world."[17] He was neither the first nor the last to do so.

"We have it in our power to begin the world over again," Paine wrote in *Common Sense*. Franklin called the new nation "an asylum . . . for those who love liberty," while Edmund Burke observed that "[a] great revolution has happened—a revolution made, not by chopping and changing of power in any one of the existing states, but by the appearance of a new state, of a new species, in a new part of the globe. It has made as great a change in all the relations, and balances, and gravitations of power, as the appearance of a new planet would in the system of the solar world."[18]

After the Treaty of Paris ended America's Revolutionary War with the British, Yale's president, Ezra Stiles, predicted,

> This great American revolution, this recent political phenomenon of a new sovereignty arising among the sovereign powers of the earth, will be attended to and contemplated by all nations. Navigation will carry the American flag around the globe itself; and display the Thirteen Stripes and New Constellation at Bengal and Canton, on the Indus and Ganges, on the Whang-Ho and the Yang-Tse-Kiang; and with commerce will import the wisdom and literature of the east.[19]

In subsequent years, presidents have sounded similar themes. America is, in Lincoln's words, "the last best hope of earth."[20] It's the product of a revolution that, Reagan explained, was the first "in the history of mankind that truly reversed the course of government . . . with three little words: 'We the people.'"[21] It's a place, George W. Bush declared, that provided not just security for "whole nations" but also "inspiration for oppressed peoples."[22] It's a nation whose founders, Obama said, "drafted a charter to assure the rule of law and the rights of man" and whose ideals "still light the world."[23]

Confident in our specialness, we have been judgmental about other systems of government. That was especially so during the Cold War, when we competed with the Soviet Union for the allegiance of Third World nations. Standing in mid-1963 before three hundred thousand exuberant people at the Berlin Wall that was to separate East from West for twenty-eight years, Kennedy said, "Freedom has many difficulties and democracy is not perfect, but we have never had to put a wall up to keep our people in, to prevent them from leaving us."[24]

Standing at the wall nearly a quarter-century later, Reagan noted that

> [i]n the 1950s, [Soviet leader Nikita] Khrushchev predicted: "We will bury you." But in the West today, we see a free world that has achieved a level of prosperity and well-being unprecedented in all human history. In the communist world, we see failure, technological backwardness, declining standards of health, even want of the most basic kind—too little food. Even today, the Soviet Union still cannot feed itself. After these four decades, then, there stands before the entire world one great and inescapable conclusion: Freedom leads to prosperity. Freedom replaces the ancient hatreds among the nations with comity and peace. Freedom is the victor.[25]

A special place. A new system of government. A tool of God. An inspiration to the world. A driver of history. All in all, a better way. No wonder the United States promotes its highest ideals to the world. It could do no less!

OF IDEALISM AND SELF-INTEREST

The modern period of U.S. human rights promotion began shortly after World War II (though Woodrow Wilson and Franklin Roosevelt built a strong foundation for it with their words and deeds). U.S. human rights promotion emerged as a central task of U.S. foreign policy along with two related developments: America's rise to global preeminence and the rise of human rights on the global agenda. More than any other nation, the United States drove human rights to a position of greater international concern. More than any other nation, the United States has used its power and influence to improve the human condition.

The United States promotes human rights for two main reasons: idealism and self-interest. Idealism flows naturally out of our revolutionary roots, our enduring values, and our sense of mission. Self-interest reflects our belief that the advance of human rights will make the world a more peaceful and more prosperous place.

Wilson was our most idealistic president—so much so that, in foreign policy circles, the terms "Wilsonianism" and idealism are often used synonymously. A political scientist and author who served as Princeton's president and New Jersey's governor before winning a three-way race for president in 1912, Wilson was bookishly smart and supremely self-confident. He had a flair for language and a self-taught talent for public oratory, and they served him well as he explained why America should enter World War I:

> We are glad . . . to fight thus for the ultimate peace of the world and for the liberation of its peoples, the German peoples included: for the rights of nations great and small and the privilege of men everywhere to choose their way of life and of obedience. The world must be made safe for democracy. Its peace must be planted upon the tested foundations of political liberty. We have no selfish ends to serve.[26]

Even before the fighting ended, Wilson unveiled his vision of a postwar world with new rules of engagement to prevent nations from ever again going to war. It had "14 Points," and they included an end to secret treaties between nations, "adequate guarantees" that would allow for a sharp reduction in "national armaments," restored or new borders and unimpeded sovereignty for a host of countries, and a "general association of nations" (i.e., League of Nations) to keep the peace and protect nations large and small.[27]

Wilson's vision died in Europe's corridors of power, where the victorious allies were more set on vengeance than utopianism. (Upon hearing that Wilson had "14 Points," French Prime Minister Georges Clemenceau reportedly sniffed that the Lord himself had only needed ten.) It also died in the halls of

Congress, where a hostile new Senate Republican majority rejected U.S. membership in the League of Nations after Wilson refused to negotiate the terms of U.S. participation with the Senate.

But Wilsonian idealism survived as a central strain of thought for subsequent presidents of both parties.

In January 1941, nearly a year before Pearl Harbor pushed America into World War II, FDR imagined a postwar world in which every human being would enjoy "four freedoms"—of speech and worship, and from want and fear.[28] In August, he joined with British leader Winston Churchill to issue the "Atlantic Charter," reflecting their joint aspiration for a postwar world. Among other things, it said that their two countries

> respect the right of all peoples to choose the form of government under which they will live; and they wish to see sovereign rights and self government restored to those who have been forcibly deprived of them. . . . They hope to see established a peace which will afford to all nations the means of dwelling in safety within their own boundaries, and which will afford assurance that all the men in all the lands may live out their lives in freedom from fear and want.[29]

Beyond the soaring words of Wilson, FDR, and their successors, however, lay a selfish motive for our foreign policy. We are driven to human rights promotion by what Obama and others have called "enlightened self-interest." We believe the spread of freedom and democracy will be good not just for other nations but also for us. It will create a more peaceful, more prosperous world that will enhance our national security and improve our own prosperity.

Our enlightened self-interest is rooted in several beliefs.

First, we believe that totalitarianism—a regime's refusal to grant human rights to its people—undermines peace, which threatens our national security.

Externally, totalitarian regimes treat other nations with the same disdain with which they treat their own people, eschewing the normal rules of engagement that maintain peace.[30] Internally, simmering populations that lack the power to change their repressive regimes will pursue more dangerous outlets for their frustrations, such as terrorism.

"A steadfast concert for peace can never be maintained except by a partnership of democratic nations," Wilson declared. "No autocratic government could be trusted to keep faith within it or observe its covenants."[31] Truman agreed, telling Congress that "totalitarian regimes imposed on free peoples, by direct or indirect aggression, undermine the foundations of international peace and hence the security of the United States."[32]

George W. Bush applied the theory to the region from which the attackers of September 11 emanated. "Sixty years of Western nations excusing and accommodating the lack of freedom in the Middle East did nothing to make us safe," he told the National Endowment for Democracy in late 2003, "because in the long run, stability cannot be purchased at the expense of liberty."[33] Upon starting his second term, he said, "[A]s long as whole regions of the world simmer in resentment and tyranny—prone to ideologies that feed hatred and excuse murder—violence will gather, and multiply in destructive power, and cross the most defended borders, and raise a mortal threat.[34]

Obama echoed the view. In his Nobel Peace Prize address of late 2009 in Oslo, he said, "[P]eace is unstable where citizens are denied the right to speak freely or worship as they please; choose their own leaders or assemble without fear" because "pent-up grievances fester, and the suppression of tribal and religious identity can lead to violence."[35]

Second, we believe that the spread of democracy makes the world a more peaceful and prosperous place because democratic nations do not make war against one another.

In a democracy, voters hold the ultimate check on their nation's foreign policy because, if dissatisfied, they can remove their leaders from office. Consequently, democracies do not tend to make war on one another because, generally speaking, people would rather be at peace than at war. As the philosopher Immanuel Kant, reportedly the first to enunciate this insight, put it, "If the consent of the citizenry is required in order to determine whether or not there will be war, it is natural that they consider all its calamities before committing themselves to so risky a game."[36]

This "democratic peace theory," in the words of democracy expert Michael McFaul, is "the closest thing we have to empirical law in the study of international relations."[37] Another expert, Bruce Russett, explained, "[D]emocratically organized political systems in general operate under restraints that make them more peaceful in their relations with other democracies." In fact, he stated, "there are no clear-cut cases of sovereign stable democracies waging war with each other in the modern international system."[38]

Democracy's role in stemming warfare has been a staple of U.S. foreign policymaking for decades. "Self-governed nations do not fill their neighbor states with spies or set the course of intrigue to bring about some critical posture of affairs which will give them an opportunity to strike and make conquest," Wilson said. "Cunningly contrived plans of deception or aggression . . . are happily impossible where public opinion commands and insists upon full information concerning all the nation's affairs."[39]

"We believe that freedom and security go together," Reagan said in Berlin, "that the advance of human liberty can only strengthen the cause of world peace."[40] Explaining America's decision to maintain global security after

World War II "with the blood of our citizens and the strength of our arms," Obama said in Oslo, "We have done so . . . because we seek a better future for our children and grandchildren and we believe that their lives will be better if others' children and grandchildren can live in freedom and prosperity."[41]

"Democratic peace theory," in fact, fueled President Clinton's "democratic enlargement" efforts (discussed in chapter 4). Speaking to the American Society of Newspaper Editors in April 1993 as he approached a meeting with Russian President Boris Yeltsin, Clinton explained how democratic advancement would benefit the United States:

> Today, our policies must also focus on relations within nations, on a nation's form of governance, on its economic structure, [and] on its ethnic tolerance. These are of concern to us, for they shape how these nations treat their neighbors as well as their own people and whether they are reliable when they give their word. In particular, democracies are far less likely to wage war on other nations than dictatorships are. Emphatically, the international community cannot seek to heal every domestic dispute or to resolve every ethnic conflict. Some are simply beyond our reach. But within practical bounds and with a sense of clear strategic priorities, we must do what we can to promote the democratic spirit and the economic reforms that can tip the balance for progress well into the next century.[42]

In particular, he said, the United States should make the "wise investment" of assisting Russia's transition to democracy because it would save U.S. lives as well as U.S. dollars that could be better spent elsewhere:

> [W]e could at last face a Europe in which no great power, not one, harbors continental designs. Think of it: land wars in Europe cost hundreds of thousands of American lives in the 20th century. The rise of a democratic Russia, satisfied within her own boundaries, bordered by other peaceful democracies, could ensure that our nation never needs to pay that kind of price again. . . . Russia's reforms are important to us because they hold one of the keys to investing more in our own future. America's taxpayers have literally spent trillions of dollars to prosecute the Cold War. Now we can reduce that pace of spending—and, indeed, we have been able to reduce that pace of spending . . . because the arms of the former Soviet Union pose a diminishing threat to us and our allies. . . . Therefore, our ability to put people first at home requires that we put Russia and its neighbors first on our agenda abroad.[43]

The democracy-peace connection has an economic component as well; when democracy helps to nourish economic growth and raise living standards, average people have too much at stake to risk war with one another.

In the late 1990s, *New York Times* columnist and author Thomas Friedman proposed what he called the "Golden Arches Theory of Conflict Prevention"—that no two nations with a McDonald's have ever fought one another because their populations would rather wait in line for hamburgers than strap on helmets and fire guns.[44] (Friedman later updated his theory by proposing the "Dell Theory of Conflict Prevention"—that no two nations that are part of a major global supply chain, such as that of computer maker Dell, will likely make war on one another because their populations don't want to jeopardize their participation in global commerce, which raises living standards.[45])

As Friedman acknowledged, his "Golden Arches" theory was a variation on an old theme. Montesquieu, the eighteenth-century French philosopher, believed a "Grand Republic" of international trade was bringing together nations and their people, which would assure peace among them. Norman Angell applied the theory to early twentieth-century Europe, writing in his 1910 classic, *The Great Illusion*, that growing commerce among the great powers would convince them not to rock the boat by going to war.[46] (Tragically, he was proved wrong four years later with the onset of World War I.)

At peace, as Clinton noted, the United States and other democracies can shift some dollars away from national security and toward domestic investment, boosting economic growth even more. The wider the circle of democratic nations, the more they can shift their defense dollars accordingly. The lower the requirement for defense dollars, the less that democracies must tax their people, leaving more money in the private sector for individuals and businesses to invest as they see fit. A post–Cold War "peace dividend" in the 1990s helped the United States bring a long era of growing federal deficits to an end and, in turn, fuel the strong economic growth of that decade.

Third, we believe that both totalitarianism and democracy are contagious, which makes the stakes of containing the former and expanding the latter that much higher.

Regarding totalitarianism, consider Truman's rationale for asking Congress for $400 million for Greece and Turkey in early 1947, after British leaders explained that their exhausted nation could no longer protect democracy in that region:

> [T]he survival and integrity of the Greek nation are of grave importance in a much wider situation. If Greece should fall under the control of an armed minority, the effect upon its neighbor, Turkey, would be immediate and serious. Confusion and disorder might well spread throughout the entire Middle East. Moreover, the disappearance of Greece as an independent state would have a profound effect upon those countries in Europe whose peoples are struggling against great difficulties to maintain their freedoms and their independence while they repair the damages of war.[47]

From such rhetoric, it is but a short step to the "domino theory," which drove U.S. intervention in Southeast Asia starting in the 1950s. "You have a row of dominoes set up," Eisenhower said in early 1954 in the first reported enunciation of the theory, "you knock over the first one and what will happen to the last one is the certainty that it will go over very quickly."[48] Kennedy and Johnson sent advisors, then troops, and then many more troops to South Vietnam because they believed that the South's defeat would threaten Laos, Thailand, Cambodia, and the rest of the region.

The domino theory proved controversial, but no more so than its flip side—that the planting of democracy in one nation can incite its spread across a region. This has also been a key component of modern U.S. foreign policymaking, but it became controversial in the aftermath of the U.S.-led invasion of Iraq in 2003, as George W. Bush sought to put his "freedom agenda" to work.

"A liberated Iraq," Bush said in February 2003, a month before the invasion, "can show the power of freedom to transform that vital region, by bringing hope and progress into the lives of millions."[49] The critics found Bush profoundly naïve to think that the Arab Middle East, a place where some combination of Western colonial power and home-grown tyranny had ruled for generations, could embrace freedom and democracy. Bush, in words with which America's founders would have been comfortable, responded that the desire for freedom is rooted deep within the human heart.

Recent history suggests Bush was not far out on a limb at all. When the Soviet-backed regimes in Eastern Europe began to fall in the late 1980s, they fell in quick succession, with an uprising in one state inspiring the people of another. So, too, did the successful uprising in Tunisia that began in late 2010 inspire the public demands for freedom and democracy that, as of this writing, also had toppled Egypt's Hosni Mubarak, Libya's Muammar Gaddafi, and Yemen's Ali Abdullah Saleh and threatened other autocrats in the region. Driven by high-minded idealism and pragmatic self-interest, the United States promotes human rights from the Balkans to Beijing—with the president applying a wide variety of tools as he leads the effort.[50]

TOOLS OF THE TRADE

To be sure, the world's most powerful nation is not the world's omnipotent nation. Though the United States retains an enormous capacity to influence events, it cannot dictate them. The world is too big and complicated, and the United States has too many other things to do at home and abroad.

Nevertheless, history demonstrates that American values and American power still matter; the former inspire others around the world to act while the latter, when deployed artfully, can help shape the course of events. For U.S. policymakers, the challenge is to know the difference between a sizeable opportunity to advance freedom and democracy and a likely disaster if it tries. Moreover, even in the case of an opportunity, a president must deftly choose among the numerous tools in his arsenal, deploying the right ones in the right ways for the right challenges at the right time.

First, a president can use perhaps his most effective tool of all—his voice.

Cynics may scoff, but words matter. "In the life of the human spirit," President Carter said, "words are action."[51] No one has a more influential "bully pulpit," no one has more power to use his words to shape events, than a U.S. president. With his words captured by global media and relayed to the far corners of our planet, a president can pressure autocrats and inspire dissidents to push ahead.

When Kennedy visited Berlin, a million Germans lined the streets from the airport to his spot at the wall, where another three hundred thousand people had gathered. When he envisioned a free Germany in the years to come, when he said that, "as a free man, I take pride in the words 'Ich bin ein Berliner,'"[52] he gave the people of that besieged city an inspiring moment that they would never forget.[53] When, twenty years later, Reagan called the Soviet Union the "evil empire," he gave hope to the prisoners in Soviet gulags that they were not forgotten, that a great power would pursue their cause.[54]

In the first decade of the twenty-first century, George W. Bush's soaring pronouncements on freedom and democracy provided a rallying cry for democratic movements, helping to bring hundreds of thousands of people into streets all over the world, to topple a handful of autocrats, and to pressure others into expanding human rights. A "Rose Revolution" in Georgia ousted a corrupt president; an "Orange Revolution" in Ukraine prevented the anointed successor to another corrupt president from taking office; and a "Cedar Revolution" in Lebanon forced Syria to end its longstanding political and military domination of that turbulent nation. Egyptian strongman Hosni Mubarak allowed democratic activist Ayman Nour to run for president, and Palestinians voted in parliamentary elections. Autocrats in Morocco, Jordan, the United Arab Emirates, Kuwait, and Saudi Arabia introduced modest democratic reforms.[55]

"Inspired by Bush's rhetoric," Michael McFaul wrote, "democratic activists in Egypt, Iran, Belarus, Syria, Russia, and Azerbaijan took chances and challenged their regimes, believing that Washington would come to their defense. They were let down."[56] Bush, McFaul said, had raised hopes of further U.S. action that did not come, leaving the activists exposed. Nowhere was that truer than in Egypt, where Mubarak later jailed Nour and Washington did little to free him. The criticism is well taken, and it makes the larger point: no one should doubt the power of a president's voice. More than any other, it is the voice that can shape history—when it's used and, alas, when it isn't.

Second, a president can promote human rights through other public expressions.

A president can send a strong signal about his priorities by, for instance, meeting or conversing with foreign dissidents who travel to Washington or, even more pointedly, meeting with dissidents when he travels to authoritarian lands. Carter wrote to iconic Soviet dissident Andrei Sakharov and met in the White House with exiled Soviet dissident Vladimir Bukovsky, while George W. Bush presented the Congressional Gold Medal to the Dalai Lama. These gestures publicly, if implicitly, rebuked the Soviet Union and China, respectively, over their human rights records.

Similarly, the U.S. Ambassador to Syria, Robert Ford, traveled across that country in 2011 during Bashar al-Assad's brutal crackdown on democracy-seeking protestors, making clear in a series of high-profile appearances that he (and, by extension, the United States) stood with the protestors and against al-Assad. He visited sites in the central and southern regions that were the scenes of protests and met with opposition leaders. Joined by ambassadors to Japan, Great Britain, and other European nations, he attended a memorial service for a human rights activist, Ghayath Mattar, who was arrested by the government and reportedly died while under torture by al-Assad's security services.[57]

Because such gestures have become standard fare in Washington, a president's refusal to make them at key moments sends another signal—that he's less interested in human rights than smooth bilateral relations with even rights-abusing regimes. President Ford refused a request by congressional anti-Soviet hardliners in 1975 that he meet with the Soviet literary giant, Aleksandr Solzhenitsyn, who was in Washington to urge stronger U.S. resistance to the Soviet empire. Similarly, President Obama refused to meet early in his term with the Dalai Lama. Ford did not want to upset Soviet leader Leonid Brezhnev before his upcoming trip to Moscow, while Obama didn't want to ruffle feathers in China before his trip to Beijing.

A president also can turn up the heat on an authoritarian regime and reassure dissidents by highlighting the findings in the State Department's annual, country-by-country human rights reports. Required by law since the mid-1970s, these reports provide page after page of graphic detail of human rights abuse, from the torture and murder of human rights activists, to the abuse of women and minorities, to the suppression of public protests, to the closure of independent newspapers. They are now a standard source of information for policymakers and human rights activists, and any president or secretary of state can promote their findings to advance the human rights cause.

Third, a president can promote human rights privately, using behind-the-scenes communications to try to sway a regime.

Along with his public vow to elevate human rights to the center of his foreign policy, Carter advocated privately on behalf of hundreds of activists and political prisoners, targeting both allies that had received U.S. military and economic assistance as well as the Soviet Union and its Eastern European satellites. Reagan continued the process, though he focused much more on the Soviet Union. Clinton and George W. Bush adopted this tactic as well.[58]

Similarly, Obama has sought "engagement" with some of America's major adversaries in efforts to improve bilateral relations and, presumably, enhance U.S. influence with the regime in power. In particular, he has sought to build a new relationship with Iran, one through which Washington would convince Tehran to end its quest for nuclear weaponry, its support of terrorism, and its suppression of human rights. That would come through private discussions among high-ranking officials on both sides. (That the effort has not borne fruit is a separate matter.)

Fourth, a president can exploit the nation's economic power to strengthen democracies and pressure rights-abusing regimes.

As noted above, Truman sought $400 million in early 1947 to help Greece and Turkey protect their democracies. A year later, he worked with Congress to enact the landmark Marshall Plan, through which the United States would provide a then-whopping $13 billion to help Western European governments rebuild their economies and, in turn, convince their people to resist the temptations of communism. He also created the modern system of U.S. foreign aid through the Mutual Security Act of 1951.

Every later president has distributed foreign aid, but policymakers have modified its structure over the years. Kennedy reformed and expanded it with the Foreign Assistance Act of 1961 and created an Alliance for Progress to "assist free men and free governments" in Latin America who were "casting off the chains of poverty." George W. Bush created the Millennium Challenge Account to reward nations with economic assistance if they demonstrated progress toward greater human rights.

While offering the enticements of foreign aid, presidents can impose the burden of economic pressure. Congress unanimously passed the Jackson-Vanik amendment to the 1974 Trade Act, which tied U.S. trade with Soviet bloc nations to their treatment of Jews and others who sought to emigrate. Jackson-Vanik played an important role in the Soviet Union's eventual demise, not only for the economic pressure that it imposed but also for the moral statement that it made. By highlighting emigration as a basic human right, it put the Soviet empire on the human rights defensive while inspiring dissidents across Eastern Europe to assert a wide variety of their own rights, including that of emigration.

Carter reduced security assistance to Ethiopia, Argentina, and Uruguay over their human rights records, and he refused to sell police equipment to China for fears that the regime would use it against that nation's dissidents. While Reagan preferred a strategy of "constructive engagement" with U.S. ally South Africa, Congress imposed economic sanctions against that nation in 1986 over its policy of apartheid toward blacks.

Fifth, a president can threaten or use military force to protect democracies and end genocide and other human rights abuses.

Through public pledges and troop deployments, the United States has protected Western Europe and Japan since World War II; during the Cold War, it sought most of all to deter the Soviet Union from crossing into Western Europe. The United States, however, also has protected South Korea since its conflict with the North in the early 1950s, and it has built regional and bilateral military alliances in Europe, Asia, Africa, the Middle East, and Latin America. As Obama said in Oslo, "The service and sacrifice of our men and women in uniform has promoted peace and prosperity from Germany to Korea, and enabled democracy to take hold in places like the Balkans."[59]

In the 1990s, George H. W. Bush sent Air Force C-130s and more than twenty-five thousand U.S. troops to help ensure famine relief in Somalia, while Clinton spearheaded NATO bombing campaigns to end Serbian atrocities in Bosnia in 1995 and Kosovo in 1999. Then in 2011, Obama joined with European leaders in a military campaign that prevented Libyan strongman Muammar Gaddafi from slaughtering the many Libyans who were seeking to end his autocratic rule. But, for reasons ranging from public disinterest to competing presidential priorities, Washington stayed on the sidelines while other horrific abuses occurred. Ford and Carter did little to prevent Pol Pot's Khmer Rouge from murdering nearly two million people in Cambodia in the late 1970s, Clinton did nothing to stop Hutu soldiers and citizens from murdering eight hundred thousand Tutsis in Rwanda in 1994, and the United States did little over the last two decades to stop a series of slaughters in Sudan that left 2.5 million people dead and millions more displaced.

Sixth, a president can support individuals and groups that are seeking to construct the building blocks of democracy in an authoritarian society, including opposition parties, labor unions, and a free press.

In the early 1980s, President Reagan and Congress created the National Endowment for Democracy (NED), which Congress funds to help promote democracy building overseas. A grant-making institution, NED provides funds largely to four affiliated organizations—National Democratic Institute for International Affairs (NDI), International Republican Institute (IRI), Center for International Private Enterprise (CIPE), and American Center for International Labor Solidarity—but also to more than 1,200 other organizations a year that are working for change in more than ninety countries.

In addition, the State Department provides funds for a host of targeted programs that support various aspects of democracy building. Some focus on nurturing a free press, others on building political parties, still others on nourishing labor unions. The State Department and other agencies also take other steps episodically. When protests erupted in Iran in 2009 against its flawed presidential election, an official in Obama's State Department asked the social networking service Twitter not to perform a planned upgrade that would have shut down the service temporarily. Demonstrators were communicating with one another and the outside world through Twitter, and this official saw an opportunity to (quietly) encourage a democratic transition in the Islamic Republic.

Critics of human rights promotion say these tools amount to misguided efforts to shape other nations' internal policies, jeopardizing U.S. interests and the advance of human rights itself. The record suggests otherwise.

"THANK YOU, AMERICA!"

Critics of U.S. human rights promotion make three main points. None of them withstands scrutiny.

First, the critics say, not everybody wants freedom and democracy. Some cultures supposedly are not amenable to Western notions of progress. Some people of some backgrounds, nourished by different political systems or practicing different religions, do not crave what we consider the blessings of modern life.

We've heard this before. We heard it after World War II, when skeptics doubted whether the United States could help formerly Nazi Germany and formerly Imperial Japan transition to freedom and democracy—until both nations built thriving economies and stable democracies, becoming strong and reliable U.S. allies. We heard it throughout the Cold War, when skeptics questioned the audience for freedom and democracy across the Soviet bloc— until populations began to stir in the late 1980s and the Soviet crack-up paved the way for democracy in Eastern Europe. We heard it about Asia, Africa, and Latin America as well—until democratic transitions toppled long-ruling autocrats.

Most recently, we heard the skeptics weigh in about the Arab world, which has long been the region that history seemed to forget. For years, it has lagged behind the world not just in political freedom, but in economic and cultural progress as well. It seemed oblivious to the march of human rights across the world. When, after September 11, President George W. Bush focused his human rights promotion efforts (his "freedom agenda") on the Arab world, critics scoffed.

Then came the Arab Spring, which (as of this writing) has toppled four dictators and prompted protests across the region. Apparently, the Arab world is not quite as different as the cynics suggested. Even Tunisians and Egyptians, Libyans and Syrians, Saudis and Jordanians, want the same basic things as other people—the freedom to choose one's leaders and pursue one's dreams. However it turns out, the Arab Spring should serve as the death knell to the notion that people in some cultures don't want or are not ready for freedom and democracy.

Second, the critics say, human rights promotion complicates other vital U.S. priorities, such as improving bilateral relations with allies and adversaries alike. A president, they say, can hardly work with the authoritarian leader of another nation when, separately, he is pressuring that leader and encouraging the democratic activists within his or her nation to push for a different form of government. By weakening a bilateral relationship in this way, a president can threaten U.S. security, trade, and other priorities.

Yes, U.S. human rights promotion can complicate U.S. relations with authoritarian regimes and even impair the cause of human rights in the short term. When, for instance, Washington enacted Jackson-Vanik, Moscow responded angrily by allowing less, not more, Jewish emigration for the next few years. But ruffled feathers within another government do not necessarily prevent Washington from making progress with that government on other issues. Nations work with one another when their strategic interests dictate that they do so. (In fact, the Soviet Union followed its reduction in Jewish emigration with a generous increase later in the decade to help convince the U.S. Senate to ratify the U.S.-Soviet SALT II arms control agreement.) Leaders of nations may dislike one another, they may resent the policies of one another, but they can set aside their differences and reach agreements that serve their national interests.

Consider two other examples from the U.S.-Soviet relationship.

At the Berlin Wall in 1963, Kennedy's critique of Soviet-led communism could not have been harsher:

> There are many people in the world who really don't understand, or say they don't, what is the great issue between the free world and the communist world. Let them come to Berlin. There are some who say that communism is the wave of the future. Let them come to Berlin. And there are some who say in Europe and elsewhere we can work with the communists. Let them come to Berlin. And there are even a few who say that it's true that communism is an evil system, but it permits us to make economic progress. "Laßt sie nach Berlin kommen." Let them come to Berlin. [60]

That was in June. A month later, culminating more than eight years of negotiations over nuclear weapons testing, "the two nations agreed to ban [nuclear] testing in the atmosphere, in space, and underwater." [61] Then, in early

August, the United States, Soviet Union, and Great Britain signed the Limited Nuclear Test Ban Treaty, barring nuclear tests in the water, the atmosphere, or outer space; allowing underground testing only as long as radioactive debris did not fall outside the boundaries of the testing nation; and pledging to work toward complete disarmament and an end to the arms race.

At the Berlin Wall in 1987, Reagan noted the signs that Soviet leader Mikhail Gorbachev was loosening Moscow's grip on society, releasing some political prisoners, allowing some foreign news broadcasts, and permitting some free enterprise. "Are these the beginnings of profound changes in the Soviet state?" Reagan asked. "Or are they token gestures, intended to raise false hopes in the West, or to strengthen the Soviet system without changing it?"

> We welcome change and openness; for we believe that freedom and security go together, that the advance of human liberty can only strengthen the cause of world peace. There is one sign the Soviets can make that would be unmistakable, that would advance dramatically the cause of freedom and peace. General Secretary Gorbachev, if you seek peace, if you seek prosperity for the Soviet Union and Eastern Europe, if you seek liberalization: Come here to this gate! Mr. Gorbachev, open this gate! Mr. Gorbachev, tear down this wall! [62]

That was in June. As in 1963, a president's strong denunciation of America's Cold War adversary did not prevent U.S.-Soviet progress on other issues. While Reagan was in West Berlin, officials from both countries were negotiating arms reductions that, Reagan believed, would ease tensions and promote peace. In December, the two leaders signed a landmark arms control treaty in Washington, the first agreement to reduce nuclear arms rather than merely limit their growth. It eliminated all U.S. and Soviet intermediate-range nuclear forces (INF) from Europe and imposed the most comprehensive verification system ever established for the two sides to monitor progress. By May 1991, the United States had scrapped nearly one thousand, and the Soviet Union nearly two thousand, missile systems. [63]

Third, the critics say, a president who promotes human rights in a particular country can hurt the cause by weakening the dissidents who are on the front lines in that country. An authoritarian regime can point to U.S. efforts and portray the dissidents as spies for, or dupes of, the United States, giving the regime an excuse to arrest and imprison the dissidents and weaken the democracy effort.

Yes, an authoritarian regime can do that. But, frankly, it can do that whether Washington has a hand in the dissidents' activities or not, whether a president is promoting their cause or not. When, for instance, democratic activists protest on the streets of Iran, the regime in Tehran routinely dismisses them as American lackeys—even when Washington has steered clear of the turmoil. [64]

The question is, what do the dissidents want? What do the opposition leaders and labor organizers, the journalists and students, who are on the front lines of battle want from the United States? They are the ones who are threatened and harassed by the regimes they criticize. They are the ones who face jail, torture, even death. They are better positioned than the critics in Washington or anywhere else to decide whether U.S. human rights promotion helps or hurts their cause.

For decades, they have answered fairly consistently. They have thanked the United States for its efforts, and they have encouraged the nation to do more, not less. By promoting human rights, dissidents say, the United States puts authoritarian regimes on the defensive, persuades average people to join budding movements for freedom and democracy, and weakens the foundation of an authoritarian society.

Mihajlo Mihajlov was a prominent dissident in communist Yugoslavia in the 1960s and 1970s who spent seven years in prison—half of it in the 1960s after writing that communist icon Vladimir Lenin had established camps for political dissidents after the Russian Revolution, the other half in the 1970s after writing critically about the government of Yugoslavian strongman Josip Broz Tito. Freed to emigrate in 1978, he came to the United States where he worked to strengthen Western support for his nation's dissidents—professors, writers, scientists, and priests who had lost their jobs due to their political beliefs, could not find other work, and were not allowed to leave. He suggested that Western intellectuals establish joint research projects and other joint ventures among scholars in the West and in Yugoslavia, helping the latter return to work. "The most frightening thing that can happen to a person," he wrote in 1978, "is to be forgotten in prison."[65]

Other dissidents echoed his sentiments during the dark days of Soviet communism. After the Soviets expelled him in 1974, Nobel laureate Aleksandr Solzhenitsyn encouraged Washington to expand its public pressure on Moscow over human rights. Vaclav Havel, the Czech playwright who became his nation's president, later thanked Washington for its support when he led the "Charter 77" movement to pressure Prague to protect human rights. So, too, did Polish labor leader Lech Walesa, who created the trade union Solidarity and went on to become the nation's first non-communist president.[66] Natan Sharansky, a Soviet dissident who spent nine years in Soviet prisons, said later that Reagan's denunciations of Moscow and calls to "tear down this wall" had "brought moral clarity to the [Cold War] and started the chain of events which led to the end of Soviet communism."[67]

Today, a new crop of dissidents cries out for America's support. "Barack Obama and his European counterparts face a moment of truth," Saad Eddin Ibrahim, a leading Egyptian democratic activist, wrote in the *Washington*

Post in early 2011 as protests mounted against Mubarak. "They can move rapidly to support the democracy activists who are putting their lives on the line in Tahrir Square, or history may never pardon them."[68]

Ibrahim, who was imprisoned three times for his political activism and never fully recovered physically from the torture he endured, is one of the most articulate and persistent advocates for U.S. human rights promotion. He founded the Ibn Khaldun Center for Development Studies in Cairo, which "trains civil society activists, publishes reports, and monitors elections," and which openly accepts grants from U.S. and European foundations, including the National Endowment for Democracy.[69] He repeatedly urged Washington to loosen its ties with Mubarak, to pressure the dictator over his human rights abuses, and to get behind the democratic activists.[70]

Ibrahim recognized that U.S. human rights promotion is not easy. He advised Washington to eschew one-size-fits-all solutions and instead adopt a "particularized," "country-by-country" approach because, for Washington, human rights promotion is far different when it comes to U.S. allies like Egypt as opposed to adversaries like Iran. In every case, he said, Washington should find out what the dissidents want. But he left no doubt that the effort is important. Referring to U.S. actions during the Cold War, he echoed Sharansky's view that the combination of U.S. pressure on Moscow and its support for the dissidents helped to bring down the Soviet empire.

Other leading dissidents in recent years have taken to the op-ed pages of leading U.S. newspapers, which they know that America's leaders read, to urge more U.S. action. These dissidents include Yang Jianli, imprisoned for five years in China, who implored Obama to pressure Chinese President Hu Jintao to free 2010 Nobel Peace Prize laureate Liu Xiaobo and other political prisoners;[71] Anwar Ibrahim, a Malaysian opposition leader, who wrote that "the U.S. must stop supporting tyrants and autocrats whether in the Middle East, Pakistan, or Southeast Asia";[72] and Russian activist Garry Kasparov, who urged Obama to more strongly support the people of Iran.

In their writings, these dissidents called mostly for the United States to exert itself morally—for Obama to use his bully pulpit and private influence to change the behavior of rights-abusing regimes. But the Arab Spring makes clear that dissidents not only benefit from but also welcome the more tangible assistance that they have received in recent years from Washington, which includes money as well as the skills to run political campaigns. In early 2011, democratic activists from Egypt, Yemen, and Jordan spoke about how previous U.S. efforts to nurture their skills in coalition-building, social networking, and other talents helped them to capitalize on the Arab Spring.

"We learned how to organize and build coalitions," Bashem Fathy, a youth leader in Egypt's 2011 uprising, said of the training he received at a 2008 technology conference in New York, which the State Department sponsored with leading technology companies.[73] Bassem Samir, who runs the

Egyptian Democratic Academy, learned about political organization, new media, and other skills through U.S.-funded programs. He visited Google's offices and was tutored by a 2008 Obama campaign specialist.[74] "[U.S. training sessions] helped me very much because I used to think that change only takes place by force and by weapons," Yemeni youth activist Entsar Qadhi said.[75] "All these efforts, by local and international organizations, paved the way for what's going on today," said Oraib al-Rantawi, a U.S.-supported Jordanian activist. "These youths didn't come from nowhere and make a revolution."[76]

Individuals and groups that helped drive the Arab Spring, including Egypt's Arab 6 Youth Movement and the Bahrain Center for Human Rights, received money and training from the National Democratic Institute for International Affairs, the International Republican Institute, and Freedom House. More than ten thousand Egyptians have participated in democracy and governance programs that were funded by the United States Agency for International Development (USAID).[77]

For these activists and others, the benefits of U.S. assistance clearly outweigh any potential for exploitation by the regime. Dissidents appreciate the help and seek more. "We need more support, and fast," Abdallah Helmy, who cofounded Egypt's Reform and Development Party, said in early 2011.[78]

Today's dissident leaders may well be tomorrow's governmental leaders. If a revolution topples an autocrat, it is these dissidents to whom a country may turn for new leadership. That's what happened in Poland and Czechoslovakia with Lech Walesa and Vaclav Havel, respectively, and it's what could happen in the Arab world. So, by assisting the dissidents, the United States is nurturing relationships that could prove fruitful at a government-to-government level down the road.

In the Middle East, U.S. human rights promotion could pay dividends with the largest audience of all: the people. Millions across that region (and elsewhere) watch what the United States does, where it lines up, and who it supports. They will remember, at a moment of possibility, where America stood.

After Iran's fraudulent election in June 2009, hundreds of thousands took to the streets in protest. In Tehran, demonstrators who were under attack by police were heard to shout: "Obama, Obama—either you're with them or you're with us."[79] Obama did little, and the regime brought things under control.

In 2011, however, Obama deployed U.S. military power to protect protestors in Libya who faced the threat of slaughter by Muammar Gaddafi. With Gaddafi hamstrung in his efforts to suppress the uprising, rebels forced him from power and sent his loyalists fleeing. Soon after, *New York Times* columnist Nicholas D. Kristof visited Tripoli and began his August 31 column this way: "Americans are not often heroes in the Arab world, but as nonstop celebrations unfold here in the Libyan capital I keep running into ordinary people who learn where I'm from and then fervently repeat variants of the same phrase: 'Thank you, America!'"[80]

CONCLUSION

U.S. human rights promotion flows naturally from America's founding and promise, its values and self-image, and its recent history. But the undertaking is difficult and, even with the best of intentions, the United States has not always done it well. Moreover, the task competes with other foreign policy priorities, so Washington has sometimes eschewed the effort even in the face of humanitarian horror.

In the ensuing chapters, we will look more closely at the history of U.S. human rights promotion—at how and why, in the period that began shortly after World War II, some presidents promoted human rights robustly while others avoided doing so. We will examine what they did, what calculations they made, and what ensued. We will discuss the conflicts and pressures that confronted Truman, Eisenhower, Kennedy, Johnson, Nixon, Ford, Carter, Reagan, Bush, Clinton, another Bush, and Obama.

We turn first to the period from Truman to Johnson, spanning the origins of the Cold War, the Truman Doctrine, the Marshall Plan, the creation of foreign aid, and popular uprisings in East Germany, Hungary, and Czechoslovakia. We will see how presidents sought to advance freedom and democracy in a turbulent world—and how America's domestic struggles with race greatly complicated the effort.

The effort began with one of the most unlikely of our modern presidents, one who assumed the job with more than a hint of trepidation.

NOTES

1. J. Hector St. John de Crevecoeur, *Letters from an American Farmer* (Philadelphia: Matthew Carey, 1793), 46–47.

2. De Crevecoeur, *Letters*, 46–47.

3. Gordon Wood, *The Idea of America: Reflections on the Birth of the United States* (New York: Penguin Press, 2011), 322.

4. Wood, *The Idea of America*, 57.

5. Thomas Paine, *Common Sense* (New York: Fall River Press, 1995), 65–66.

6. Governor John Winthrop, "A Model of Christian Charity," 1630.

7. John F. Kennedy, Address to the Joint Convention of the General Court of the Commonwealth of Massachusetts, January 9, 1961.

8. Ronald Reagan, Farewell Address to the Nation, January 11, 1989.

9. John F. McManus, "A Republic, If You Can Keep It," *New American*, November 6, 2000.

10. Thomas Jefferson, Inaugural Address, March 4, 1801.

11. Abraham Lincoln, Gettysburg Address, November 19, 1863.

12. John Adams, *Dissertation on the Canon and Feudal Law*, quoted in Ted Widmer, *Ark of the Liberties: America and the World* (New York: Hill and Wang, 2008), 47.

13. Andrew Jackson, Farewell Address to the Nation, March 4, 1837.

14. Widmer, *Ark*, 171.

15. Widmer, *Ark*, 298.

16. Barack Obama, Inaugural Address, January 20, 2009.

17. De Crevecoeur, *Letters*, 46–47.

18. Widmer, *Ark*, 58.

19. Widmer, *Ark*, 65.

20. Abraham Lincoln, State of the Union Address, December 1, 1862.

21. Reagan, Farewell Address.

22. George W. Bush, Address at the Twentieth Anniversary of the National Endowment for Democracy, United States Chamber of Commerce, November 6, 2003.

23. Obama, Inaugural Address.

24. John F. Kennedy, Address to the People of West Berlin, June 26, 1963.

25. Ronald Reagan, Address to the People of West Berlin, June 12, 1987.

26. Woodrow Wilson, Address to a Joint Session of Congress, April 2, 1917.

27. Woodrow Wilson, Address to a Joint Session of Congress, January 8, 1918.

28. Franklin D. Roosevelt, Address to a Joint Session of Congress, January 6, 1941.

29. Franklin Roosevelt and Winston Churchill, "The Atlantic Charter," August 1941.

30. This link between a totalitarian regime's domestic and international behavior has been a staple of geopolitical thinking in the United States and elsewhere for decades. Speaking to the UN General Assembly in 1948, Secretary of State George Marshall said, "Governments which systematically disregard the rights of their own people are not likely to respect the rights of other nations and other people and are likely to seek their objectives by coercion and force in the international field." Sandy Vogelgesang, "Diplomacy of Human Rights," *International Studies Quarterly*, vol. 23, no. 2 (June 1979): 236. Decades later, a successor of Marshall, Madeleine Albright, said that "regimes that run roughshod over the rights of their own citizens may well show similar disregard for the rights of others. Such governments are more likely to spark unrest by persecuting minorities, sheltering terrorists, running drugs or secretly building weapons of mass destruction." Barbara Ann J. Rieffer and Kristan Mercer, "U.S. Democracy Promotion: The Clinton and Bush Administrations," *Global Society*, vol. 19, no. 4 (October 2005): 391. Soviet dissident Andrei Sakharov used to say, "A country that does not respect the rights of its own people will not respect the rights of its neighbors." Natan Sharansky, *The Case for Democracy* (New York: PublicAffairs, 2004), 3. Sharansky himself put it this way: "The world cannot depend on leaders who do not depend on their own people." Sharansky, *Case*, xix.

31. Wilson, Joint Session, April 2, 1917.

32. Harry S. Truman, Address to a Joint Session of Congress, March 12, 1947.

33. Bush, National Endowment for Democracy.

34. George W. Bush, Inaugural Address, January 20, 2005.

35. Barack Obama, Address at the Nobel Peace Prize Ceremony, December 10, 2009.

36. Sean M. Lynn-Jones, "Why the United States Should Spread Democracy," Discussion Paper 98–07, Center for Science and International Affairs, Harvard University (March 1998): 17.

37. Jack Levy, "Domestic Politics and War," in *The Origin and Prevention of Major Wars*, eds. Robert Rotberg and Theodore Rabb (New York: Cambridge University Press, 1989), 88, as cited in Michael McFaul, *Advancing Democracy Abroad: Why We Should and How We Can* (Lanham, MD: Rowman & Littlefield, 2010), 59.

38. Bruce Russett, *Grasping the Democratic Peace: Principles of a Post–Cold War World* (Princeton, NJ: Princeton University Press, 1993), 11, as cited in McFaul, *Advancing*, 59.

39. Wilson, Joint Session, April 2, 1917.

40. Reagan, West Berlin.

41. Obama, Nobel Peace Prize Ceremony.

42. William Jefferson Clinton, "A Strategic Alliance with Russian Reform," Address to the American Society of Newspaper Editors, Annapolis, Maryland, April 1, 1993.

43. Clinton, "A Strategic Alliance."

44. Thomas L. Friedman, *The Lexus and the Olive Tree* (New York: Farrar, Straus and Giroux, 1999), 248–75.

45. Thomas L. Friedman, *The World Is Flat* (New York: Farrar, Straus and Giroux, 2005).

46. Friedman, *Lexus*, 249.

47. Truman, Joint Session.

48. Widmer, *Ark*, 258.

49. George W. Bush, Address at the American Enterprise Institute, February 26, 2003.

50. George Mason University's Peter T. Leeson and West Virginia University's Andrea M. Dean sought to evaluate the domino theory more comprehensively through the experiences of 130 countries between 1900 and 2000. They found that, in fact, democracy tends to spread geographically—its advance in one country raises the chance of its advance in a neighboring country. They say, however, that the impact of a democratizing nation tends to be less powerful than the theory's biggest boosters suggest. Peter T. Leeson and Andrea M. Dean, "The Domino Theory: An Empirical Investigation," www.peterleeson.com/domino_theory.pdf.

51. Jimmy Carter, Commencement Address at Notre Dame University, May 22, 1977.

52. Kennedy, West Berlin.

53. As discussed in chapter 2.

54. As discussed in chapter 4.

55. McFaul, *Advancing*, 5–6.

56. McFaul, *Advancing*, 152.

57. Associated Press, "Syria: U.S. Envoy Mourns Activist," *New York Times*, September 14, 2011; Max Boot, "Confirm Robert Ford as Syrian Ambassador," *Los Angeles Times*, September 23, 2011; Human Rights Now, "Syrian Activist Ghayath Mattar Killed in Detention—Show Your Solidarity," Amnesty International USA Web Log, http://blog.amnestyusa.org/iar/syrian-activist-ghayath-mattar-killed-in-detention-show-your-solidarity.

58. Roberta Cohen, "Integrating Human Rights in U.S. Foreign Policy," Brookings Institution, April 2008, 4.

59. Obama, Nobel Peace Prize Ceremony.

60. Kennedy, West Berlin.

61. "Nuclear Test Ban Treaty," John F. Kennedy Presidential Library and Museum, www.jfklibrary.org/JFK/JFK-in-History/Nuclear-Test-Ban-Treaty.aspx.

62. Reagan, West Berlin.

63. "Intermediate-Range Nuclear Forces [INF]," Federation of American Scientists, www.fas.org/nuke/control/inf/index.html.

64. At a late 2009 conference, "Advancing & Defending Democracy," Jeff Gedmin, then-president of Radio Free Europe/Radio Liberty, asked Ali Afshari, an activist for democratic reform in Iran, "[O]ne thing one frequently hears about Iranian oppositionists is that if they get too much help from the West or the wrong sort of help from the West, they're tainted; it's manipulated by the regime; it's not productive, it's counterproductive. Is that true, or are there guidelines or limits that you would advise people in Washington, for example?" Afshari replied, "No, I don't believe that, because the regime always uses that. For example, if you follow the policy of the regime, since 30 years ago, every time a regime sentences—a [member of the opposition, the] regime condemn[s] the opposition as [an] agent of the U.S." See "Voices of Freedom: A Conversation with Dissidents," from "2009 FPI Forum: Advancing & Defending Freedom," September 21–22, 2009, Foreign Policy Initiative, www.foreignpolicyi.org/advancing-and-defending-democracy/voices-of-freedom-a-conversation-with-dissidents.

65. Mihajlo Mihajlov, "Notes of a Survivor," *New Leader*, July 31, 1978, as cited in Arthur M. Schlesinger Jr., "Human Rights and the American Tradition," *Foreign Affairs*, vol. 57, no. 3 (1978): 15.

66. James P. Rubin, "The Principle of the Thing," *Newsweek*, December 5, 2009.

67. "The View from the Gulag: An Interview with Natan Sharansky," *Weekly Standard,* June 21, 2004.

68. Saad Eddin Ibrahim, "Mubarak Must Leave to Save Egypt," *Washington Post,* February 4, 2011.

69. Michael Rubin, "Is American Support for Middle Eastern Dissidents the Kiss of Death?" American Enterprise Institute, Middle Eastern Outlook, December 2006.

70. Saad Eddin Ibrahim, "Obama Is Too Friendly with Tyrants," *Washington Post,* June 15, 2010.

71. Yang Jianli, "Stand Up for Rights, Mr. Obama," *Washington Post,* January 19, 2011.

72. Anwar Ibrahim, "Will Tunisia Be the First Domino?" *Wall Street Journal,* January 26, 2011.

73. Ron Nixon, "U.S. Groups Helped Nurture Arab Uprisings," *New York Times,* April 14, 2011.

74. Charles J. Hanley, "US Training Quietly Nurtured Young Arab Democrats," Huffington Post, March 12, 2011, www.huffingtonpost.com/huff-wires/20110312/ml-mideast-a-little-help.

75. Nixon, "U.S. Groups."

76. Hanley, "US Training."

77. Nixon, "U.S. Groups"; Hanley, "US Training."

78. Hanley, "US Training."

79. Jim Hoagland, "Listen to the Dissidents," *Washington Post,* November 8, 2009.

80. Nicholas D. Kristof, "Thank you, America!" *New York Times,* August 31, 2011.

Chapter Two

Laying the Groundwork: From Truman to LBJ

World War II was over, but America would have little time to bask in the glory of victory. A new enemy soon emerged, and a new "Cold War" divided the world between two superpowers with vastly different ideas about political and civil liberties, the role of government, and the organization of society. With the Soviet Union imposing its hegemony over Eastern Europe and threatening to expand further, the United States would have to meet the challenge of defending freedom and democracy.

Harry S. Truman put the building blocks of U.S. human rights promotion in place, enunciating a U.S. commitment to support "free peoples" who were facing threats from internal and external forces, strengthening the devastated Western European democracies with a bold plan of financial assistance, and establishing a new tool of government called "foreign aid." John Kennedy picked up the mantle both rhetorically and financially. He defended freedom with landmark addresses in Washington and West Berlin, and he reshaped foreign aid with a bold plan that focused assistance more squarely on promoting economic growth and democratic government.

In the early decades of the Cold War, however, the United States also learned the limits of human rights promotion. It could not be everywhere or do everything, nor could it risk a military confrontation with the Soviet Union even as Moscow crushed uprisings for more political and economic freedom behind the Iron Curtain. Washington could not, for instance, realistically stop Moscow from reimposing its will on East Germany in 1953 after worker strikes and riots, on Hungary in 1956 after democratic protests, and on Czechoslovakia in 1968 after the "Prague Spring" of political reform that threatened the premise of communist rule. In the Hungarian case, the United States also learned the risks inherent in human rights promotion. After the broadcasts of Radio Free Europe encouraged the democratic activists to press on and suggested that Washington would intervene, the United States stood aside when Soviet troops arrested, charged, tried, and executed many of the trouble-makers, nourishing an anti-American bitterness across Hungary that would linger for years to come.

U.S. human rights promotion also suffered from the mismatch between America's ideals and its behavior at home. Race, an issue that had dogged America since its founding, took its place at the center of the Cold War. While the United States trumpeted its belief that, in the words of its Declaration of Independence, "all men are created equal" and endowed with unalienable rights to "Life, Liberty and the pursuit of Happiness," it was refusing those rights to its darker-skinned citizens. Lynchings, mob beatings, and other violence against blacks tarnished America's image on the world stage; threatened U.S. relations with countries across Asia, Africa, and Latin America; and gave the Soviet Union a major tool of propaganda as it competed with the United States for the loyalty of nations across the Third World. As Presidents Truman, Eisenhower, Kennedy, and Johnson took steps to advance civil rights, they were keenly aware that race was an albatross around the neck of U.S. foreign policy.

A PRELUDE TO HUMAN RIGHTS

It was late in the afternoon of April 12, 1945. Vice President Truman had finished presiding in his largely ceremonial role as president of the Senate and was about to have drinks in the office of House Speaker Sam Rayburn, a pal from Truman's days as a senator from Missouri. White House secretary Steve Early called Rayburn to ask that he tell Truman to return quickly to the White House. By the time Truman arrived at Rayburn's office, Early had already tracked him down. Truman turned to say goodbye, muttered "Jesus Christ and General Jackson" out of fears of what he might find at the White House, and rushed to the waiting car.

Directed upstairs to President Roosevelt's private quarters, Truman was met by Eleanor Roosevelt.

"Harry, the president is dead," Eleanor said.

"Is there anything I can do for you?" Truman asked the new widow.

"Is there anything we can do for you, Harry?" she replied. "For you are the one in trouble now."

Truman felt the same way. "I'm not big enough. I'm not big enough for this job," he told his friend, Vermont senator George Aiken, the next day. "I feel like I have been struck by a bolt of lightning," he said by phone to perhaps his closest friend, John W. Snyder, vice president of the First National Bank of St. Louis. After a lunch on Capitol Hill, he told reporters, "Boys, if you ever pray, pray for me now. I don't know whether you fellows ever had a load of hay fall on you, but when they told me yesterday what had happened, I felt like the moon, the stars and all the planets had fallen on me. I've got the most terribly responsible job a man ever had."[1]

His fears reflected more than personal insecurity. Professionally speaking, Truman was ill prepared for the challenges ahead. He had met only twice with Roosevelt in the eighty-three days in which he was vice president, and their conversations had been inconsequential. He knew nothing of FDR's thinking on issues related to a postwar world, nor did he even know about the Manhattan Project to build the atomic bomb (a bomb that Truman would use several months later to force Japan's surrender).

But if he lacked knowledge about U.S. plans and capacity, Truman had an unmistakable instinct about America's new adversary in the Cold War. In mid-1941, as the Soviet Union was battling fiercely to rebuff a Nazi invasion, he told a reporter, "If we see that Germany is winning we ought to help Russia and if Russia is winning we ought to help Germany and that way let them kill as many as possible, although I don't want to see Hitler victorious under any circumstances. Neither of them thinks anything of their pledged word."[2] The events that immediately followed World War II did nothing to change his mind, as Allied victory over the Axis Powers was replaced by U.S.-Soviet tensions over the postwar world. The free elections that Soviet leader Josef Stalin had promised for Eastern Europe were not occurring, with the Soviets installing puppet governments there instead.

Just eleven days after Truman assumed the presidency, Soviet Foreign Minister Vyacheslav Molotov, who was on his way to San Francisco for the United Nations founding conference, dropped by the White House to see Truman about the U.S.-Soviet dispute over Poland. Truman thought Stalin had agreed to free elections there, but Stalin was installing a communist government. Truman dressed down Molotov bluntly, expressing his unhappiness with Soviet actions in Eastern Europe. A startled Molotov blurted, "I have never been talked to like that in my life." Without missing a beat, Truman replied, "Carry out your agreements and you won't be talked to like that."[3]

So, Truman had no illusions about the daunting challenges ahead. On one hand, he needed to prevent the mounting U.S.-Soviet tensions from escalating into another world war—a war that many officials in Washington and average Americans across the country not only feared but also expected. On the other hand, he needed to protect the United States and its interests abroad, to support the ravaged democracies of Western Europe and fend off the expansionary impulses of Soviet-led communism, and to build a postwar architecture that would promote the advance of freedom and democracy.

FDR had spoken eloquently about his dreams for the future. In his State of the Union Address of January 1941, he envisioned a postwar world that guaranteed "four freedoms" for all people, wherever they lived, whatever their current plight:

> The first is freedom of speech and expression—everywhere in the world. The second is freedom of every person to worship God in his own way—everywhere in the world. The third is freedom from want, which, translated into world terms, means economic understandings which will secure to every nation a healthy peacetime life for its inhabitants—everywhere in the world. The fourth is freedom from fear, which, translated into world terms, means a world-wide reduction of armaments to such a point and in such a thorough fashion that no nation will be in a position to commit an act of physical aggression against any neighbor—anywhere in the world.[4]

FDR would have no opportunity to bring this world to pass. After complaining of a headache on that monumental day in early 1945, he collapsed and died of a cerebral hemorrhage while sitting behind a desk at his retreat in Warm Springs, Georgia. It would be left to his successor to build a better world after the horrors of a second world war. It would be left to Truman—a short, bespectacled, unassuming haberdasher from Kansas City, Missouri, by way of Lamar, Grandview, and Independence—to craft the vision, build the architecture, and enunciate the doctrine that would advance human rights.

The landmark moment came on March 12, 1947, as Truman addressed a joint session of Congress.

TRUMAN'S DOCTRINE

Great Britain had ruled the world for most of the previous century, with such far-flung holdings that, it was said, "The sun never sets on the British Empire." But by the late 1940s, after a world war in which it had first stood alone against a Nazi blitzkrieg and then joined the United States and Soviet Union to defeat the Axis Powers, the once-proud empire was tired and broke. It could harbor no realistic hope of reclaiming its glory. In late winter of 1947, British leaders sent word to Washington that their nation could no longer play its longstanding global role and provide the needed financial support for Greece and Turkey, which were desperate for assistance.[5] If those nations on the Mediterranean Sea were to remain in the camp of free nations, the United States would have to provide the aid.

The tectonic plates of international relations were shifting, with leadership of the free world passing from London to Washington—if the latter would grab it. Truman's top aides agreed that it must do so. "The United

Kingdom had historically served as the gyroscope of world order, managing the international economic system, keeping the sea-lanes open, and protecting the balance of power in the chief geostrategic theaters of the world," historian Walter Russell Mead explained. "Truman administration officials agreed that the Great Depression and World War II could in large part be blamed on the United States' failure to take up the burden of global leadership as the United Kingdom declined. The Soviet disruption of the balance of power in Europe and the Middle East after World War II was, they believed, exactly the kind of challenge to world order that the United States now had to meet."[6]

Truman knew the stakes, but he faced long odds for rallying his nation around a larger global role. For one thing, the Democratic president was facing a Congress that was now in Republican hands after mid-term congressional elections of a year earlier—elections before which the GOP had asked Americans whether they had "had enough" of postwar inflation and more than a decade of Democratic rule. For another, Truman was facing a public that increasingly found him wanting, an inadequate successor to FDR, ill fit for the job. "To err is Truman" was a popular slogan of the day.

Moreover, Americans were plainly weary of global involvement. As they had done before and would do again after engaging in war, the American people sought to turn their attention to the more mundane tasks of work and family. "I can state in three sentences what the 'popular' attitude is toward foreign policy today," Assistant Secretary of State Dean Acheson told the Maryland Historical Society in November 1945. "1. Bring the boys home. 2. Don't be a Santa Claus. 3. Don't be pushed around."[7] The long-time diplomat and presidential advisor, Averill Harriman, put it more succinctly, saying Americans wanted to "go to the movies and drink Coke."[8]

In early 1947, Truman met with congressional leaders to outline the international challenges and seek their support for an aggressive U.S. global posture. Attendees included Michigan's Republican senator, Arthur Vandenberg, chairman of the Senate Foreign Relations Committee. Vandenberg had been a strident isolationist, one who believed U.S. entry into World War I had been a disaster and who had encouraged U.S. neutrality in the 1930s as the countries of Europe prepared for war. But Vandenberg had since undergone a public conversion from isolationism to global involvement. During the meeting, he told Truman that he supported his effort. But he also said that, if the president hoped to win congressional support for the effort, he needed to do something else: "make a personal appearance before Congress and scare the hell out of the country."[9]

And so, in March 1947, twenty-three months to the day after he had assumed the presidency, Truman took his case to the people. Speaking in the House chamber to a joint session of Congress, he reviewed the situation in Greece, a country that was ravaged by the retreating Nazi forces at the end of

World War II, that desperately needed financial and other assistance, and that was threatened "by the terrorist activities of several thousand armed men, led by communists, who defy the government's authority at a number of points, particularly along the northern boundaries."[10] He reviewed the situation in Turkey, which also desperately needed financial support.

"One of the primary objectives of the foreign policy of the United States," Truman explained, putting the crises of Greece and Turkey into a broader context,

> is the creation of conditions in which we and other nations will be able to work out a way of life free from coercion. This was a fundamental issue in the war with Germany and Japan. Our victory was won over countries which sought to impose their will, and their way of life, upon other nations. . . . We shall not realize our objectives, however, unless we are willing to help free peoples to maintain their free institutions and their national integrity against aggressive movements that seek to impose upon them totalitarian regimes. This is no more than a frank recognition that totalitarian regimes imposed on free peoples, by direct or indirect aggression, undermine the foundations of international peace and hence the security of the United States. [11]

The world, Truman went on, was now divided between two forms of governance—in essence, two different visions for human rights:

> One way of life is based upon the will of the majority, and is distinguished by free institutions, representative government, free elections, guarantees of individual liberty, freedom of speech and religion, and freedom from political oppression. The second way of life is based upon the will of a minority forcibly imposed upon the majority. It relies upon terror and oppression, a controlled press and radio, fixed elections, and the suppression of personal freedoms. [12]

With so much at stake, Truman argued, the United States must step up. In what would become known as the Truman Doctrine, he declared, "I believe that it must be the policy of the United States to support free peoples who are resisting attempted subjugation by armed minorities or by outside pressures. I believe that we must assist free peoples to work out their own destinies in their own way."[13]

It was a defining moment for U.S. human rights promotion. Truman proposed bold U.S. leadership, sustained support for fledgling democracies, and determined opposition to the spread of totalitarianism. "The free peoples of the world look to us for support in maintaining their freedoms," he declared. "If we falter in our leadership, we may endanger the peace of the world—and we shall surely endanger the welfare of our own nation."[14] Truman's vision echoed Wilson's call to "make the world safe for democracy," but it also proved more durable. For while Wilson's dream largely died in the corridors of Congress and the power centers of Europe, Truman's vision laid the groundwork upon which presidents would build for years to come.

Also laying the groundwork upon which later presidents would build, Truman asked Congress for $400 million to assist Greece and Turkey over the course of fifteen months. Those dollars would prove a precursor to a category of annual spending known as "foreign aid," the military and economic assistance that every subsequent president and Congress have allocated routinely to scores of nations in order to advance U.S. interests. Foreign aid has been a key tool of human rights promotion ever since. The nation's leaders allocate it to strengthen free and democratic nations and to support groups that are working for freedom and democracy in authoritarian lands. They also deny aid to authoritarian governments to pressure those governments to change their ways.

Before foreign aid became a regular piece of the federal budget, however, Truman asked Congress for a separate, temporary, but huge program of aid for the struggling democracies of Western Europe. The proposal was so big, it seemed so out of tune with public desires to focus the nation's resources on domestic needs, that Truman would pursue an extraordinary strategy for making it public.

MARSHALL'S PLAN

Truman was a savvy political operative. He had ascended the ranks of local and state officialdom through the Pendergast machine that ruled Kansas City and Jackson County, Missouri. He understood that, in politics, authorship matters. A polarizing or unpopular figure, which the president clearly was in early 1947, would have less of a chance to pry big bucks out of a Republican-controlled Congress than an esteemed, larger-than-life public servant.

And so it was that Secretary of State George C. Marshall came to stand before the graduating class of Harvard University on June 5, 1947. Marshall had served as the Army's chief of staff during World War II and was FDR's top military advisor. Churchill had labeled him the "organizer of victory."[15] In the popular imagination, he was a larger-than-life figure, above politics and beyond reproach. Walking to the graduation ceremony, surrounded by Harvard officials bedecked in robes, he wore a three-piece suit, a handkerchief in his breast pocket, and a solemn look on his face.

In strikingly blunt remarks, he termed the "world situation . . . very serious," described the "dislocation of the entire fabric of European economy" from the loss of life and destruction of cities, factories, mines, and railroads, and concluded that "the rehabilitation of the economic structure of

Europe quite evidently will require a much longer time and greater effort than had been foreseen."[16] The people of Europe needed food and fuel, and their governments were forced to use their scarce cash to buy it, rather than invest in their countries' reconstruction, Marshall explained. The demands of these nations would continue for the next several years to outstrip their ability to pay, so Europe needed additional assistance to get back on its feet. Only the United States could provide it.

This, Marshall said, would be a partnership between the United States and Europe. Rather than impose its own solution on Europe, Washington would work with its counterparts in London, Paris, and other capitals to draft a program that would most effectively spur a European economic revival. Once the program was in place, the United States would provide the requisite financial aid to support it. Washington would help any nation that would cooperate in this venture, not just the Western European allies but the Soviet Union and its satellites as well. (The Soviet bloc declined the offer.)

As Truman did in enunciating his doctrine and requesting aid for Greece and Turkey, Marshall placed his plan in the context of broader U.S. interests. European recovery would not just provide new markets for American goods, strengthening America's economy. It would make the world a safer, more peaceful place, which would strengthen America's national security. In essence, U.S. economic and financial aid would promote freedom and democracy, advancing human rights and peace in the process.

> Aside from the demoralizing effect on the world at large and the possibilities of disturbances arising as a result of the desperation of the people concerned, the consequences to the economy of the United States should be apparent to all. It is logical that the United States should do whatever it is able to do to assist in the return of normal economic health in the world, without which there can be no political stability and no assured peace.[17]

It was an enormous request. In the legislation that he sent Congress in late 1947, Truman proposed $17 billion for the four years from April 1948 to June 30, 1952.[18] That would come on top of the $10 billion to $20 billion in emergency aid that the United States had already provided to its Western European allies since the end of World War II. Truman was seeking an enormous increase in federal spending not to invest at home but to rescue other nations on a continent that was an ocean away.[19]

The president and his aides clearly thought that Western Europe's future was at stake, that its governments might collapse if they could not respond to the widespread hardship, that the desperate citizens of France, Italy, and elsewhere who lacked food and shelter could well opt for communism if they did not see more tangible benefits from Western-style capitalism. In America, where isolationist fever was running high and people were focused on home and family, this was no easy sell. But, after months of wrangling,

Congress came through, enacting a slimmed-down version of the Marshall Plan in the early spring of 1948, providing $13 billion to Europe through the end of 1951.[20]

It was an undisputed success. By the time the Marshall Plan was fully implemented, the economies of Western Europe had grown significantly beyond their pre-war levels—and, over the next two decades, Western Europe would enjoy the fruits of sustained prosperity and rising living standards. At a time of severe hardship and political vulnerability for tens of millions of people across Western Europe, the United States came through with a dramatic program of aid that did more than rescue their devastated economies. In the end, it protected their human rights as well.

To be sure, the Marshall Plan was an extraordinary example of U.S. largesse. (In later decades, proponents of great causes—e.g., saving the earth from environmental degradation or saving America's cities from creeping decay—often tried to elevate their cause by calling for a second "Marshall Plan" of some kind.) But if the sums have not been matched since by any single piece of global assistance, the idea of allocating financial assistance to advance freedom and strengthen democracy was one that would take root and endure.

As the Marshall Plan was ending in 1951, Congress was creating the architecture for the more permanent program of foreign aid, one that came to fruition with the Mutual Security Act of 1951 and its operating arm, the Mutual Security Agency.[21] Progress ensued. The Foreign Operations Administration, created in 1953 as an independent agency and directed by Harold Stassen to centralize all federal economic and military aid programs, was merged a year later into the State Department's International Cooperation Administration. Foreign aid grew more sophisticated and more targeted over time. The Mutual Security Act of 1954 originated the concepts of "development assistance, security assistance, a discretionary contingency fund, and guarantees for private investments."[22] Also that year, policymakers implemented the Food for Peace program. The Mutual Security Act of 1957 laid the foundation for a new Development Loan Fund to provide loans in local currency, which neither the Export-Import Bank nor other donors were offering.

From those earliest days, foreign aid has been integral to U.S. foreign policy and, as such, has reflected its overarching goals. From the mid-1940s to the late 1980s, policymakers allocated foreign aid mostly to fight the Cold War as effectively as possible. After the Soviet collapse, George H. W. Bush and Clinton steered foreign aid to address the regional challenges of their tenures. In the aftermath of September 11, George W. Bush and Obama shifted aid significantly to the war on terror.[23]

As the 1950s ended, however, foreign aid was adrift. It would take a new man in the Oval Office to give it a more focused purpose.

KENNEDY UPS THE ANTE

Campaigning for president, John F. Kennedy issued a battle cry to "get this country moving again." Once in office, he exuded energy and promised action. On human rights, he built on the foundations laid by Truman and maintained by Eisenhower, drawing sharp and dramatic distinctions between the free and communist worlds and refashioning foreign aid so that it could better advance U.S. efforts to promote freedom and democracy and build stronger U.S. ties to the Third World.

From Truman's description of a world split between two dramatically different visions of government and society, from his critique of totalitarianism as a fundamentally destabilizing force in world affairs, and from his call for U.S. human rights promotion in the interests of morality and national self-interest, it was but a short rhetorical step to some of Kennedy's most stirring moments. Two of his best came less than three weeks apart, in June 1963—five months before the young president was gunned down.

Speaking about peace at American University in Washington, he said, "As Americans, we find communism profoundly repugnant as a negation of personal freedom and dignity," adding, "The communist drive to impose their political and economic system on others is the primary cause of world tension today. For there can be no doubt that, if all nations could refrain from interfering in the self-determination of others, the peace would be much more assured."[24]

Then, on a windswept day in Germany, Kennedy delivered perhaps the most stirring call for human rights of any American president.

Berlin was the most dangerous flashpoint of the Cold War.[25] It was where the Soviet Union imposed a blockade on the city's western section in 1948, hoping to pressure the United States to abandon the city, and where Truman ordered an airlift of food and supplies that continued for eleven months until Moscow reopened the gates.[26] It was where Moscow, seeking to stem the tide of Germans who were leaving the communist East for the free West, built the Berlin Wall in 1961. It was where East and West faced one another most dramatically, and where the superpowers almost came to military blows.

West Berliners were thrilled by Kennedy's visit. "To catch a glimpse of their American hero, Berliners were hanging from trees and lampposts and standing on rooftops and balconies. The Red Cross, which had mobilized to handle casualties in the crowd, would report that more than a thousand people fainted."[27]

Kennedy first toured the Berlin Wall, which must have incited a swirl of emotions within him. The Soviets had constructed it on his watch, but at the time the president was as relieved as he was outraged. He had been worrying that the U.S.-Soviet stand-off over Berlin could trigger a war. He also had concluded that, with so many people fleeing East Germany for West Berlin, the Soviets understandably would have to do something to stop the flow or East Germany would collapse, followed by Poland and the rest of the Eastern European satellites. Just days before the Soviets built it, Kennedy told an aide, Walt Rostow, that a wall was a real possibility. After it arose, he said, "It's not a very nice solution, but a wall is a hell of a lot better than a war."[28]

When Kennedy took the stage for his speech, three hundred thousand were waiting to hear him. The grainy black-and-white video from that day shows the president leaning forward somewhat awkwardly from behind his podium; perhaps his ailing back was acting up. He stood with his arms bent at the elbow, his hands in front of him, both of them clutching the index cards that contained his remarks.

"Two thousand years ago," Kennedy began with a slow, dramatic cadence, "two thousand years ago, the proudest boast was 'civis Romanus sum [I am a Roman citizen].' Today, in the world of freedom, the proudest boast is 'Ich bin ein Berliner [I am a Berliner].'"[29] After rousing cheers, Kennedy continued:

> There are many people in the world who really don't understand, or say they don't, what is the great issue between the free world and the communist world. Let them come to Berlin. [Cheers] There are some who say that communism is the wave of the future. Let them come to Berlin. [Cheers] And there are some who say in Europe and elsewhere we can work with the communists. Let them come to Berlin. [Cheers] And there are even a few who say that it's true that communism is an evil system, but it permits us to make economic progress. "Laßt sie nach Berlin kommen." Let them come to Berlin! [Cheers][30]

"Freedom has many difficulties," Kennedy next acknowledged, "and democracy is not perfect. But, we have never had to put a wall up to keep our people in, to prevent them from leaving us."[31] "You live in a defended island of freedom," he told the people of West Berlin, "but your life is part of the main."

> So let me ask you, as I close, to lift your eyes beyond the dangers of today to the hopes of tomorrow, beyond the freedom merely of this city of Berlin, or your country of Germany, to the advance of freedom everywhere, beyond the wall to the day of peace with justice, beyond yourselves and ourselves to all mankind. Freedom is indivisible, and when one man is enslaved, all are not free. When all are free, then we can look forward to that day when this city will be joined as one, and this country, and this great Continent of Europe, in a peaceful and hopeful globe. When that day finally comes, as it will, the people of West Berlin can take sober satisfaction in the fact that they were in the front

lines for almost two decades. All free men, wherever they may live, are citizens of Berlin, and, therefore, as a free man, I take pride in the words: Ich bin ein Berliner. [32]

The words were stirring; the delivery, magnificent. It was a moment that many in the crowd would remember for the rest of their lives. But, as Kennedy knew, stirring words were but one element of human rights promotion. Words could inspire those around the world who sought more freedom and democracy. Words could put authoritarian governments on the defensive. Words alone, however, could not improve the lives of hundreds of millions of people around the world whose loyalties were the object of fierce U.S.-Soviet competition. Dollars were important as well.

By the time Kennedy assumed office, congressional and public support for foreign aid was falling. Kennedy, however, was committed to this tool of human rights promotion, so he proposed a dramatic overhaul. The foreign aid bureaucracy was too fragmented, he argued, while the purposes behind different programs were sometimes contradictory, other times obsolete. Foreign aid remained an important element of national security, he said, an important way to promote freedom and democracy. We needed not less of it, he said, but more. The problem was that, as structured, it wasn't working.

"[T]here is no escaping our obligations," Kennedy said, in words that echoed the twin motives of morality and self-interest that Truman had articulated.

> [O]ur moral obligations as a wise leader and good neighbor in the interdependent community of free nations—our economic obligations as the wealthiest people in a world of largely poor people, as a nation no longer dependent upon the loans from abroad that once helped us develop our own economy—and our political obligations as the single largest counter to the adversaries of freedom. To fail to meet those obligations now would be disastrous; and, in the long run, more expensive. For widespread poverty and chaos lead to a collapse of existing political and social structures which would inevitably invite the advance of totalitarianism into every weak and unstable area. Thus our own security would be endangered and our prosperity imperiled. A program of assistance to the underdeveloped nations must continue because the nation's interest and the cause of political freedom require it. [33]

Kennedy's call to arms led to the landmark Foreign Assistance Act of 1961, which created the United States Agency for International Development (USAID) to coordinate all economic assistance programs. The legislation called for a Development Loan Fund; a Development Grant Fund; a guaranty program that has since become the Overseas Private Investment Corporation; a supporting assistance program that has since become the Economic Support Fund; and a contingency fund. The act steered the focus of foreign aid to long-term projects that would promote economic growth and democratic government, with each project tailored to the particular circumstances of individual nations and with the entire effort designed to prevent the spread of communism.

In later years, foreign aid would continue to prove controversial despite the many efforts to update and improve it, to adjust its components to the twists and turns of U.S. foreign policy. In every era, many Americans questioned why Washington was helping other nations when the United States had its own unmet needs, from urban decay and rural poverty to failing schools and crumbling roads. Presidents and Congresses would battle mightily over foreign aid, proving the adage that "where you stand depends on where you sit." A president (as the nation's chief diplomat) would routinely seek more foreign aid to advance the nation's global goals than Congress (a collection of lawmakers, each focused on the parochial concerns of constituents) would want to provide.

Foreign aid, however, was hardly the only, or even the most, controversial tool of human rights promotion. It paled in comparison to the wrenching question of whether the nation should use military force to assist the people of foreign lands who were seeking freedom and democracy—and, if so, when.

THE CHALLENGE OF INTERVENTION

Presidents enunciate foreign policy doctrines that set goals and outline conditions for U.S. action, military or otherwise.

As we have seen, Truman established a policy of "support[ing] free peoples who are resisting attempted subjugation by armed minorities or by outside pressures." Kennedy vowed that America would "pay any price, bear any burden, meet any hardship, support any friend, oppose any foe, to assure the survival and the success of liberty."[34] Carter pledged, after the Soviets invaded Afghanistan in December 1979, that "an attempt by any outside force to gain control of the Persian Gulf region will be regarded as an assault on the vital interests of the United States of America, and such an assault will be repelled by any means necessary, including military force."[35] George W. Bush announced, after September 11, that "from this day forward, any nation that continues to harbor or support terrorism will be regarded by the United States as a hostile regime."[36]

Doctrines are one thing, their application in particular situations sometimes quite another, however. U.S. action carries risks, and presidents calibrate risks against rewards, weigh short-term versus long-term goals, assess the national appetite for aggressiveness, and consider the nation's financial and military resources. When risks outweigh rewards, U.S. efforts to carry human rights promotion to its logical end—to use military force to support the people of other nations who are facing repression—can fall by the wayside. Even the world's greatest military power has to pick its spots carefully.

As the Cold War took shape in the late 1940s, Truman pursued a version of the "containment" strategy that senior State Department official George Kennan propounded in his "long telegram" from Moscow in February 1946 and then in an anonymous essay in *Foreign Affairs* in July 1947.[37] In the latter, he wrote,

> [I]t is clear that the main element of any United States policy toward the Soviet Union must be that of a long-term, patient but firm and vigilant containment of Russian expansive tendencies . . . it will be clearly seen that the Soviet pressure against the free institutions of the Western world is something that can be contained by the adroit and vigilant application of counterforce at a series of constantly shifting geographical and political points, corresponding to the shifts and maneuvers of Soviet policy, but which cannot be charmed or talked out of existence.[38]

Though it did not formally accept Soviet hegemony over Eastern Europe—indeed, much of U.S. foreign policy for four decades was designed to weaken Moscow's grip on its satellites—Washington would not use force to topple the puppet governments. What it would do, instead, was "contain" Soviet efforts to expand its sphere of influence beyond the postwar borders. Sending U.S. troops to protect South Korea and South Vietnam from communist takeovers from the north was one thing. Sending them to free the people of East Germany, Hungary, or Czechoslovakia was quite another.

It was June 1953. Moscow was still distracted by Stalin's death of three months earlier when trouble broke out in one of the supposed "worker paradises" of the Soviet sphere, this one in East Germany. Seeking to boost a weak national economy that was producing far less food and other goods than East German families wanted, the government raised production quotas for workers; in essence, they would work harder for the same pay. Thousands gathered in Berlin to protest, and protests soon spread to more than four hundred cities, towns, and villages across the country. As the demonstrations swelled in size, participants expanded their demands from the economic to the political. They called for free elections and chanted such threatening slogans as "Death to Communism" and "Love Live Eisenhower."[39]

It was the first serious internal threat to Soviet-backed rule in Eastern Europe, and East Germany's government seemed to be losing control. Moscow awoke from its post-Stalin slumbers and sent tanks and troops to quell the uprising, opening fire and killing many demonstrators. Before long, the demonstrations ended and order was restored. West Germany, expressing a familial affinity with its brethren to the east, commemorated the uprising by establishing a national holiday for June 17. Over the years, German writers, poets, and singers have paid homage to the uprising. Though crushed in brutal fashion, it sent an important signal across both the free and communist worlds that perhaps the Soviet grip on its satellites was not as strong as many had assumed.

In Washington during the uprising, anti-Soviet hardliners pushed for aggressive action, with some officials even seeking to "encourage elimination of key puppet officials." But President Eisenhower feared that overly aggressive action within the Soviet sphere risked a U.S. war with its Cold War adversary. Human rights would have to take a back seat to peace. Washington spoke out forcefully against Moscow's actions, provided some covert aid to the rebels, and launched a food distribution program that brought significant relief to East Germany's people. But Washington would go no further.

Three years later, Moscow faced an even more serious threat, this one from Hungary. The new Soviet leader, Nikita Khrushchev, had consolidated his authority in the Kremlin, pushing aside other aspirants to replace Stalin. In February 1956, he denounced Stalin in a speech to a closed session of the Soviets' Communist Party, launching the "de-Stalinization" policy that brought hope for more freedom and democracy across Eastern Europe and prompted demonstrations in Poland and Hungary.[40] Momentum accelerated in Hungary, in particular, where demonstrations expanded and the public grew emboldened. Students, workers, and soldiers battled with the nation's secret police and with Soviet troops, neither of whom could quell the protests. By October, rebel forces were achieving inspiring, even unfathomable, victories on the ground, often defeating Soviet forces while using only kitchen utensils for weapons.

Rather than dampen public expectations for more freedom, Hungary's government fueled the fire. It released thousands of political prisoners and, in late October, selected the popular Imre Nagy as prime minister. Even more surprising, Moscow eventually seemed resigned to the changes. Upon assuming office, Nagy asked Khrushchev to remove Soviet troops from Hungary and the latter agreed, pulling the Soviet army out of Budapest within days. On October 31, the state-run Soviet newspaper, *Pravda*, published a declaration that promised more equality between the Soviet Union and its satellites. "[T]he Soviet Government," it read, "is prepared to enter into the appropriate negotiations with the government of the Hungarian People's Republic and other members of the Warsaw Treaty on the question of the presence of Soviet troops on the territory of Hungary." Western observers were flabbergasted, with CIA Director Allen Dulles calling Moscow's promise "a miracle."[41]

There would be no miracle, however. De-Stalinization was one thing; a threat to Soviet hegemony was quite another. Moscow grew concerned that the unrest would spread across Eastern Europe, threatening the edifice of Soviet control, and that the West would view Soviet inaction as a sign of weakness. By the time Nagy announced in early November that he would pull Hungary out of the Warsaw Pact and appealed for UN and Western help to guarantee Hungary neutrality, Soviet leaders had decided to reverse course. In the early morning of November 4, Moscow sent its forces into Hungary. The air force bombed Budapest while more than one thousand tanks entered the capital by land. The fighting largely ended within days, with the democratic forces defeated and tens of thousands killed. Nagy sought asylum in Yugoslavia's embassy in Budapest. Promised that he would face no retribution, he left the embassy, only to be immediately arrested by Soviet forces, flown to Romania, and later tried and executed. In the ensuing years, the Soviet-backed government executed or imprisoned thousands more. The mere mention of Nagy's name in public could bring severe punishment.

Eisenhower, who would win a sweeping reelection just two days after the Soviet invasion, faced the same dilemma as with East Germany. Anti-Soviet hardliners within and outside his administration again pushed for action. But here as well, the United States could do little that would help the rebels succeed—short of risking war with the Soviet Union. "And he was not prepared to go that far," Malcolm Byrne wrote later, "nor even, for that matter, to jeopardize the atmosphere of improving relations with Moscow that had characterized the previous period."[42] It was another prudent, though painful, compromise on human rights.

Then it was Czechoslovakia's turn, this time in 1968. That January, Alexander Dubcek replaced long-time communist hardliner Antonin Novotny as first secretary of the Czechoslovak Communist Party, and he promised "radical reforms and 'socialism with a human face.'" By summer, the government had lifted censorship, allowing for open discussion in newspapers, magazines, and literary journals. The reform movement became known as the "Prague Spring" and, as in East Germany and Hungary in the previous decade, the movement seemed to threaten the very *raison d'être* of Soviet rule. The West was delighted, the Soviet bloc enraged. Moscow's allies in East Germany, Poland, and other Eastern European nations pressured the Kremlin to act.[43]

In the early morning hours of August 21, a half-million troops from the Soviet Union, Bulgaria, East Germany, Hungary, and Poland moved on Czechoslovakia.[44] On state radio, Dubcek's government made clear that it had not invited them in. In Prague, people waved Czech flags and makeshift signs that read, "Go Home" and "Why Are You Shooting At Us?" Some residents climbed on the incoming tanks, demanding to know why they were there. Among them was Czechoslovakia's most famous athlete, Emil Zatopek, the distance runner who had broken world records and won Olympic gold. State radio went underground, broadcasting for several days while Soviet soldiers searched for its location.[45]

Before long, Warsaw Pact troops had restored order, leaving 108 dead and almost 500 injured.[46] The new Soviet-backed government imposed what became known as the "normalization." The Soviets seized Dubcek and the other Communist Party leaders, flew them to Moscow, kept them under house arrest, and forced them to sign the Moscow Protocols, "which legitimized the Soviet occupation and annulled all the reforms of the Prague Spring." The authorities then asked millions of average people across the country to sign statements that welcomed Moscow's "brotherly" assistance; those who refused lost their jobs, party memberships, and other benefits. Soviet troops remained in Czechoslovakia for the next two decades to prevent further trouble.

At the time, U.S.-Soviet relations were warming. President Johnson had met the previous year with Soviet Premier Alexei Kosygin in Glassboro, New Jersey, nurturing what came to be called the "spirit of Glassboro." As Richard V. Allen, foreign policy coordinator for the 1968 Republican presidential candidate, Richard Nixon, wrote later, "In the West, and especially in the United States, most pundits, specialists, and policymakers had agreed that the Soviets would not dare risk the universal condemnation that would accompany such a drastic course. Most believed the Soviets would not put at risk the economic, trade, and other benefits that détente conferred."[47] Nevertheless they did, simply because Moscow could not afford to lose control of a country within its sphere. For all the old reasons and now for a new one—its own troubles in Vietnam—the United States could do little as the Soviet Union suppressed any talk of greater human rights.

Three uprisings. Three defeats. Moscow maintained control, reinforcing Soviet-style communism over Eastern Europe and denying freedom and democracy to tens of millions of people for years to come. The United States largely stood back. For all its talk of advancing human rights, for all of FDR's vision of a postwar world of "four freedoms," for all of JFK's promise to "pay any price, bear any burden," Washington had no realistic way to push any of the uprisings over the goal line without risking war with Moscow. It would settle for exploiting the example of Moscow's behavior in the continuing U.S.-Soviet competition for friends across the Third World.

With regard to Hungary, Washington came under fierce attack over more than its military inaction. The problem was the signals that the United States had sent to the protestors through other channels. The U.S. government had long sought to weaken Soviet control over Eastern Europe through TV and radio broadcasts, and it created the Voice of America in 1942, Radio Free Europe in 1949, and Radio Liberty in 1951 for that purpose.[48] They were designed to give Eastern Europeans access to the news and information that they were denied under communist rule. In the heady days of Hungary's insurrection, some of Radio Free Europe's broadcasts suggested that Washington would provide more support. When the Soviets stepped in and Washington did not, the Hungarian people were bitterly disappointed, leaving a trail of anger that lingered for decades.[49]

Later, Radio Free Europe was concerned enough about the criticism that it launched an internal investigation. In a report dated December 5, 1956, its political adviser, William Griffith, wrote that while he found "few genuine violations of policy," he noted several instances in which broadcasts encouraged the Hungarian people to continue fighting, provided instructions on how to do so, and implied that U.S. help was on the way.[50]

"If the Soviet troops really attack Hungary," a November 4 broadcast stated, "if our expectations should hold true and Hungarians hold out for three or four days, then the pressure upon the government of the United States to send military help to the Freedom Fighters will become irresistible. . . . The reports from London, Paris, the U.S. and other Western reports show that the world's reaction to Hungarian events surpasses every imagination. In the Western capitals, a practical manifestation of Western sympathy is expected at any hour."[51]

It was not the last time that Washington would encourage others to join an uprising, offer hints of U.S. intervention, and leave blood on its hands by standing back as the authorities responded with violence. As discussed in chapter 4, it would happen again in 1991 when the United States led an international coalition to push Iraq out of Kuwait and U.S. leaders encouraged the Iraqi people to remove Saddam Hussein from power—only to stand aside when Saddam slaughtered the would-be revolutionaries.

Though failures in their day, the uprisings in East Germany, Hungary, and Czechoslovakia proved important down the road. They built a moral case against communism, tarnished Moscow's global reputation, exposed the inherent instability of authoritarian rule, nourished a constituency for protest behind the Iron Curtain, and left a legacy on which the protestors' successors would build. The brave workers and farmers, housewives and students, of 1953, 1956, and 1968 laid the foundation for the uprisings of later years in Czechoslovakia, Poland, and elsewhere that culminated in the overthrow of communist rule in the late 1980s.

Where Washington could provide neither troops nor dollars to promote human rights, it would hope to set an example for the world by promoting its ideals. When, however, the United States did not live up to those ideals at home, it faced charges of hypocrisy, delivering a severe blow to its human rights promotion efforts. On no problem did the charge of hypocrisy stick more forcefully than that of race.

PERILS OF A "GOLDFISH BOWL"

When you think about the civil rights movement, the name John Foster Dulles[52] does not often come to mind.

Born on February 25, 1888, in Washington, DC, the eldest son of a Presbyterian minister, Dulles was a Phi Beta Kappa graduate of Princeton University who later received his law degree from George Washington Law School and served as an international lawyer with the prestigious New York firm of Sullivan & Cromwell. With his uncle, Robert Lansing, serving as Woodrow Wilson's secretary of state, Dulles caught the bug of public service. Wilson appointed him legal counsel to the U.S. delegation to the Versailles peace talks after World War I, where he worked under his uncle. He was chief foreign policy advisor to Thomas E. Dewey, the Republican presidential candidate, in 1944 and an advisor to influential Republican senator Arthur H. Vandenberg. He attended the United Nations founding conference in San Francisco in 1945, helped write the preamble to the UN Charter, and served as a U.S. delegate to the General Assembly in 1946, 1947, and 1950. Dewey, New York's governor, appointed him to fill a vacant U.S. Senate seat in 1949, but he lost his subsequent electoral bid to win the seat outright.

Dulles was one of America's leading Cold War hardliners. In his 1950 book, *War or Peace*, he argued that the nation should replace "containment" with a policy of rolling back the Soviet empire and liberating its people. Eisenhower appointed Dulles secretary of state, a position he held from 1953 until 1959 and from which he built a series of regional alliances through which the United States pledged with other nations to take collective action to confront aggression (presumably, Soviet-driven aggression). He did not reserve his animus only for Soviet communism, however; he allegedly refused to shake hands with Communist China's Zhou En Lai at the 1954 Geneva Conference on Indochina.

But in late 1957, it was a high-profile civil rights battle in Little Rock, Arkansas, that had Dulles "sick at heart." Nine students sought to enroll at Central High School and Arkansas Governor Orval Faubus refused their entrance, tapping the National Guard to enforce his decision. Newspapers around the world closely monitored the drama, and Moscow exploited it by painting the United States as an ideological hypocrite—not a beacon of human rights, but instead a human rights violator that deserved global condemnation. "This situation [is] ruining our foreign policy," Dulles told Attorney General Herbert Brownell by phone. "The effect of this in Asia and Africa will be worse for us than Hungary was for the Russians."[53]

Race had long dogged the United States. Though America was founded upon a declaration that "all men are created equal," it took a civil war before the nation extended the principle constitutionally to enslaved blacks. After that war, blacks faced a new era of sanctioned discrimination as "Jim Crow" laws denied them political freedom and social equality across the South. Not even U.S. participation in two world wars, each framed as a fight for freedom and democracy, would convince America's white majority to allow people of color to partake fully in the opportunities accorded by a free society.

Race demanded the serious attention of every president in the first two decades after World War II—not just as a domestic issue, but also because of its impact on America's global standing. Truman, Eisenhower, Kennedy, and Johnson were men of different backgrounds, with different perspectives on the problem of race. Each, however, became keenly aware of the global impact of the marches and sit-ins, the protests and riots, and the violence and bloodshed that swept the nation during what's known as the Civil Rights Era. Each sought more racial harmony as an essential tool of foreign policy. As Mary L. Dudziak wrote in one of her ground-breaking essays on the subject, "[T]his foreign policy angle, this Cold War imperative, was one of the critical factors driving the federal government's postwar civil rights efforts."[54]

The challenge emerged soon after the war ended. In the late 1940s, a wave of racial violence swept the South. That black soldiers who had fought to defend America were among the victims was not just disgusting but, frankly, embarrassing. In 1946, a sergeant was beaten and blinded in both eyes by the police chief of Aiken, South Carolina. The chief was indicted but then acquitted, evoking cheers in the courtroom. Blacks were killed by angry mobs for having the effrontery to vote or to fight with whites.

The world watched in horror. The *Fiji Times & Herald* wrote, "[H]undreds of thousands of negroes exist today in an economic condition worse than the out-and-out slavery of a century ago."[55] A columnist in Ceylon argued that "the colour bar is the greatest propaganda gift any country could give the Kremlin in its persistent bid for the affections of the coloured races of the world."[56] Of race relations in America's South, an Indian newspaper wrote, "The farther South one travels, the less human the Negro status becomes, until in Georgia and Florida it degenerates to the level of the beast in the field."[57]

Making matters worse, some foreign dignitaries who visited the United States were subject to racial discrimination, which only fed the flames of anti-American hostility across the Third World. Arriving in Biloxi, Mississippi, to attend an agricultural conference, Haiti's secretary of agriculture was, for "reasons of color," denied a room at the same hotel as the other participants. He also could not eat in the hotel restaurant with the other guests. The Haitian official returned home without attending the conference, dressed down a U.S. embassy official upon his return, and lodged an official complaint with the United States. One socialist-leaning Haitian newspaper blasted America for the mismatch between its ideals and its actions, asking in an editorial, "[C]an serious people still speak of American democracy?"[58]

The Soviet Union sought to exploit America's troubles across Asia and Africa, citing stories in U.S. newspapers. *Trud*, a Soviet newspaper, described "the increasing frequency of terrorist acts against negroes," which included "the bestial mobbing of four negroes by a band of 20 to 25 whites" in Monroe, Georgia. In addition, it relayed an incident near Linden, Louisiana, where "a crowd of white men tortured a negro war veteran, John Jones, tore his arms out and set fire to his body. The [American] papers stress the fact that the murderers, even though they are identified, remain unpunished." *Trud* wrote that Southern blacks lived under "[s]emi-slave forms of oppression and exploitation" and that the movement for racial equality was engendering "exceptional fury and resistance" in the United States.[59] Buttressing Soviet efforts to exploit America's racial troubles, other U.S. critics (both foreign and domestic) used the United Nations as a forum through which to air grievances. One such critic was America's leading advocacy group for African Americans, the National Association for the Advancement of Colored People.

The Truman administration and, in particular, its State Department sought to rebuff the negative international publicity that America's civil rights struggle generated. Officials wrote articles for foreign newspapers across the Third World, and the department sponsored trips for U.S. blacks to reassure foreign audiences that race relations were improving in the United States and that U.S.-style democracy was dramatically more humane than Soviet-style communism. At home, meanwhile, U.S. foreign policy officials tried to shape laws, policies, and court decisions in ways that would improve civil rights and thus remove the albatross of race relations around the neck of America's global image.

In 1946, then-Acting Secretary of State Dean Acheson put the matter in stark terms in a letter to the chair of the federal Fair Employment Practices Committee:

> The existence of discrimination against minority groups in this country has an adverse effect upon our relations with other countries. . . . An atmosphere of suspicion and resentment in a country over the way a minority is being treated in the United States is a formidable obstacle to the development of mutual understanding and trust between the two countries. We will have better international relations when these reasons for suspicion and resentment have been removed.[60]

The Truman administration weighed in on pending civil rights court cases, filing amicus curiae (friend of the court) briefs that "stressed to the Supreme Court the international implications of U.S. race discrimination."[61] In a brief on school desegregation, the Justice Department quoted Acheson's contention that "[d]uring the past six years, the damage to our foreign relations attributable to [the race problem] has become progressively greater" and concluded with the following quote from Truman: "If we wish to inspire the people of the world whose freedom is in jeopardy, if we wish to restore hope to those who have already lost their civil liberties, if we wish to fulfill the promise that is ours, we must correct the remaining imperfections in our practice of democracy."[62]

Succeeding Truman in 1953, Eisenhower sought to boost America's image a year later by capitalizing on the Supreme Court's landmark decision in *Brown v. Board of Education*, which declared that separate schools for the races were inherently unequal. The administration pushed the news out aggressively, particularly across the communist world, through the Voice of America. Newspapers around the world praised the decision. As Dudziak put it, "*Brown* helped to undercut the more powerful anti-American arguments."[63]

Three years later, however, the school confrontation that had Secretary of State Dulles "sick at heart" played out in Little Rock. Henry Cabot Lodge, the U.S. ambassador to the United Nations, wrote to Eisenhower that "I can see clearly the harm that the riots in Little Rock are doing to our foreign relations." When the vice president and Mrs. Nixon toured South America a year later, "Mrs. Nixon was grabbed by the arm by a youth who shouted 'Little Rock, Little Rock!' and suggested that the Vice President was responsible for 'torturing little black boys' there."[64]

Eisenhower, seeking to uphold federal law and end a crisis that was giving America another international black eye, sent Army paratroopers to protect the black students as they enrolled. Strikingly, in an address to the nation to explain his actions, Ike concluded on an international note:

> At a time when we face grave situations abroad because of the hatred that communism bears toward a system of government based on human rights, it would be difficult to exaggerate the harm that is being done to the prestige and influence, and indeed to the safety, of our nation and the world. Our enemies are gloating over this incident and using it everywhere to misrepresent our whole nation. We are portrayed as a violator of those standards of conduct which the peoples of the world united to proclaim in the Charter of the United Nations. There they affirmed "faith in fundamental human rights" and "in the dignity and worth of the human person" and they did so "without distinction as to race, sex, language or religion."

Kennedy also was keenly aware of the global implications of U.S. domestic policy. Asked about Little Rock in his second presidential debate with Nixon in late 1960, he said:

> We sit on a conspicuous stage. We are a goldfish bowl before the world. We have to practice what we preach. We set a very high standard for ourselves. The Communists do not. They set a low standard of materialism. We preach in

the Declaration of Independence and in the Constitution, in the statement of our greatest leaders, we preach very high standards; and if we're not going to be charged before the world with hypocrisy we have to meet those standards.

It was a cross that he would also bear. In the early 1960s, foreign diplomats of color who drove Maryland's Highway 40 between Washington and New York often could not eat in Maryland restaurants. A new ambassador from Chad who was driving south to present his credentials to Kennedy stopped for gas and was turned away when he tried to buy a cup of coffee. When a black delegate to the United Nations landed in Miami on his way to New York, he could not enter the airport restaurant, and instead received a sandwich wrapped in waxed paper and a canvas stool on which to sit in the corner of the hangar.[65]

Kennedy responded with an eye on America's global audience. Upon learning of the problems along Highway 40, he established an Office of Special Protocol in the State Department that, among other things, pushed successfully for a Maryland law to end discrimination in "public accommodations." He sent troops in 1962 to ensure that James Meredith, a black student, could attend the University of Mississippi. A year later, with Birmingham, Alabama's police chief, "Bull" Connor, using fire hoses and dogs on the more than one thousand black children and teenagers who were marching for civil rights, Kennedy directed his aides to work with local officials "to desegregate facilities in large department stores, redress employment discrimination, and release jailed civil rights demonstrators." When, in 1963, Alabama Governor George Wallace dramatically stood in the doorway to block integration at the University of Alabama, Kennedy again sent aides to resolve the matter quietly.[66]

Kennedy's address to the nation on civil rights, which he delivered just hours after two black students enrolled at the University of Alabama, is considered among his finest speeches. It cited the Bible, asked Americans to look into their hearts, and called for federal legislation to desegregate public facilities. While issuing a moral call to action, Kennedy put the issue in international terms as well:

> Today, we are committed to a worldwide struggle to promote and protect the rights of all who wish to be free. And when Americans are sent to Vietnam or West Berlin, we do not ask for whites only. . . . We preach freedom around the world, and we mean it, and we cherish our freedom here at home, but are we to say to the world, and much more importantly, to each other that this is the land of the free except for the Negroes; that we have no second-class citizens except Negroes; that we have no class or caste system, no ghettoes, no master race except with respect to Negroes?[67]

With an eye on not just Birmingham, but also on cities and villages across Asia, Africa, and Latin America, Kennedy's answer was clear.

CONCLUSION

After World War II, the United States quickly learned the promise and peril of human rights promotion.

Proud of its ideals, confident in the role that destiny had assigned to it, the United States enunciated the intellectual case and created the governmental architecture to promote human rights as a central element of its Cold War strategy. With the rhetorical foundation that Wilson and FDR laid, Truman and Kennedy used the full force of their "bully pulpit" to make the case for U.S.-led freedom and democracy. Meanwhile, America's economy generated the wealth to enable Washington to bail out Western Europe through the Marshall Plan and create a permanent system of foreign aid that would enable U.S. leaders to help allies and pressure adversaries in order to promote human rights.

Human rights promotion, however, was but one priority of U.S. foreign policy, and the nation was forced to sacrifice it more than once when faced with larger issues of national security. Yes, Washington could speak loudly and allocate dollars liberally. But however much it sympathized with the people of Eastern Europe, it could not risk a military confrontation with Moscow by sending troops to help the people of East Germany, Hungary, or Czechoslovakia overthrow their governments. The United States learned something else during this period. In promoting its ideals abroad, it invited scrutiny and, in turn, criticism from the global community when its practices at home did not measure up. Bigotry and discrimination against African Americans, both *de jure* and *de facto*, gave America a black eye on the world stage. It made America's job of selling itself and its ideals, and of promoting human rights around the world, that much more difficult.

The years from Truman to LBJ represent just the first stage of postwar U.S. human rights promotion. To be sure, the presidential rhetoric, the foreign policy doctrines, the aid dollars, and the other tools that Washington deployed to promote human rights all proved enormously important as the United States sought to advance the spread of freedom and democracy. But the modern era of U.S. human rights promotion really began in the early to mid-1970s. That period, which is the focus of the next chapter, brought new laws and new institutions in and out of government to promote human rights, push progress, and monitor results. The progress was driven largely by a broad public rejection of the foreign policy "realism" of Presidents Nixon and Ford and their foreign policy guru, Henry Kissinger, which sought to significantly reduce the role of U.S. human rights promotion in U.S. foreign policy. It also was driven by the growing evidence of, and focus on, the humanitarian horrors that dominated so much of the world at that time.

NOTES

1. Robert Dallek, *Harry S. Truman* (New York: Henry Holt, 2008), 17–18; Robert J. Donovan, *Conflict and Crisis: The Presidency of Harry S. Truman* (New York: W. W. Norton, 1977), 3–17.

2. *New York Times*, June 24, 1941, p. 7, as cited in Donovan, *Conflict*, 36.

3. Public Broadcasting Service, "Interview: Walter LaFeber, Historian," *American Experience*, www.pbs.org/wgbh/amex/truman/filmmore/it_1.html.

4. Franklin D. Roosevelt, Address to a Joint Session of Congress, January 6, 1941.

5. John Lewis Gaddis, *The Cold War: A New History* (New York: Penguin Press, 2005), 31.

6. Walter Russell Mead, "The Tea Party and American Foreign Policy," *Foreign Affairs* (March/April 2011).

7. Greg Behrman, *The Most Noble Adventure: The Marshall Plan and the Time When America Helped Save Europe* (New York: Free Press, 2007), 15. Of Acheson's three popular priorities, Behrman adds, "The last seemed a distant number three."

8. Behrman, *Most Noble*, 15.

9. Julian E. Zelizer, *Arsenal of Democracy: The Politics of National Security—From World War II to the War on Terrorism* (New York: Basic Books, 2010), 68.

10. Harry S. Truman, Address to a Joint Session of Congress, March 12, 1947.

11. Truman, Joint Session.

12. Truman, Joint Session.

13. Truman, Joint Session.

14. Truman, Joint Session.

15. George C. Marshall Museum, www.virginia.org/Listings/Museums/GeorgeCMarshall-Museum.

16. "The 'Marshall Plan' Speech at Harvard University," June 5, 1947, Organization for Economic Co-operation and Development, www.oecd.org/document/10/0,3746,en_2649_201185_1876938_1_1_1_1,00.html.

17. "The 'Marshall Plan' Speech."

18. Behrman, *Most Noble*, 139.

19. In today's Washington, where the White House and Congress spend more than $3.5 *trillion* a year on a wide array of domestic and defense programs, a presidential request to spend $17 billion on anything—especially in the area of foreign aid—would face considerable skepticism. Coming in 1947, the request was almost mind-boggling. That year, the federal government spent about $35 billion for *everything* it did. Office of Management and Budget, *Historical Tables*, www.whitehouse.gov/omb/budget/Historicals.

20. "In today's dollars," Greg Behrman writes, "the sum equals roughly $100 billion, and as a comparable share of U.S. Gross National Product it would be in excess of $500 billion." Behrman, *Most Noble*, 4.

21. U.S. Agency for International Development, "USAID History," www.usaid.gov/about_usaid/usaidhist.html.

22. U.S. Agency for International Development, "USAID History."

23. Curt Tarnoff and Marian Leonardo Lawson, "Foreign Aid: An Introduction to U.S. Programs and Policy," Congressional Research Service, April 9, 2009.

24. John F. Kennedy, Commencement Address at American University, June 10, 1963.

25. As outlined in Frederick Kempe, *Berlin 1961: Kennedy, Khrushchev, and the Most Dangerous Place on Earth* (New York: G. P. Putnam's Sons, 2011).

26. Andrei Cherny, *The Candy Bombers: The Untold Story of the Berlin Airlift and America's Finest Hour* (New York: P. G. Putnam's Sons, 2008).

27. Kempe, *Berlin 1961*, 499.

28. Kempe, *Berlin 1961*, 488; James M. Markham, "A Lot Better Than A War," *New York Times*, February 8, 1987.

29. John F. Kennedy, Address to the People of West Berlin, June 26, 1963.

30. Kennedy, West Berlin.

31. Kennedy, West Berlin.

32. Kennedy, West Berlin.

33. U.S. Agency for International Development, "USAID History."

34. John F. Kennedy, Inaugural Address, January 20, 1961.

35. Jimmy Carter, State of the Union Address, January 23, 1980.

36. George W. Bush, Address to a Joint Session of Congress, September 20, 2001.

37. To be fair, however, Kennan believed that the version pursued by Truman and subsequent presidents was too militaristic in tone.

38. George F. Kennan (signed as "X"), "The Sources of Soviet Conduct," *Foreign Affairs* (July 1947).

39. Malcolm Byrne, ed., "Uprising in East Germany, 1953," National Security Archive Electronic Briefing Book, June 15, 2001, www.gwu.edu/~nsarchiv/NSAEBB/NSAEBB50.

40. BBC, "1956: Soviet Troops Overrun Hungary," http://news.bbc.co.uk/onthisday/hi/dates/stories/november/4/newsid_2739000/2739039.stm.

41. Malcolm Byrne, "The 1956 Hungarian Revolution," Central European University Press, 2002, www.gwu.edu/~nsarchiv/NSAEBB/NSAEBB76.

42. Byrne, "1956 Hungarian Revolution."

43. Richard V. Allen, "Richard Nixon, LBJ, and the Invasion of Czechoslovakia," *Hoover Digest*, January 30, 1999, www.hoover.org/publications/hoover-digest/article/6425. See also Radio Prague, "The Prague Spring," Radio Prague's History Online Virtual Exhibit, http://archiv.radio.cz/history/history14.html.

44. John Pike, "Soviet Invasion of Czechoslovakia," Global Security, October 18, 2009, www.globalsecurity.org/military/world/war/czechoslovakia2.htm.

45. Jeremy Bransten, "Forty Years Ago, the Tanks Rolled into Czechoslovakia," Radio Free Europe, August 19, 2008, www.rferl.org/content/Forty_Years_Ago_The_Tanks_Rolled_Into_Czechoslovakia/1192247.html.

46. The figure comes from the Institute for the Study of Totalitarian Regimes, in Prague, as cited by Bransten, "Forty Years Ago."

47. Allen, "Richard Nixon."

48. In later years, Washington would create Radio Free Asia for China and Radio Marti for Cuba. Radio Free Europe/Radio Liberty would create Radio Free Iraq (which became Radio Sawa) and for Iran, Radio Farda. See Michael McFaul, *Advancing Democracy Abroad: Why We Should and How We Can* (Lanham, MD: Rowman & Littlefield, 2010), 18–19.

49. Byrne, "1956 Hungarian Revolution."

50. William Griffith, "Policy Review of Voice for Free Hungary Programming, October 23–November 23, 1956," December 5, 1956.

51. Griffith, "Policy Review."

52. The brother of CIA director Allen Dulles, referenced above.

53. Mary L. Dudziak, "The Little Rock Crisis and Foreign Affairs: Race, Resistance, and the Image of American Democracy, *Southern California Law Review*, vol. 70, no. 6 (September 1997): 1690. I am indebted to Ms. Dudziak for her ground-breaking research on this aspect of U.S. foreign policy, both through this article as well as several others that she has written, as the ensuing endnotes make clear.

54. Mary L. Dudziak, "Desegregation as a Cold War Imperative," *Stanford Law Review*, vol. 41 (1988): 119.

55. Dudziak, "Desegregation," 81.

56. Dudziak, "Desegregation," 83.

57. Dudziak, "Desegregation," 85.

58. Dudziak, "Desegregation," 90–91.

59. Dudziak, "Desegregation," 88–89.

60. Dudziak, "Desegregation," 101.

61. Dudziak, "Desegregation," 103.

62. Dudziak, "Desegregation," 111–12.

63. Dudziak, "Desegregation," 118.

64. Dudziak, "The Little Rock Crisis," 1694.

65. Mary L. Dudziak, "Birmingham, Addis Ababa, and the Image of America: International Influence on U.S. Civil Rights Politics in the Kennedy Administration," in *Window on Freedom: Race, Civil Rights, and Foreign Affairs 1945–1988*, ed. Brenda Gayle Plummer (Chapel Hill: University of North Carolina Press, 2003), 186.

66. Dudziak, "Birmingham," 187–91.

67. John F. Kennedy, Address to the Nation on Civil Rights, June 11, 1963.

Chapter Three

The Perfect Storm: From Nixon to Ford

"The president proposes and Congress disposes." As the adage suggests, the president sets the national agenda, outlining his priorities in an annual State of the Union address and fleshing them out in legislative proposals. Presidents drive efforts to expand civil rights (Lincoln and LBJ); create frameworks to rebuild the economy (FDR, Reagan, and Obama); enunciate doctrines to reshape foreign policy (Monroe, Teddy Roosevelt, and Truman); and launch wars in response to attack (Madison, FDR, and George W. Bush) or to counter aggression (Wilson, Truman, George H. W. Bush, and Clinton). Congress is largely a reactive body, with a cacophony of voices and a multitude of committees that respond to presidential plans by holding hearings and drafting bills. On occasion, however, Congress rises up to grab the agenda from a president who has lost the public's confidence. That's what happened in the mid-1970s on the issue of U.S. human rights promotion.

Republicans Richard Nixon and Gerald Ford (and their hugely influential aide, Henry Kissinger) conducted a foreign policy of realism that seemed cold-blooded and valueless. Under it, the nation would aspire to nothing grander than its own security, would do whatever it took to protect its friends and topple its enemies, and would consort with whatever dastardly regime would serve its purposes—no matter how odious, no matter how brutal. The policy provoked a backlash on Capitol Hill, where a Democrat-run Congress launched a multipronged effort to force Nixon and Ford to change course, constructing a new architecture of U.S. human rights promotion for those and future presidents.

To be sure, congressional Democrats were driven by more than revulsion to Nixon-Ford realism. Their actions were the outgrowth of a "perfect storm" of events that included the Vietnam War, where U.S. military and diplomatic actions showcased the mismatch between America's ideals and its behavior;

crackdowns on human rights by Latin American dictators and military rulers with whom the United States was aligned; horrors in Cambodia, Vietnam, and elsewhere; and revelations about the Soviet Union that came to light through, for instance, the 1973 publication of Aleksandr Solzhenitsyn's *The Gulag Archipelago.*

Congress held dozens of hearings to highlight the issue of human rights and, over the objections of Nixon, Ford, and Kissinger, enacted legislation that expanded the State Department's role in monitoring human rights violations around the world, restricted Washington from providing foreign aid to countries that violated the human rights of their people, and tied trade with the Soviet bloc to its willingness to let Jews and other oppressed people emigrate. Meanwhile, organized labor publicized human rights violations and helped labor activists in authoritarian lands; the Helsinki Accords put the human rights policies of Moscow and its satellites more squarely on the international agenda; and a host of nongovernmental organizations (NGOs) burst forth to monitor human rights around the world and pressure the United States to shape its policies accordingly.

All told, the mid-1970s represented a dividing line in human rights promotion, transforming the task into a more tangible, more operational element of U.S. foreign policy. With new laws and new institutions in and out of government to promote human rights, push progress, and monitor results, human rights has since become a more central element of U.S. foreign policy—whether any particular president wants it to be or not. Presidents now face pressure from what amounts to a human rights industry.

THE SETTING

The mid-1970s were a troubled time in America. A great nation had lost a bit of its luster at home and abroad.

At home, years of turmoil had taken their toll. Civil rights marches and urban riots, Birmingham and Watts, Malcolm X and the Black Panthers, Haight Ashbury and Woodstock, hippies and yippies, drugs and rock, Kent State and Attica, and the murders of John and Bobby Kennedy and Martin Luther King—all of it fed fears that the country was unraveling. The Pentagon Papers and Watergate, Nixon's resignation and Ford's pardon—all of it dampened the "ask what you can do for your country" idealism that Kennedy had stirred, nurturing a deep public cynicism about politics and government that endures to this day.[1] The economy struggled, raising fears that America's best years had come and gone. After a quarter-century of rising living standards after World War II, during which Americans moved from crowded cities to plush suburbs and tapped an expanding array of creature comforts, progress stalled in the early 1970s and households struggled to get ahead.

Overseas, the nation seemed spent. The United States gradually left Vietnam, its final departure marked by the telling photo of a U.S. helicopter fleeing with U.S. and South Vietnamese personnel as North Vietnamese forces overran the South. The My Lai Massacre, in which U.S. soldiers gunned down hundreds of unarmed civilians, and such popular anti-war movies of the late 1970s as *The Deer Hunter*, *Apocalypse Now*, and *Coming Home* helped cement public views that U.S. involvement in Vietnam was misguided from the start. More broadly, U.S. power seemed to be ebbing in comparison to its Cold War rival, the Soviet Union. An Arab oil embargo in 1973 (and a second oil crisis in 1979) put the nation at the mercy of hostile forces half-a-world away. After Vietnam, the nation turned inward, as the voices of isolationism gathered steam and the nation focused on its domestic challenges. *M*A*S*H**, the popular anti-war sitcom, began an eleven-year run in 1972.

Nor, during these turbulent times, was the world growing more hospitable to American values. To be sure, the two decades that followed World War II had brought what political scientist Samuel P. Huntington called a "second wave" of democratization. U.S. efforts had helped cement freedom and democracy in West Germany, Japan, Italy, Austria, and South Korea, while democracy came or returned to, among other places, Greece, Turkey, Uruguay, Brazil, Costa Rica, Argentina, Colombia, Peru, and Venezuela. But, starting in the early 1960s, a "reverse wave" took root, with authoritarianism returning in a big way to Latin America, in particular. Military regimes altered or replaced democracies in Peru, Brazil, Bolivia, Argentina, Uruguay, and Chile. Democracies also suffered reversals in Pakistan and India, South Korea and the Philippines, Greece and Turkey.

"The global swing away from democracy in the 1960s and early 1970s was impressive," Huntington wrote. "In 1962, by one count, thirteen governments in the world were the product of coups d'état; by 1975, thirty-eight were. By another estimate one-third of 32 working democracies in the world in 1958 had become authoritarian by the mid-1970s. In 1960 nine of ten South American countries of Iberian heritage had democratically elected governments; by 1973, only two, Venezuela and Colombia, did."[2]

The world also witnessed a few landmark instances of humanitarian horror. In Cambodia, Pol Pot's Khmer Rouge, which ruled the country from 1975 to 1979, launched a monstrous effort to turn back the clock, evacuating cities and forcing hundreds of thousands of urban dwellers to the countryside. Through a program of mass starvation, political execution, religious persecution, and torture, the Khmer Rouge killed an estimated 1.7 million (a fifth) of the nation's 8 million people.[3] In Vietnam, hundreds of thousands of "boat people" died on the seas while fleeing the horrors of their nation, where the communist North followed its victory over the South in 1975 with a broad-scale campaign of murder, torture, and imprisonment.[4] Many of those lucky enough to survive the seas in their rickety boats met further humanitarian horror in refugee camps. In East Timor, Indonesia invaded the tiny colony in late 1975 on the pretense of preventing a communist takeover, and its campaign of genocide and a resulting famine claimed 150,000 lives.[5]

Presidents often personify the tenor of their nation, and Richard Nixon was no exception. Elected by a sliver in 1968 and reelected in a landslide four years later, he was perhaps the perfect symbol of a cynical and embittered America. He was a driven politician who had lost his run for president in 1960 (when critics asked, "Would you buy a used car from this man?") and then for California governor in 1962 (after which he told reporters that "you won't have Nixon to kick around anymore"). He won the presidency in 1968 only after the Democratic Party imploded at its angry national convention in Chicago and disgruntled liberals refused to back the party's nominee, Hubert Humphrey. Nixon was awkward in person and unconvincing on TV. With his deep-set eyes and brooding manner, he seemed altogether shifty. He hated the media and assumed that enemies were encircling him. That a scandal would later drive him from office seems quite fitting.

Fitting as well, Nixon's views about America's place in the world mirrored the diminished expectations of his time. Though a hard-core Cold Warrior in his earlier days, by the early 1970s Nixon had come to believe that the United States had entered a period of decline,[6] one in which it would be just one of several great powers. "[I]nstead of just America being number one in the world from an economic standpoint, the preeminent world power, and instead of there being just two super powers," Nixon told media executives in mid-1971, "when we think in economic terms and economic potentialities, there are five great power centers in the world today"—the United States, Europe, the Soviet Union, China, and Japan.[7] Even more striking, he told *Time* magazine in early 1972:

> We must remember the only time in the history of the world that we have had any extended period of peace is when there has been balance of power. It is when one nation becomes infinitely more powerful in relation to its potential competitor that the danger of war arises. So I believe in a world in which the United States is powerful. I think it will be a safer world and a better world if we have a strong, healthy United States, Europe, Soviet Union, China, Japan, each balancing the other, not playing one against the other, an even balance.[8]

In Nixon's view, America's era of unchallenged predominance was over. The nation would have less power to impose its will abroad. It would succeed by competing economically and cooperating diplomatically. Among the things it would most certainly *not* do was promote human rights.

REALISM TO THE RESCUE

Scholars have long struggled to explain the frameworks and patterns of American foreign policy.

Walter Russell Mead suggested that U.S. foreign policymakers come in four varieties: Hamiltonians, who seek U.S. integration into the global economy; Wilsonians, who advance U.S. values around the world for moral and selfish reasons; Jeffersonians, who eschew crusades abroad and focus on U.S. domestic challenges; and Jacksonians, who focus U.S. policy on strengthening national and economic security.[9] John Lewis Gaddis argued that notions of preemption, unilateralism, and hegemony, with which George W. Bush was associated and for which he was much maligned, have been constant themes of U.S. foreign policy from our earliest days.[10] Others categorize U.S. foreign policy along the lines of liberal internationalism, neoconservatism, and other frameworks.

But perhaps the most pervasive divide—indeed, the "fundamental fault line" of U.S. foreign policy, in the words of Council on Foreign Relations President Richard Haass[11]—is between realists and idealists. To oversimplify, realists counsel that the United States should single-mindedly pursue its "national interest" and avoid the temptation of nobler goals, while idealists seek to use U.S. power and influence to make the world a better place. This realist-idealist "template" dates back at least to the early twentieth century, with Teddy Roosevelt personifying the former, Woodrow Wilson the latter.[12] TR sought to build the nation's global footprint while eschewing efforts to better mankind,[13] while Wilson sought U.S. entry into World War I to help make the world "safe for democracy."[14]

The doctrine of realism, or strains of it, have pervaded the views of presidents and foreign policy thinkers ever since. Franklin Roosevelt mixed the idealism of his call for all humans to enjoy "four freedoms"[15] with a realist vision of a postwar world in which the great powers would ensure collective security through a United Nations. George Kennan, the father of "containment," was an unapologetic realist, as was Reinhold Niebuhr, the postwar theologian and Democratic Party guiding light. More recently, realism has been closely associated with Nixon and Ford (and, as we will see, George H. W. Bush and Barack Obama).

Realism is no uniquely American doctrine, however. Its most famous practitioner of the last two centuries may have been Austria's Prince Metternich, who spearheaded an alliance of Austria, Russia, Prussia, Great Britain, and France after the fall of Napoleon that managed to keep the peace among Europe's leading powers for more than three decades after 1815. The European leaders at the turn of the twentieth century also were realists who thought that, with their balanced power and intertwined economies, they had found the formula for long-term continental stability. (That was before an assassin shattered their dreams by gunning down Austria's Archduke Franz Ferdinand and his wife in Sarajevo in 1914, triggering the events that led to World War I.)

Academically, realism is perhaps best exemplified by the writings of political scientist Hans J. Morgenthau, who provided a classic enunciation in his 1951 book, *In Defense of the National Interest*: "Forget the sentimental notion that foreign policy is a struggle between virtue and vice, with virtue bound to win. Forget the utopian notion that a brave new world without power politics will follow the unconditional surrender of wicked nations. Forget the crusading notion that any nation, however virtuous and powerful, can have the mission to make the world over in its own image."

"Remember," Morgenthau additionally advised,

> that the golden age of isolated normalcy is gone forever and that no effort, however great, and no action, however radical, will bring it back. Remember that diplomacy without power is feeble, and power without diplomacy is destructive and blind. Remember that no nation's power is without limits, and hence that its policies must respect the power and interests of others. Remember that the American people have shown throughout their history that they are able to face the truth and act upon it with courage and resourcefulness in war, with common sense and moral determination in peace. And, above all, remember always that it is not only a political necessity, but also a moral duty for a nation to always follow in its dealings with other nations but one guiding star, one standard for thought, one rule for action: The National Interest. [16]

That Morgenthau would describe the pursuit of "The National Interest" as "a moral duty" is noteworthy, for it is on morality where realism is most controversial. With "The National Interest" serving as its "one guiding star," "one standard for thought," "one rule for action," realism seems profoundly amoral, cold and uninspiring, hardly worthy of a nation that views itself as a beacon for others. Singularly focused on "The National Interest," the practice of realism makes the United States seem decidedly un-special, a nation that does only what every other nation does—protect its own interests.

Realists would disagree. Morgenthau explained the moral underpinnings of his foreign policy vision this way:

> [I]t still remains true, as it has always been true, that a nation confronted with the hostile aspirations of other nations has one prime obligation—to take care of its own interests. The moral justification for this prime duty of all nations—for it is not only a moral right but also a moral obligation—arises from the fact that if this particular nation does not take care of its interests, nobody else will. [17]

If so, then the dispute between idealists and realists is less over goals than means. Both would like to see a better world. Idealists are more confident about America's ability to help fashion it, while realists worry more about the costs of doing so. By promoting the cause of human rights, realists fear that the United States might destabilize friendly regimes and possibly find them replaced by far more hostile governments that are no better on the human rights front. By intervening militarily to help democratic forces, realists fear, the United States can find itself bereft of money and troops to protect itself.

"Both the need for intervention and the chances for successful intervention are much more limited than we have been led to believe," Morgenthau wrote in early 1967 as domestic opposition to America's role in Vietnam was growing.

> Intervene we must where our national interest requires it and where our power gives us a chance to succeed. The choice of these occasions will be determined not by sweeping ideological commitments nor by blind reliance upon American power but by a careful calculation of the interest involved and the power available. If the United States applies this standard, it will intervene less and succeed more.[18]

All presidents are realists to some extent, for none have the luxury to pursue idealism in all cases and in all of its purity. Threats to national security, regional stability, and access to natural resources force even the most idealistic presidents to set aside their lofty goals for another day.

At the same time, most of our post–World War II presidents have been partly idealists as well. Though cold-blooded in the interest of U.S. national security when necessary, they have also sought to build a better world when possible. Truman created the Marshall Plan to rescue a devastated Western Europe after World War II; George H. W. Bush sent more than twenty-five thousand troops to Somalia as part of a United Nations effort to provide famine relief; Clinton dispatched U.S. warplanes to bomb Serbian forces in order to stop ethnic cleansing in the Balkans; and Obama joined with European leaders in military action to protect Libyan rebels who were threatened with slaughter by strongman Muammar Gaddafi.

Nixon and Ford, however, were exceptions to the postwar rule, for they offered no nod to the more idealistic strain of U.S. policymaking. They pursued the national interest as they saw it—period. They cavorted with Western leaders and Third World dictators alike as long as it served U.S. interests. They eschewed public calls to advance human rights and to pressure other regimes to improve their human rights records, saying that America should not interfere in the internal affairs of another state and that U.S. leaders could accomplish more through private diplomacy than public name-calling.

As Nixon put it in 1973: "[T]he 'national interest' is the only proper concern of this nation's foreign policy, and the 'national interest' should be narrowly construed to exclude moral commitments or 'causes' that do not promise a clear, direct, predictable payoff in increased security or prosperity for the nation."[19]

Behind the scenes, the president practiced what he preached. "I cannot remember an occasion," recalled the long-time Soviet foreign minister, Andrei Gromyko, when Nixon "launched into a digression on the differing social structures of our states. He always presented himself as a pragmatist uninterested in the theoretical aspects of an issue, a man who preferred to keep discussions on a purely practical level."[20] Nixon pursued the same policy of pragmatism toward China, telling Mao Zedong, "What is important is not a nation's internal political philosophy. What is important is its policy toward the rest of the world and toward us."[21]

Throughout Latin America at the time, repressive regimes in Argentina, Chile, Brazil, Uruguay, and elsewhere were arresting, detaining, and torturing political opponents and others who threatened their rule.[22] Nixon and Ford hardly seemed to notice. With broader geopolitical concerns in mind, they boosted military aid not only to Chile but also to other brutal but friendly regimes around the world—Indonesia, Iran, and the Congo, for instance— evoking complaints that those governments were using the aid to repress their people.[23] In fact, researchers have found that "under presidents Nixon and Ford foreign assistance was directly related to levels of human rights violations, i.e. more aid flowed to regimes with higher levels of violation."[24]

The Cold War continued to shape all U.S. foreign policy and, on this front, Nixon and Ford followed a policy of "détente" with Moscow. It reflected the belief that, as Ford said later, "we recognized differences, domestically and internationally, with the Soviet Union, but that it was better to solve problems than to have confrontations."[25] Problem-solving required some measure of working relationship between the super powers. Consequently, Nixon and Ford avoided actions that would upset Soviet leaders and, in the process, threaten progress on arms control and other matters of potential cooperation.

Nixon and Ford were ably assisted by an intellectual comrade-in-arms who was perhaps the most powerful U.S. foreign policy advisor of modern times.

KISSINGER AS LIGHTNING ROD

Henry Kissinger was the perfect foil for his critics. Rather than defuse conflict and seek accommodation, he dug in his heels. Rather than narrow the gap between realism and the visions of his adversaries, he widened it further. He was as sure of himself as he was disdainful of his critics, and he did nothing to hide his arrogance. (Once, a man approached him at a large Washington dinner and said, "Dr. Kissinger, I want to thank you for saving the world." Kissinger replied, "You're welcome."[26])

"We deal with governments as they are," Kissinger said at his Senate confirmation hearings in 1973 when Nixon appointed him secretary of state, after he had run the National Security Council for four years. "I believe it is dangerous for us to make the domestic policy of countries around the world a direct objective of American foreign policy. . . . The protection of basic human rights is a very sensitive aspect of the domestic jurisdiction of . . . governments."[27]

That may have been the clearest statement of Kissingerian realism, but it was not his only memorable pronouncement on the subject. At different times, he referred to human rights as "easy slogans," "empty posturing," "sentimental nonsense," and "malarkey."[28] He called the State Department officials who expressed interest in human rights "bleeding hearts," "theologians," and "people who have a vocation for the ministry."[29] He ordered David Popper, the U.S. ambassador to Chile, to "cut out the political science lectures" after Popper raised human rights concerns with Chilean officials.[30] Blocking the State Department's release of a report to Congress on the human rights records of U.S. foreign aid recipients, he explained, "Neither the U.S. security interest nor the human rights cause would be served" by fingering other nations for "public obloquy."[31] When Congress reacted in anger, forcing a human rights agenda on Kissinger and the two administrations he served, the result was an inter-branch "battle royale" (as discussed below).

That Kissinger adhered so strongly to the dictates of realism has baffled at least some of his critics. They point to his roots—a Jew who fled Nazi Germany as a teen in 1938, just before the horrors of World War II and the Holocaust—and wonder why he has not displayed a greater sensitivity to oppressed people, including Jews, or promoted the use of U.S. military power to address their suffering where it could make a difference. In late 2010, the Nixon presidential library and museum released Oval Office tapes on which Kissinger is heard telling Nixon in 1973, "The emigration of Jews from the Soviet Union is not an objective of American foreign policy. And if they put Jews into gas chambers in the Soviet Union, it is not an American concern. Maybe a humanitarian concern." Nixon agreed, replying, "I know. We can't blow up the world because of it."[32]

Kissinger's supporters, however, say his realism is an understandable by-product of the frightening world that he fled. The lesson that he took from Hitler's rise, they say, is that "revolutions," such as Nazism, are dangerous and chaotic, and that they can replace democratic mores with authoritarian brutality. If so, then the best way to protect human rights is to promote a world of stability among great powers so that no would-be revolutionary, such as Hitler, arises to destabilize. In Kissinger's time, it would be the United States and Soviet Union that, while competing around the world, would simultaneously maintain global stability and rein in would-be revolutionaries.

Of Kissinger, Robert D. Kaplan wrote, "he preserved what he saw as the legitimate order, in which the Soviet Union was both contained and accepted, so that revolutionary chaos was confined to the edges of the superpower battlefield, in the Third World."[33] It was, of course, this "acceptance" of the Soviet Union that long made Kissinger the bête noire of hard-core conservatives who wanted not to collaborate with Moscow but to defeat it, not to manage the Cold War but to win it. That Kissinger did not foresee the Soviet collapse of later years did nothing to raise his esteem in conservative circles.

Either way, Kissingerian realism had real consequences on the human rights front, according to Daniel Patrick Moynihan, who served as Nixon's ambassador to India and Ford's ambassador to the United Nations before beginning his long service as a U.S. senator from New York. In "The Politics of Human Rights," his August 1977 essay in *Commentary*, Moynihan noted that, due to America's silence, by 1976 "human rights had disappeared so completely from the councils of the West that a newcomer to the field might well never have heard the issue even discussed."[34]

Moynihan's experience at the United Nations in 1975 was particularly telling. That year, the General Assembly had passed one resolution calling for unconditional amnesty for all political prisoners in South Africa and a second one calling for the same thing in Chile. Moynihan then brought a resolution before the General Assembly's "Third Committee" for a world-wide amnesty for political prisoners. The ambassador, no novice when it came to America's enemies, expected opposition from the Soviet bloc. But with the United States largely silent on human rights issues for years by then, he could not even build support for the resolution among Western democracies. Western leaders decided that the virtues of promoting human rights were not worth the cost of ruffled feathers with their Iron Curtain adversaries within the UN's cozy confines.

By the mid-1970s, lawmakers had had enough. They sought to pressure Nixon, Ford, and Kissinger to change direction. The fruits of their labor would shape U.S. human rights promotion for decades to come.

CONGRESS ERUPTS

It was late 1974 and Kissinger was talking to Assistant Secretary of State William D. Rogers, describing congressional efforts to reshape U.S. foreign policy: "It is a problem of the whole foreign policy that is being pulled apart, pulling it apart thread by thread, under one pretext or another."[35]

By then, lawmakers had used public hearings and other tools of communication to convince Americans that the United States should reassert its values around the world, and they also had inserted human rights promotion into the laws that governed U.S. foreign policy. Leaders of the effort included Representatives Donald Fraser and Tom Harkin and Senators Jacob Javitz, Hubert Humphrey, Edward Kennedy, Alan Cranston, James Abourezk, and Henry "Scoop" Jackson. Lawmakers' efforts were fueled by revulsion over what they viewed as valueless realism; by the larger struggle at the time between an "imperial presidency" (as Arthur Schlesinger Jr. titled his 1973 book)[36] and a Congress that sought to reassert its role in the policy process; and by the 1974 congressional elections that brought to Washington a new class of Democratic "Watergate babies," many of whom wanted to elevate human rights to a more prominent place in U.S. foreign policy.[37]

Nixon, Ford, and Kissinger would not back down for at least two reasons. First, they harbored no second thoughts about how they were conducting U.S. foreign policy. Second, they did not want to let what was, in their minds, an out-of-control legislature usurp their executive authority.

Fraser, a liberal Democrat from Minnesota, chaired the House Foreign Affairs Subcommittee on International Organizations and Movements. From August to December 1973, his panel held fifteen hearings and heard from more than forty witnesses—current and former government officials, members of Congress, lawyers, scholars, and officials from nongovernmental organizations. One key product was a landmark report, *Human Rights in the World Community: A Call for U.S. Leadership*, which the subcommittee issued in March 1974, urging the United States to elevate human rights to a more central role in its foreign policy. It represented a clear rebuke to Nixonian realism. "The human rights factor is not accorded the high priority it deserves in our country's foreign policy," the report declared.

> Too often it becomes invisible on the vast foreign policy horizon of political, economic, and military affairs. Proponents of pure power politics too often dismiss it as a factor in diplomacy. Unfortunately, the prevailing attitude has led the United States into embracing governments which practice torture and unabashedly violate almost every human rights guarantee pronounced by the world community. Through foreign aid and occasional intervention—both covert and overt—the United States supports those governments. Our relations

with the present Governments of South Vietnam, Spain, Portugal, the Soviet
Union, Brazil, Indonesia, Greece, the Philippines, and Chile exemplify how
we have disregarded human rights for the sake of other assumed interests.[38]

The subcommittee acknowledged that Washington could not, and should not,
respond to every human rights violation around the world. Nor should it
make human rights the sole, or even the top, consideration of U.S. foreign
policy. Nevertheless, the panel wrote, Washington should raise the profile of
human rights as part of its foreign policy for reasons of both idealism and
self-interest. Idealistically, "[r]espect for human rights is fundamental to our
own national traditions." Selfishly, "disregard for human rights in one country can have repercussions in others,"[39] such as when human rights horrors
serve as precursors for regional instability or for wars in which the United
States is forced to participate. As discussed in chapter 1, this two-sided
rationale for U.S. human rights promotion—idealism and self-interest—pre-
dated the subcommittee and would far outlast it.

Nixon and Ford did not willingly follow all of the panel's recommenda-
tions, nor did they welcome other advice from lawmakers. So, when necessary, the panel (and Congress at large) moved from offering advice to imposing requirements. Congressional efforts fell into three buckets: (1) elevating
the role of human rights within the federal bureaucracy, specifically at the
State Department; (2) tying military and economic aid to the human rights
performance of a potential recipient; and (3) linking trade between the United
States and the Soviet bloc to its willingness to let Jews and other oppressed
people emigrate.

On the bureaucratic front, *Human Rights in the World Community* called
for, among other things, an Office for Human Rights in the State Department's Bureau of International Organization Affairs, an assistant legal adviser on human rights in the department's Legal Adviser's Office, and an officer
for human rights affairs in each of State's regional bureaus. Kissinger, hoping to release some steam from an angry congressional balloon, agreed in
early 1975 to appoint a coordinator for human rights and humanitarian affairs
for Deputy Secretary of State Robert Ingersoll's office. (President Carter
later elevated the position to assistant secretary of state and gave it more
staff.) Kissinger also appointed the assistant legal adviser and the officers for
human rights affairs for the geographic bureaus.[40]

Congress also imposed a requirement, however, that Kissinger strongly
opposed and with which he refused to comply—that the administration provide annual reports on human rights in other countries. In the face of Kissinger's intransigence, an angry Congress toughened the requirement a year later,
requiring the administration to provide a report on any country that would

receive U.S. aid. In later decades, Congress expanded the requirement to all countries, the reports grew more robust and useful, and they became a standard resource for policymakers and human rights activists over time.[41]

On the aid front, Congress attached increasingly tight strings to foreign aid, starting with requests that the administration deny aid to human rights abusers and, after administration refusals, legal requirements that it do so. From the 1973 Foreign Assistance Act, urging the administration to provide no military or economic aid to regimes that held political prisoners, Congress moved in the 1974 version of the law to urge the administration to cut or end all military aid to any regime that "engages in a consistent pattern of gross violations of internationally recognized human rights."

In 1975, Congress added economic aid to the foreign aid that's subject to human rights determinations (due to fears that rights-abusing regimes were using economic aid more to help themselves than their populations). A year later, Congress further strengthened the human rights–related restrictions on foreign aid. Over time, Congress gave the president less wiggle room to avoid such mandates and gave itself more power to overrule him. Nevertheless, Ford used his flexibility to maintain military aid for rights-abusing regimes in Argentina, Haiti, Indonesia, Iran, Peru, and the Philippines.[42]

On the trade front, Congress unanimously passed the Jackson-Vanik amendment to the 1974 Trade Act, which conditioned U.S. trade with the Soviet bloc on its willingness to let Jews and other oppressed people emigrate. Jackson-Vanik deserves a closer look because, perhaps as well as any other post–World War II measure, it crystallized the fundamental questions that lie at the heart of U.S. human rights promotion: How should the United States balance its short- and long-term foreign policy goals? How should it balance human rights promotion against other foreign policy goals, such as trade expansion? How should it weigh the views of political dissidents in authoritarian lands? What role should moral principle play in shaping U.S. global relations?

SOVIET JEWS AND U.S. TRADE

Jackson-Vanik climaxed a long struggle by Jewish and human rights groups to raise consciousness, in the United States and elsewhere, of Moscow's treatment of Jews and other oppressed people and its refusal to let them emigrate.[43]

In August 1972, in the midst of U.S.-Soviet détente and warming relations, Moscow announced that those seeking to leave the Soviet Union would have to pay an exorbitant "education reimbursement fee"—supposedly to reimburse the nation for the education that they had received but in reality to give Moscow another tool to prevent a "brain drain" of home-grown talent.[44] Later that year, Senator Henry "Scoop" Jackson and Representative Charles A. Vanik introduced legislation to deny "most favored nation" status—in essence, normal trade relations with the United States—to "non-market economies" that denied their people the right to emigrate.

The Soviets withdrew the fee in the face of global condemnation. Jackson and Vanik, however, moved ahead anyway because Moscow continued to severely restrict Jewish and other emigration. To Jackson, Vanik, and other proponents of the measure, the issue was broader than the fee; it was the basic human right to emigrate.[45] The 1948 Universal Declaration of Human Rights stated that "everyone has the right to leave any country, including his own, and to return to his country."[46] The United Nations included similar language in the International Covenant on Civil and Political Rights and in the Convention on the Elimination of All Forms of Discrimination against Women, which the General Assembly adopted in 1976 and 1979, respectively. (Though the Soviet Union did not sign the Universal Declaration, it signed the other two documents.[47])

"Freedom of movement," scholar Thomas M. Magstadt argued,

> is the most fundamental right of all because it is the right of last resort, the escape clause in every citizen's contract with the state. Although no one should ever have to choose between state-imposed silence and self-imposed exile, those with something to say who are denied a platform can seek refuge in a place more hospitable to free speech. By the same token, citizens denied the right to cast a meaningful ballot can vote with their feet. Finally, people who are persecuted by the state for their convictions can, figuratively speaking, follow Moses out of the political wilderness in search of the Promised Land.[48]

"The right to emigrate," Magstadt additionally wrote,

> is implicit in the concept of citizenship, which denotes voluntary membership in a political association in return for collective protection of rights. At an absolute minimum, therefore, citizens must have the right to terminate membership in the state. When individuals who feel deprived of certain rights essential to their self-fulfillment in their native land are denied the chance to seek it elsewhere, they possess none of the attributes of genuine citizens. Involuntary residents are, at best, subjects.[49]

Strongly opposed to the Jackson-Vanik legislation and determined to convince Congress to reject it, Nixon and Kissinger warned that it would backfire by prompting Soviet leaders to restrict emigration further in order to show that Washington could not force Moscow to change its ways.[50] Also opposed were U.S. business leaders who hoped to expand trade with the Soviet bloc. At meetings with lawmakers that were arranged by U.S. business groups, Soviet officials sought to weaken congressional support for Jackson-Vanik by explaining how the United States would benefit from expanded U.S.-Soviet trade. Soviet leader Leonid Brezhnev joined the effort during his visit to Washington in June 1973.

In the short run, Nixon and Kissinger proved prophetic. Soviet leaders responded to Jackson-Vanik, which was tucked into the broader 1974 Trade Act that President Ford signed in early 1975, by letting fewer Jews emigrate, not more. Jewish emigration, which had jumped from 8,000 in total from 1965–1970 to 35,000 in 1973 alone, fell to 21,000 in 1974 and 13,000 in 1975. (Then, after rising in the late 1970s when Moscow sought U.S. ratification of the SALT II Treaty, it fell to almost nothing in the early 1980s.) Not until Mikhail Gorbachev took power in 1985, promoting *glasnost* (governmental openness) and *perestroika* (political and economic restructuring) did Jews enjoy the right to leave for Israel, the United States, or elsewhere in great number.[51]

But for its proponents, Jackson-Vanik was a key piece of a broader, longer-term initiative to undermine the legitimacy of Soviet rule. Soviet dissident Andrei Sakharov viewed it that way, which explains why he issued an "open letter" to Congress in September 1973 to urge its adoption. He turned Nixon and Kissinger's pursuit of détente on its head, arguing that the "minimal right" of emigration was essential for "mutual trust" between the two superpowers. To reject Jackson-Vanik, he wrote, would amount to "a betrayal of the thousands of Jews and non-Jews who want to emigrate, of the hundreds in camps and mental hospitals, of the victims of the Berlin Wall."[52]

Years later, another leading Soviet dissident, Natan Sharansky, argued that Jackson-Vanik played a major role in the Soviet collapse. In his 2004 book, *The Case for Democracy*, he explained:

> Thanks to the Jackson amendment, the sands in the hourglass of the Soviet's fear society were running out. The regime was again facing a lose-lose proposition. With each additional emigrant allowed to leave, the level of fear inside the Soviet Union fell. At the same time, every obstacle that the authorities placed in the path of free emigration was reducing the likelihood of an enervated fear society winning the fruits of cooperation with the West. The Soviet Union was finally being unmasked before the eyes of the entire free world. They could continue to violate the rights of their own people, but it now would come with an expensive price tag.[53]

In Washington, Jackson-Vanik's proponents agreed. Richard Perle, the anti-Soviet hardliner who drafted the measure as a Jackson staffer, later called it "arguably the most important piece of legislation in the century," noting its "galvanizing effect on millions of Soviet citizens—Jews and non-Jews—who understood that people in the West . . . were willing to stand with people seeking freedom."[54] More broadly, Senator Gordon Smith said that Jackson-Vanik "actualized the notion that human rights are not the province of any country's 'domestic internal policy.'"[55]

With Jackson-Vanik, the United States weighed in on a central issue of human rights. In mid-1975, a thin, bearded Russian with a sharp pen and an anguished voice urged Washington to do much, much more.

LABOR STEPS UP

"Today, in this grave hour in human history, when the forces arrayed against the free spirit of man are more powerful, more brutal and more lethal than ever before, the single figure who has raised highest the flame of liberty heads no state, commands no army, and leads no movement that our eyes can see."[56]

The date: June 30, 1975. The place: Washington, DC. The speaker: AFL-CIO President George Meany. The occasion: Meany's introduction of Aleksandr Solzhenitsyn, the Soviet dissident who had been deported from his native land a year earlier. Solzhenitsyn became a literary giant with the 1962 publication of his *A Day in the Life of Ivan Denisovich*, a novel about a Soviet prison inmate. He won the Nobel Prize for literature in 1970, three years before publication of perhaps his most famous work, *The Gulag Archipelago*, a history of the Soviet gulag in more than three hundred thousand words.

Organized labor had long played an important role in U.S. human rights promotion. It positioned itself squarely on the anti-totalitarian side soon after World War II. With progressives split between President Truman and fellow Democrat Henry Wallace, the latter of whom was loudly blaming the United States for the emerging Cold War, labor's leadership decided to purge its ranks of communists and communist sympathizers.[57] Labor's alignment with Truman's anti-totalitarianism and against Wallace's communist sympathizing did more than help Truman win reelection in 1948. It set the stage for labor's important backing of U.S. human rights promotion and its behind-the-scenes work to help labor activists in authoritarian lands (such as Poland in the 1980s) for decades to come.[58]

Solzhenitsyn delivered two speeches to the AFL-CIO that summer. Following the one referenced above, he spoke to the group on July 9 in New York City where he was introduced by Lane Kirkland, then the group's secretary-treasurer who would later replace Meany as president. Three years later, Solzhenitsyn delivered the commencement address at Harvard University. In these speeches and others, he warned the West about the unrelenting threat from the Soviet Union and chastised his listeners for their creeping weakness in the struggle between freedom and totalitarianism.

Solzhenitsyn was no fan of détente, which he viewed as Western appeasement of a clever, brutal, aggressive, and expansionist enemy that was on the march while the West retreated. By giving the Soviet Union the food to feed its people and the technology to fuel its economy, Solzhenitsyn warned, the United States was empowering Moscow to expand its empire. Détente, he said, was "a process of shortsighted concessions; a process of giving up, and giving up and giving up and hoping that perhaps at some point the wolf will have eaten enough."[59]

"The course of history—whether you like it or not—has made you the leaders of the world," he told the AFL-CIO in his first oration. "Your country can no longer think provincially. Your political leaders can no longer think only of their own states, of their parties, of petty arrangements which may or may not lead to promotion. You must think about the whole world, and when the new political crisis in the whole world will arise . . . the main decisions will fall anyway on the shoulders of the United States of America."[60]

America, he went on in language that presaged Reagan's description of the Soviet Union as the "evil empire," needed to see the world with clear eyes:

> It is almost a joke now in the Western world, in the 20th century, to use words like "good" and "evil." They have become almost old-fashioned concepts, but they are very real and genuine concepts. . . . [W]e have to recognize that the concentration of world evil and the tremendous force of hatred is there and it's flowing from there throughout the world. And we have to stand up against it and not hasten to give to it, give to it, give to it, everything that it wants to swallow.[61]

Freedom, Solzhenitsyn explained in his second speech to the AFL-CIO nine days later in New York, is not free. It brings moral responsibility and demands selflessness: "I understand that you love freedom, but in our crowded world you have to pay a tax for freedom. You cannot love freedom just for yourself and quietly agree to a situation where the majority of humanity over the greater part of the globe is being subjected to violence and oppression."[62]

Freedom also demands vigilance: "I understand, it's only human that persons living in prosperity have difficulty understanding the necessity of taking steps—here and now, in a state of prosperity—to defend themselves. That even in prosperity one must be on guard."[63]

The West was basing its security on the false hopes of détente, he warned. It was investing less in arms to defend itself and in research to better understand the Soviet Union. Rather than a road to greater U.S.-Soviet cooperation over the long run, he said, détente was a path to Western defeat.

With Solzhenitsyn in Washington for his first AFL-CIO speech, anti-Soviet hardliners (including Republican Senators Jesse Helms and Strom Thurmond, Democratic Senator Henry "Scoop" Jackson, and Republican Representative Jack Kemp) tried to arrange a meeting between President Ford and the dissident. Ford's chief of staff, a young Dick Cheney, strongly supported the idea. But Ford was scheduled to meet soon with Soviet leader Leonid Brezhnev in Moscow. Committed to détente, advised by Kissinger, and concerned that a meeting with Solzhenitsyn would ruffle feathers in the Kremlin, Ford refused.[64]

Though fiercely criticized by conservative hardliners and liberal human rights activists, Ford did not seem unsure of his decision. Behind the scenes, he called Solzhenitsyn a "goddamn horse's ass," a "Slavophile and a Czarist" who was "far right of Goldwater," a writer who "isn't as good as Tolstoy," and someone who "wanted to visit the White House primarily to publicize his books and drum up lecture dates." Of his treatment by Moscow, Ford said, "at least [the regime] let Solzhenitsyn and his family out." In an earlier era, he noted, "the punishment was liquidation."[65]

Ford's critics included the leaders of a burgeoning human rights industry that, in the ensuing years, would play an increasingly vital role in forcing the issue of human rights onto policymakers and the public.

NGOS STEP OUT

In the 1970s, labor's efforts were buttressed by a host of new private entities, known as nongovernmental organizations (NGOs), that were born or rose to greater prominence on the singular issue of human rights.

The groups monitored human rights around the world; launched fact-finding missions on which they talked to lawyers, religious leaders, and the families of political prisoners; built ties to human rights groups in authoritarian lands; mounted letter-writing campaigns on behalf of prisoners; and shared what they discovered with one another, with members of Congress, and with others who disseminated the information through their own channels. The more they did, the more that lawmakers, journalists, and others looked to them for information, enhancing their status and moving human rights up the agenda of national concern.

Some of these NGOs are household names today, but in the mid-1970s they were plowing new ground and creating a new industry. As Kenneth Cmiel, perhaps the leading scholar of human rights NGOs, put it, "United States human rights activists, in tandem with partners around the world, devised ways to collect accurate accounts of some of the vilest behavior on earth that no one had bothered to document before. They invented ways to move this information to wherever activists had some chance to shame and pressure the perpetrators. Theirs was a politics of the global flow of key bits of fact."[66]

Over time, this new industry would benefit greatly from the sweeping changes in media and communications that would soon come, raising its profile, power, and relevance. Rather than disseminate information and commentary alone, activists could increasingly provide images (i.e., pictures and video) of human rights horror that, with the advent of round-the-clock news, social media, and the Internet, would reach Americans and their leaders in real time. Rather than read about human rights abuses and later see pictures that confirmed earlier reports, Americans increasingly received images from violent government crackdowns on peaceful protests *as they were happening*.

Then (as now), perhaps the leading human rights NGO was Amnesty International (AI), which was founded in London in 1961 and expanded to the United States four years later. After both the parent organization and its U.S. branch almost closed in the 1960s due to managerial and financial problems, they both stabilized themselves and expanded greatly in the human rights–conscious 1970s. The U.S. branch grew from 6,000 to 35,000 members between 1970 and 1976; from one part-time staffer in 1970 to a staff of fourteen and offices in New York, San Francisco, Chicago, Washington, DC, and elsewhere a decade later; and from two local chapters to more than one hundred by 1976. A year after its 1976 opening, AI's Washington office was "a whirlwind of activity" that included meetings with State Department officials and lawmakers and briefings for business and religious leaders who were about to meet with ambassadors from human rights–abusing regimes.[67]

Beyond AI, what had been a trickle of human rights activity in 1970 became a deluge by the end of the decade. The Ford Foundation began to underwrite human rights efforts in 1973, providing funds for, among others, academics in South America who were fired from their jobs by the military dictators who ruled their countries. The Rockefeller Foundation and others soon joined in. The Lawyers Committee for Human Rights was born in 1975 and Human Rights Watch arrived three years later. By the late 1970s, more than two hundred groups were working on human rights and more than fifty were lobbying in Washington. These groups and others launched publications through which to disseminate their findings, including the *Index of Censorship*, *Human Rights Bulletin*, and *Checklist of Human Rights Documents*. While collecting information across national borders, the groups helped the political dissidents with whom they were communicating to create their own organizations that would monitor human rights in their countries.

As the NGOs rose to prominence and their work became more central to the human rights debate in Washington, administration officials and lawmakers developed ties to them, using their information and communications channels. In one celebrated case, Ronald Palmer, the State Department's deputy coordinator for human rights, secretly visited AI's London headquarters to enlist its help in circumventing Kissinger's opposition to elevating human rights promotion within U.S. foreign policy. He suggested that the group draft questions that lawmakers could ask the State Department, which was legally required to answer all inquiries from lawmakers within two days. Meanwhile, several House members used AI's research when they complained to Georgetown University about its decision to award an honorary degree to the sister of the Shah of Iran.

It was not just the private sector, however, that was creating organizations to monitor human rights. In 1976, activists approached U.S. Representative Millicent Fenwick—an eccentric, pipe-smoking Republican from New Jersey who was the model for Lacey Davenport of Garry Trudeau's long-running comic strip, *Doonesbury*—about creating an independent government agency to monitor human rights behind the Iron Curtain. Before long, a new U.S. Helsinki Commission began to monitor compliance with a 1975 multinational agreement that, over time, would shake the foundation of the Soviet empire.

"BEYOND OUR WILDEST IMAGINATIONS"

Leonid Brezhnev thought he had scored a diplomatic coup that would strengthen the Soviet empire for years to come.

The United States, Canada, and Western European nations had met in the summer of 1975 with the Soviet Union and its Eastern European bloc at the Conference on Security and Cooperation in Europe. On August 1, thirty-five nations signed the "Final Act" in Helsinki, the capital of Finland. The Soviet side had initiated the conference as a way to improve East-West relations during this period of détente, and it was the Soviet side that boasted the most when the pact was signed. That's because the Helsinki Accords called for these nations to respect the borders of one another, and for such borders to change only by peaceful means.

To the Soviets, that meant the United States was officially abandoning its long-held dream of rolling back the Soviet post–World War II absorption of Eastern Europe. Brezhnev "had looked forward . . . to the publicity he would gain . . . when the Soviet public learned of the final settlement of the postwar boundaries for which they had sacrificed so much."[68]

U.S. critics agreed. Ronald Reagan, the hero to hard-core conservative Republicans who would challenge Ford in the GOP presidential primaries a year later, thought the accords constituted an American sell-out, if not a sign of surrender in the battle among competing ideologies. So, too, did the Senate Democratic hawk, Henry "Scoop" Jackson, who was gearing up for his own presidential run. So, too, did many Americans of Eastern European descent who understood the oppression under which their brethren were living. So, too, did the *New York Times* and the *Wall Street Journal*, both of which criticized Ford for traveling to Helsinki. So, too, did Solzhenitsyn, who called Helsinki "an amicable agreement of diplomatic shovels" that, behind the Iron Curtain, "will bury and pack down corpses still breathing in a common grave."[69]

But the accords included another set of provisions in Article 7 (also known as the "Third Basket") that would produce the kind of long-term—indeed cataclysmic—change within the Soviet bloc that not even the most optimistic proponents could have anticipated. It called for all signatories to respect human rights and basic freedoms within their borders. No one, of course, expected Soviet leaders and their Eastern European puppets to respect these provisions. But sometimes words provide opportunities for others to exploit.

The following spring, a group of dissidents within the Soviet Union decided to do what no one could have anticipated—try to hold Moscow to its words. Soviet physicist Yuri Orlov invited a small group of dissidents to gather on May 12, 1976, at the apartment of perhaps the most famous Soviet dissident of all, Andrei Sakharov. Among the small group on hand were Sakharov's wife, Elena Bonner, and Natan Sharansky. They decided to establish an organization, the Moscow Helsinki Group (MHG), to monitor Soviet compliance with Helsinki's human rights provisions.

Courage proved contagious. Across Eastern Europe, other MHG-like groups sprung up—in Lithuania, Ukraine, Georgia, Armenia, Poland, Czechoslovakia, and elsewhere. In the coming years, such organizations would arise in thirty-seven nations. MHG also inspired the creation of offshoot organizations within the Soviet Union, such as the Working Commission to Investigate the Use of Psychiatry for Political Purposes and the Christian Committee for the Defense of the Rights of Religious Believers.

Among the more important MHG-inspired groups in Eastern Europe was Czechoslovakia's Charter 77, whose name was taken from the four-page document that its leaders had crafted. Published in January 1977, it referred to Helsinki's human rights provisions in its first paragraph and then provided a bill of particulars against the regime for violating its terms. The Helsinki Accords publication, it said, "reminds us with new urgency how many fundamental civil rights for the time being are—unhappily—valid in our country only on paper." Although the authorities detained Vaclav Havel and other leading dissidents when they sought to deliver Charter 77 to the government and confiscated the original draft, copies made their way to several leading Western newspapers and were relayed back to the Czechoslovakian people through Radio Free Europe and the Voice of America. The group pressed for change in the years ahead, issuing reports on the government's human rights abuses—even as the government sentenced Havel and five other charter leaders to up to five years in prison for subversion and harassed others among the 242 original charter signatories.

Helsinki produced a more generalized fervor for freedom and democracy, one that extended beyond the particulars of its human rights provisions. In Poland, Lech Walesa later recalled, Helsinki encouraged workers to come together and form an independent trade union to defend their rights. In East Germany, Helsinki prompted more people to seek permission to leave for the West.

Of the many new groups, MHG was particularly gutsy—considering the way Moscow normally treated its trouble-makers. MHG gathered information from Soviet citizens about human rights violations and drafted reports that it sent to the Supreme Soviet Presidium and to Moscow's embassies in all thirty-five Helsinki nations. The group held press conferences during which it gave the reports to foreign journalists who wrote them up in newspapers around the world.

Behind the Iron Curtain, the human rights cat was out of the authoritarian bag, leaving Moscow in a tough spot. "Documents show that initially the KGB [the Soviet Union's internal security police force] was cautious about suppressing the growing human rights movement out of concern for," among other things, détente.[70] Nevertheless, the threat to domestic tranquility was clearly on the minds of Soviet leaders, enough that then-KGB head Yuri Andropov wrote a report on the issue to the party's Central Committee in late 1975. "The state security organs [of the Soviet Union and its satellites] are undertaking measures to study the situation . . . and to monitor the actions of those who are developing anti-Soviet designs," Andropov wrote. "Guided by the requirements of Soviet laws, the KGB is decisively disrupting the most dangerous crimes against the state."[71]

Before long, Soviet leaders had had enough of MHG. Threats to Soviet stability and the regime's legitimacy were growing too great. Moscow went after the Helsinki-inspired trouble-makers, arresting first Orlov and fellow dissident Alexander Ginzburg, then Sharansky and Malva Landa. Soviet leaders also drained MHG's ranks by allowing some members to leave the Soviet Union. New members replenished MHG's numbers to some extent, but repression and targeted emigration enabled Moscow to achieve its goal. "By the end of 1981," MHG itself wrote, "only [three] MHG members were free—Elena Bonner, Sophia Kallistratova, and Naum Meiman."[72] A year later, the group announced that it was disbanding (though it returned in later years).

Repression would not prove effective forever. Helsinki and the activities that it spurred ignited a new public consciousness on the issue of human rights both in the West and, more importantly, across the Soviet empire. The more groups there were to monitor human rights, issue reports, and publicize violations, the more that citizens came forward to volunteer more data, making the reports ever-richer. The greater the focus on human rights, the more that activists of different stripes (e.g., would-be labor leaders) sought to carve out rights about which they were most concerned.

Helsinki did not bring down the Soviet empire by itself. But in concert with other factors—Reagan's arms build-up, Soviet economic failures, and Mikhail Gorbachev's efforts to reform Soviet communism from within—Helsinki played a hugely important role. As William G. Hyland, a former top U.S. foreign policy official who later served as editor of *Foreign Affairs* magazine, wrote, "If it can be said that there was one point when the Soviet empire began to crack, it was at Helsinki."[73]

President Ford later claimed some measure of clairvoyance, suggesting that U.S. leaders knew full well that Helsinki could generate the kind of long-term pressure that would help bring the Soviet empire to its knees. "The Helsinki Accords were pretty broad," he told an interviewer from the National Security Archive, "but the one issue that was important to the United States was the elevation of human rights, so that the Soviet Union and its communist allies had to recognize that human rights were of equal importance [to the other provisions] across the board." In fact, he went on to say:

> We in the United States, and our Western allies I'm sure, were hopeful that that provision would bring about the kind of uprisings that did take place in the Warsaw Pact nations, Hungary, Czechoslovakia, Poland, and even in the Soviet Union itself. History I think is going to recognize that the Helsinki Accord was one of the great diplomatic achievements in the past, in this current century.[74]

That history will recognize Helsinki as a great diplomatic achievement seems indisputable. That the United States and its allies truly harbored expectations that it could inspire the uprisings that ensued across the Warsaw Pact seems more like revisionist history. What's probably more accurate is what Robert Gates, then serving on Ford's National Security Council, wrote years later about the human rights provisions: They "yielded benefits to us beyond our wildest imaginations."[75]

CONCLUSION

By the second half of the 1970s, a new architecture of U.S. human rights promotion was in place across the public and private sectors. New laws and mandates, pursued by more people in more offices, combined to elevate the issue of human rights for both policymakers and the public. The presidents who would follow Nixon and Ford faced heightened expectations that, rather than eschew issues of human rights, they would incorporate human rights concerns into their foreign policy.

The four presidents who presided in the last quarter of the twentieth century took vastly different approaches to the challenge. Partly, their responses were shaped by the particular problems that they confronted. Mostly, however, they were shaped by the distinctly different views that these presidents held about the global challenges facing the United States, how it should respond, and where human rights concerns should fit in.

The first man to address the issue of human rights in this new environment was a former peanut farmer from Georgia.

NOTES

1. In a telling exchange right after JFK's murder, columnist Mary McGrory told Daniel Patrick Moynihan, then a Labor Department official, "We'll never laugh again." Moynihan replied, "Heavens, we'll laugh again. It's just that we'll never be young again." Steven R. Weisman, ed., *Daniel Patrick Moynihan: A Portrait in Letters of an American Visionary* (New York: PublicAffairs, 2010), 70.

2. Samuel P. Huntington, *The Third Wave: Democratization in the Late Twentieth Century* (Norman: University of Oklahoma Press, 1991), 21. Huntington cites S. E. Finer, *The Man on Horseback: The Role of the Military in Politics*, 2nd ed. (Harmondsworth: Penguin Books, 1976), 223; and Sidney Verba, "Problems of Democracy in the Developing Countries," Remarks, Harvard-MIT Joint Seminar on Political Development, October 6, 1976, 6.

3. Cambodian Genocide Program, Yale University, www.yale.edu/cgp.

4. VietKa.com, Archives of Vietnamese Boat People, www.vietka.com.

5. Ben Kiernan, "War, Genocide, and Resistance in East Timor, 1975–99: Comparative Reflections on Cambodia," Genocide Studies Program, Yale University, www.yale.edu/gsp/east_timor/03-263_Ch_09.pdf; Richard Just, "Yet Another Disgrace," *New Republic*, November 28, 2010.

6. Nixon was not the first public figure to predict America's decline, nor would he be the last. Predictions of decline, which tend to crystallize in intellectual circles about once a generation, date back literally to the time of America's founding (when Europeans widely expected the "American Experiment" to fail). Declinism has even appeared during periods in which U.S. power seemed ascendant. Though the United States emerged from World War II as an economic and military behemoth, unchallenged on the world's stage, John Dos Passos nevertheless wrote in *Life* magazine in early 1946, "We've lost the peace." Over the ensuing decade, Mao's victory in China, America's stalemate in Korea, and Moscow's launch of Sputnik did nothing to reassure the declinists. More recently, declinism has returned. As I write these words in early 2012—with the economy weak, budget deficits soaring, and the military stretched—opinion leaders are once again predicting that U.S. power will decline and the future will belong to a rising China. But U.S. decline is no more inevitable today than it has ever been. Whether the nation retains its strength at home and its influence overseas will be determined less by historical forces than by the decisions we make. Will we strengthen our economy, rein in our deficits, and invest in our future, or will we let our problems mount, sapping our strength in the process? We retain the power to chart our course.

7. Richard Nixon, Remarks to Midwestern News Media Executives, Kansas City, Missouri, July 6, 1971.

8. Cited in Alastair Buchan, "A World Restored?" *Foreign Affairs* (July 1972).

9. Walter Russell Mead, *Special Providence: American Foreign Policy and How It Changed the World* (New York: Routledge, 2002).

10. John Lewis Gaddis, *Surprise, Security, and the American Experience* (Cambridge, MA: Harvard University Press, 2004).

11. Quoted in Ryan Lizza, "The Consequentialist: How the Arab Spring Remade Obama's Foreign Policy," *New Yorker*, May 2, 2011.

12. Ted Widmer, *Ark of the Liberties: America and the World* (New York: Hill and Wang, 2008), 158.

13. "Ordinarily," Roosevelt said at one point, "it is very much wiser and more useful for us to concern ourselves with striving for our own moral and material betterment here at home than to concern ourselves with trying to better the condition of things in other nations." Arthur M. Schlesinger Jr., "Human Rights and the American Tradition," *Foreign Affairs*, vol. 57, no. 3, (1978): 5.

14. Woodrow Wilson, Address to a Joint Session of Congress, April 2, 1917.

15. As noted previously, FDR in early 1941 outlined his vision of a world in which everyone would enjoy freedom of speech and of worship and the freedom from want and from fear.

16. Hans J. Morgenthau, *In Defense of the National Interest: A Critical Examination of American Foreign Policy* (New York: Alfred A. Knopf, 1951), as quoted in J. Peter Pham, "What Is in the National Interest? Hans Morgenthau's Realist Vision and American Foreign Policy," *American Foreign Policy Interests*, vol. 30 (2008): 258.

17. Morgenthau, *National Interest*, as quoted in Pham, "What Is in the National Interest?" 259.

18. Hans J. Morgenthau, "To Intervene or Not to Intervene," *Foreign Affairs*, vol. 45, no. 3 (April 1967), as quoted in Pham, "What Is In the National Interest?" 6–7.

19. Clair Apodaca, *Understanding U.S. Human Rights Policy* (New York: Routledge, 2006), 31.

20. Robert Gates, *From the Shadows* (New York: Simon & Schuster, 2006), 85.

21. Michael McFaul, *Advancing Democracy Abroad: Why We Should and How We Can* (Lanham, MD: Rowman & Littlefield, 2010), 12, citing William Burr, ed., *The Kissinger Transcripts: The Top Secret Talks with Beijing and Moscow* (New York: New Press, 1999), 64.

22. Kenneth Cmiel, "The Emergence of Human Rights Politics in the United States," *Journal of American History*, vol. 86, no. 3 (December 1999).

23. Representative Donald Fraser, a Minnesota Democrat who chaired the House Foreign Affairs Subcommittee on International Organizations and Movements, for instance, said, "[M]ilitary aid to a regime which practices torture was simply wrong on its face, [because] it enhanced the power of that government to remain in control and repress its own citizens." Donald M. Fraser, "Human Rights and U.S. Foreign Policy," *International Studies Quarterly*, vol. 23, no. 2 (June 1979): 179, as cited in Barbara Keys, "Kissinger, Congress, and the Origins of Human Rights Diplomacy," *Diplomatic History*, vol. 34, no. 5 (November 2010): 835.

24. Michael Stohl, David Carleton, and Steven E. Johnson, "Human Rights and U.S. Foreign Assistance from Nixon to Carter," *Journal of Peace Research*, vol. 21, no. 3 (1984).

25. National Security Archive, "Episode 16: Détente, Interview with Gerald Ford," www.gwu.edu/~nsarchiv/coldwar/interviews/episode-16/ford1.html.

26. "Historical Notes: How Kissinger Handled a War," *Time*, July 1, 1974.

27. Keys, "Kissinger, Congress," 829.

28. Keys, "Kissinger, Congress," 828.

29. Keys, "Kissinger, Congress," 837.

30. Roberta Cohen, "Integrating Human Rights in U.S. Foreign Policy," Brookings Institution, April 2008, 2.

31. Cohen, "Integrating," 3.

32. Adam Nagourney, "In Tapes, Nixon Rails about Jews and Blacks," *New York Times*, December 10, 2010.

33. Robert D. Kaplan, "Kissinger, Metternich, and Realism," *Atlantic Monthly*, June 1999.

34. Daniel Patrick Moynihan, "The Politics of Human Rights," *Commentary* (August 1977).

35. Keys, "Kissinger, Congress," 839.

36. Arthur M. Schlesinger Jr., *The Imperial Presidency* (New York: Popular Library, 1973).

37. Keys, "Kissinger, Congress," 825–26.

38. United States House Foreign Affairs Subcommittee on International Organizations and Movements, *Human Rights in the World Community: A Call for U.S. Leadership*, March 27, 1974, 9.

39. United States House Foreign Affairs Subcommittee on International Organizations and Movements, *Human Rights*, 9.

40. Apodaca, *Understanding*, 33; Lincoln Bloomfield, "From Ideology to Program to Policy: Tracking the Carter Human Rights Policy," *Journal of Policy Analysis and Management*, vol. 2, no. 1 (Autumn 1982): 4.

41. Apodaca, *Understanding*, 75.

42. Apodaca, *Understanding*, 34–42; Bloomfield, "From Ideology," 4.

43. The dramatic story is told thoroughly in Gal Beckerman's *When They Come for Us, We'll Be Gone: The Epic Struggle to Save Soviet Jewry* (New York: Houghton Mifflin Harcourt, 2010).

44. David C. Speedie, "Jackson-Vanik: A Bridge to the 20th Century," Carnegie Council, March 30, 2010, www.carnegiecouncil.org/resources/articles_papers_reports/0046.html.

45. For Jackson, the issue was a particularly personal one. He told his colleagues, "I would not be in this chamber today if Norway, the country of my parents' birth, had practiced the sort of emigration policy that the Soviet Union has today." As cited in William Korey, "Jackson-Vanik: Its Origin and Impact as Russia Nears 'Graduation,'" *Harriman Review*, vol. 14, nos. 1–2 (November 2002): 2.

46. Universal Declaration of Human Rights, Article 13, No. 2.

47. Thomas M. Magstadt, "Emigration and Citizenship: Implications for Soviet-American Relations," Cato Institute, Policy Analysis No. 70, May 2, 1986; the United Nations Department of Public Information, "Short History of CEDAW Convention," www.un.org/womenwatch/daw/cedaw/history.htm.

48. Magstadt, "Emigration and Citizenship."

49. Magstadt, "Emigration and Citizenship."

50. In his *Years of Upheaval* (Boston: Little, Brown, 1982), Kissinger wrote that Soviet leaders "could not possibly change their policies in response to an act of a capitalist legislature." Cited in Korey, "Jackson-Vanik," 1.

51. Magstadt, "Emigration and Citizenship."

52. Korey, "Jackson-Vanik," 5.

53. Natan Sharansky, *The Case for Democracy* (New York: PublicAffairs, 2004), 122–23.

54. "U.S.-Russian Relations: The Legacy of Jackson-Vanik," *Centerpoint*, March 2010, www.wilsoncenter.org/article/us-russian-relations-the-legacy-jackson-vanik.

55. Gordon Smith, Remarks, United States Senate, April 10, 2002.

56. Internet Archive, "Solzhenitsyn: The Voice of Freedom," www.archive.org/details/SolzhenitsynTheVoiceOfFreedom.

57. Peter Beinart, *The Good Fight: Why Liberals—and Only Liberals—Can Win the War on Terror and Make America Great Again* (New York: HarperCollins, 2006), 13.

58. See chapter 4.

59. Internet Archive, "Solzhenitsyn."

60. Internet Archive, "Solzhenitsyn."

61. Internet Archive, "Solzhenitsyn."

62. Internet Archive, "Solzhenitsyn."

63. Internet Archive, "Solzhenitsyn."

64. In a telling comment, Kissinger could hardly muster any criticism of Moscow on human rights grounds even after the Soviets deported Solzhenitsyn in 1974, saying only that "the necessity for détente—does not reflect approbation of the Soviet domestic structure." United States House Foreign Affairs Subcommittee on International Organizations and Movements, *Human Rights*, 11.

65. Paul Kengor, "Summer of Appeasement: When Ford Snubbed Solzhenitsyn," *American Spectator*, October 8, 2010.

66. Cmiel, "Emergence," on which I relied heavily for this section of the chapter.

67. Cmiel, "Emergence."

68. John Lewis Gaddis, *The Cold War: A New History* (New York: Penguin Press, 2005), 190.

69. History Commons, "Profile: Alexander Solzhenitsyn," www.historycommons.org/searchResults.jsp?searchtext=alexander+solzhenitsyn&events=on&entities=on&articles=on&topics=on&timelines=on&projects=on&titles=on&descriptions=on&dosearch=on.

70. National Security Archive, "The Moscow Helsinki Group 30th Anniversary: From the Secret Files," Electronic Briefing Book No. 191, www.gwu.edu/~nsarchiv/NSAEBB/NSAEBB191/index.htm.

71. Yuri Andropov, "Committee for State Security, at the USSR Council of Ministers, December 29, 1975, No. 3213-A," as posted by the National Security Archive, www.gwu.edu/~nsarchiv/NSAEBB/NSAEBB191/1975-12-29%20Andropov.pdf.

72. Moscow Helsinki Group, "English Language Page, Moscow Helsinki Group (Public Group of the Assistance of the Implementation of Helsinki Accords in the USSR, Moscow Group "Helsinki")," www.mhg.ru/english/18E49C2.

73. Quoted in Gates, *From the Shadows*, 87.

74. National Security Archive, "Episode 16: Détente."

75. Gates, *From the Shadows*, 89.

Chapter Four

Cold War Victory and Beyond: From Carter to Clinton

In the last quarter of the twentieth century, presidents responded in profoundly different ways to the heightened public expectations of U.S. human rights promotion that the Nixon-Ford years helped to nurture. Jimmy Carter promised to put human rights at the very center of his foreign policy. Ronald Reagan viewed the Soviet Union as the world's greatest human rights abuser, so he associated the advance of human rights with his efforts to weaken the Soviet empire. George H. W. Bush, a foreign policy realist, was far less interested in promoting human rights than in ensuring global stability, sacrificing the former at the altar of the latter. Bill Clinton, who viewed foreign policy largely through an economic prism, sought to advance human rights by expanding the community of free and democratic nations.

Not only were these presidents very different from one another but so were the challenges they faced. This quarter-century was a time of profound change both for the United States and the world. In the late 1970s, the United States had the look of a declining power, with an uncertain resolve to continue checking the Soviet Union. A mere decade later, it was the Soviet empire that was collapsing, ending decades of global bipolarity and leaving the United States as the world's sole superpower. As the 1990s began, U.S. officials were seeking an appropriate vision for post–Cold War global affairs. By the end of the decade, Washington was trumpeting U.S.-led freedom and democracy as the wave of the future (as Moscow had once trumpeted Soviet-led communism).

On this canvass of sweeping change, U.S. human rights promotion continued to operate within tangible limits of benefit and risk. Though Carter had pledged an "absolute" commitment to human rights, larger geopolitical concerns would force him to compromise. Though Reagan had sought not just to "contain" the Soviets but also to roll back their empire, he tried less to weaken Moscow directly than through its satellites in Eastern Europe and its allies in Central America. Bush led an international coalition of nations that reversed Iraq's 1990 invasion of Kuwait, but he mistakenly raised expectations that Washington would help Iraqis oust Saddam Hussein from power and then refused to intervene when Saddam slaughtered those who had tried. Bush and Clinton differed greatly in their foreign policy outlooks, but they both used military force in the 1990s to halt humanitarian horror thousands of miles from home—showing that neither could escape the heightened public expectations that, in such circumstances, the United States should act.

WILSONIAN DREAMS, SELECTIVE ENFORCEMENT

If Richard Nixon personified the cynicism of his time, Jimmy Carter symbolized a collective desire to rise above it. Nixon had tarnished the nation with Watergate; Carter embodied religious purity. Nixon had lied; Carter promised never to do so. Nixon and Ford were men with long histories in Washington; Carter was a one-term governor with no national experience. Nixon's presidency seemed imperial; Carter sought to bring it down to earth by carrying his own bags, curtailing limousines for cabinet members, and selling the presidential yacht. Most important for our purposes, Nixon and Ford eschewed human rights promotion, arguing that it would unduly complicate U.S. foreign policy; Carter promised to make human rights the centerpiece of his foreign policy.

If, as we have said, the battle between realists and idealists is the "fundamental fault line" of U.S. foreign policy, then Carter planned to reposition foreign policy on a strikingly new place across that line, replacing hard-core realism with dreamy idealism. The Democratic Party had paved the way for the new Democratic president. From the conservative wing, Senator Henry "Scoop" Jackson worked with Representative Charles Vanik to enact the Jackson-Vanik amendment to the 1974 Trade Act, inserting a strong moral voice into U.S. foreign policy (as discussed in the previous chapter). From the liberal wing, activist Sam Brown played a major role in crafting what became the 1976 Democratic Party platform's strong commitment to human rights, calling for an end of U.S. aid for any regime that abused rights.[1]

"Our commitment to human rights must be absolute," Carter proclaimed in his inaugural address in January 1977, adding that "we will not behave in foreign places so as to violate our rules and standards here at home, for we know that the trust which our nation earns is essential to our strength." "Because we are free," he went on, "we can never be indifferent to the fate of freedom elsewhere. Our moral sense dictates a clear-cut preference for those societies which share with us an abiding respect for individual human rights."[2]

Four months later, Carter outlined his foreign policy vision more fully at Notre Dame University, where he described "the strands that connect our actions overseas with our essential character as a nation."

> I believe we can have a foreign policy that is democratic, that is based on fundamental values, and that uses power and influence, which we have, for humane purposes. . . . Because we know that democracy works, we can reject the arguments of those rulers who deny human rights to their people. We are confident that democracy's example will be compelling, and so we seek to bring that example closer to those from whom in the past few years we have been separated and who are not yet convinced about the advantages of our kind of life. We are confident that the democratic methods are the most effective, and so we are not tempted to employ improper tactics here at home or abroad. . . . For too many years, we've been willing to adopt the flawed and erroneous principles and tactics of our adversaries, sometimes abandoning our own values for theirs. We've fought fire with fire, never thinking that fire is better quenched with water. This approach failed, with Vietnam the best example of its intellectual and moral poverty. But through failure we have now found our way back to our own principles and values, and we have regained our lost confidence. . . . First, we have reaffirmed America's commitment to human rights as a fundamental tenet of our foreign policy.[3]

Early on, Carter seemed true to his word. He criticized Moscow over human rights, exchanged letters with Soviet dissident Andrei Sakharov, and welcomed exiled Soviet dissident Vladimir Bukovsky to the White House. His State Department protested publicly when Czechoslovakian authorities cracked down on Charter 77, the nation's leading human rights group, and it defended Sakharov publicly in his battle with Soviet authorities. Carter nominated human rights activist Patricia M. Derian as coordinator for human rights and humanitarian affairs, elevated the post to assistant secretary of state, and increased her staff. Derian expanded the annual, country-specific human rights reports that Congress had mandated in law under Nixon and Ford, and Carter made these reports a reason for ending aid to five Latin American countries. *New York Times* columnist Anthony Lewis beamed that Carter "is giving not just Americans but people in the West generally a sense that their values are being asserted again, after years of silence in the face of tyranny and brutality."[4] By 1978, the International League of Human Rights reported that, due to Carter's high-profile efforts, the focus on human rights around the world had intensified markedly.[5]

Carter and his team sought to "institutionalize the process of decision-making on human rights within the U.S. government." The administration sent directives to all U.S. ambassadors around the world, making them personally responsible for pursuing U.S. concerns with rights-abusing regimes; established an Interagency Working Group on Human Rights and Foreign Assistance; incorporated the issue of human rights into most of its major strategy papers and statements of objectives; assigned a National Security Council staffer to focus on human rights; and required that each State Department bureau have a full-time human rights officer. Human rights played a role in administration decisions on whether to provide aid to other nations through the U.S. foreign aid and food assistance programs, the Overseas Private Investment Corporation, the Export-Import Bank, and major international financial institutions over which Washington exerted a strong influence.[6]

Carter, however, had set a high bar—too high, in fact. In foreign affairs, America's commitment to human rights could never be "absolute." Human rights promotion was a tenet of foreign policy that would necessarily compete with other priorities—the Cold War, regional stability, bilateral relations, and so on. Carter's absolutist language left him vulnerable to charges of hypocrisy when he continued U.S. support for regimes in Tehran, Manila, and elsewhere that were abusing human rights; when he eased his criticism of Soviet abuses while pursuing a U.S.-Soviet arms control agreement; and when he downplayed human rights problems in China in the interests of improved U.S.-China relations.[7]

Nixon and Ford had endured severe criticism for providing foreign aid to human rights–abusing governments, but the distribution of U.S. foreign aid did not change dramatically under Carter. "We are forced to conclude that Jimmy Carter did not actually usher in a new era of United States foreign policy with respect to the distribution of U.S. foreign assistance," scholars Michael Stohl, David Carleton, and Steven E. Johnson wrote. In his first year, they found, Carter reduced aid to only three of fifty-seven countries "found guilty of gross violations," cut off military aid to only eight countries during the entirety of his term, and restored aid to a human rights–compromised government in El Salvador at the end of his tenure.[8]

Carter's own deputy assistant secretary of state for human rights and security assistance later wrote,

> [T]he Carter Administration exhibited a remarkable degree of tentativeness and caution, so that its pursuit of human rights goals was anything but "single-minded." Relatively few governments were considered to be "engaged in a consistent pattern of gross (human rights) violations." Security assistance was actually cut off to even fewer, because other U.S. interests were often found to outweigh human rights concerns under the exception for "extraordinary circumstances."[9]

The gap between promise and action was even starker on the foreign policy crises that dominated Carter's tenure—nowhere more so than with Iran.

Washington had had a long and complicated relationship with Tehran. Through the CIA (and with the help of British intelligence), the United States helped to orchestrate the 1953 coup that overthrew popularly elected Prime Minister Mohammad Mosaddeq, enabling the Shah (Mohammad Reza Pahlavi) to return after a brief exile in Rome and stoking anti-American resentment among Iranians for years to come. In November 1977, the Shah visited Carter in Washington, and on New Year's Eve Carter returned the favor, visiting the Shah in Tehran. There, Carter toasted him heartily, describing Iran as "an island of stability in one of the more troubled areas of the world."

Stable? Yes. But the Shah also was an iron-fisted autocrat who, through his internal security force, the SAVAK, brutalized his opponents, including Iranians who sought to bring democracy to their land. As the Iranian Revolution gathered force through 1978, the Carter administration was divided over how to respond. Some of Carter's advisors urged him to press the Shah to crack down on the movement, while others wanted the administration to reach out to opposition leaders who would likely form a future government. [10] From the left, Carter was criticized for not abandoning the rights-abusing Shah. From the right, he was lambasted for not sticking with a reliable U.S. ally and thus sending an unfortunate signal to other U.S. allies who might face their own challenges down the road. (Carter's refusal to stick with another U.S. ally, Nicaraguan strongman Anastasio Somoza, who faced his own insurgency at the time, further angered the right.)

When the Shah fled Iran for good in January 1979, Carter refused to grant him asylum. When Carter changed his mind, allowing the Shah temporary asylum in October of that year to receive cancer treatment, he angered the revolutionaries in Iran who had toppled him. A month later, militants stormed the U.S. embassy, taking more than sixty U.S. employees, holding fifty-two of them hostage for 444 days, and launching a political crisis that would dominate the rest of Carter's term.

Also in November 1979, a Georgetown University professor published a seminal essay on Carter's foreign policy in the pages of *Commentary*. Rare is the article that changes history, but this one may have done so. Titled "Dictatorships and Double Standards" and penned by Jeane J. Kirkpatrick, it came to the attention of Ronald Reagan, front-runner for the Republican presidential nomination in 1980. It encapsulated the conservative case against Carter, and it prompted Reagan to later appoint Kirkpatrick as U.S. ambassador to the United Nations and a member of his cabinet.

"The failure of the Carter administration's foreign policy is now clear to everyone except its architects," she began with a biting judgment,

> and even they must entertain private doubts, from time to time, about a policy
> whose crowning achievement has been to lay the groundwork for a transfer of
> the Panama Canal from the United States to a swaggering Latin dictator of

Castroite bent [Omar Torrijos]. In the thirty-odd months since the inauguration of Jimmy Carter as President there has occurred a dramatic Soviet military buildup, matched by the stagnation of American armed forces, and a dramatic extension of Soviet influence in the Horn of Africa, Afghanistan, Southern Africa, and the Caribbean, matched by a declining American position in all these areas. The U.S. has never tried so hard and failed so utterly to make and keep friends in the Third World. [11]

The problem, she wrote, was Carter's apparent sympathy for left-wing dictatorships over those of the right. [12] In Iran and Nicaragua, as in other places under earlier presidents,

the American effort to impose liberalization and democratization on a government confronted with violent internal opposition not only failed, but actually assisted the coming to power of new regimes in which ordinary people enjoy fewer freedoms and less personal security than under the previous autocracy— regimes, moreover, hostile to American interests and policies. . . . At best we will have lost access to friendly territory. At worst the Soviets will have gained a new base. And everywhere our friends will have noted that the U.S. cannot be counted on in times of difficulty and our enemies will have observed that American support provides no security against the forward march of history. [13]

Carter's actions, she argued, flowed from a foreign policy outlook that was both wrong and dangerous to U.S. interests. For starters, she instructed, right-wing autocracies can evolve into democracies over time, but history provides no example of a "revolutionary 'socialist' or Communist society" doing the same. But Carter did not know how to effectively encourage such transformation on the right. Viewing change in right-wing autocratic societies as inevitable and desirable, he helped to usher it in, only to see those regimes replaced by left-wing dictatorships with a decidedly anti-American bent. But, she wrote, Carter ignored human rights abuses among communist or other left-wing autocrats and did nothing to seek liberalization within them. "The President," she summed, "continues to behave as before—not like a man who abhors autocrats but like one who abhors only right-wing autocrats." [14]

At Notre Dame, Carter expressed relief that "we are now free of that inordinate fear of communism which once led us to embrace any dictator who joined us in that fear." Nevertheless, the United States was gathering growing evidence throughout 1979 that the Soviet Union was planning a military operation in Afghanistan, where internal turmoil was threatening Soviet interests. The question was not whether Moscow would act; it was how big the operation would be. At the time, Carter was committed to Senate ratification of the U.S.-Soviet SALT II treaty, so he preferred not to focus heavily on what might occur. (He had previously tamped down his public criticism of Moscow over human rights in order to secure the U.S.-Soviet agreement in the first place.) The Soviets opted for a major operation in late

December (which, among other things, sank the SALT II treaty in the Senate). The president expressed surprise, telling ABC's *World News Tonight*, "[T]his action of the Soviets has made a more dramatic change in my opinion of what the Soviets' ultimate goals are than anything they've done in the previous time I've been in office."[15]

Carter lost his bid for reelection in 1980, unable to overcome the burdens of a weak economy and a sense of drift in U.S. foreign affairs. His presidency points up the inherent limits of U.S. human rights promotion—and the problems that a president will create by promising far more than he can reasonably deliver. Unlike Carter, his successor would not be surprised by unsavory Soviet behavior.

COLD WAR VICTORY

Natan Sharansky had already been languishing for three years in Soviet prisons for promoting human rights when Ronald Reagan assumed the presidency. The short, chubby Jew from the Soviet town of Stalino knew little about the tall, slim Presbyterian from California by way of Tampico, Illinois, but what he and his fellow inmates *did* know gave them little reason to hope that Reagan would promote human rights.

"Remember," Sharansky recalled later, "we accepted it as a given that Jimmy Carter was the world's great human rights advocate. . . . All we knew about Reagan was that he was a poorly regarded actor, and after living for so long in an Orwellian world where play-acting was all we ever experienced from our own leaders, the very fact that Reagan was an actor, I will say, left us far more concerned than encouraged at first."[16]

That changed dramatically in March 1983. Speaking to the National Association of Evangelicals in Orlando, Florida, Reagan criticized the growing calls in the West for a U.S.-Soviet "freeze" on nuclear weapons, which he thought would put the United States at a military disadvantage. It would reward the Soviets for their recent arms build-up, prohibit the United States and its allies from modernizing their defenses, and leave the West vulnerable to attack—all while doing nothing to curb Moscow's expansionist desires.

For Reagan, however, the issue was not solely one of national security. It was one of human rights as well. America, he said, "has been the story of hopes fulfilled and dreams made into reality. Especially in this century, America has kept alight the torch of freedom, but not just for ourselves but for millions of others around the world." The Soviet Union was a place of "totalitarian darkness" where "they preach the supremacy of the state, declare its omnipotence over individual man, and predict its eventual domination of all peoples on the earth." The United States could not fall behind the

Soviets militarily nor ignore their expansionism because the fate of free peoples everywhere was at stake. With that in mind, Reagan issued a plea to the religious leaders: "I urge you to beware the temptation of pride—the temptation of blithely declaring yourselves above it all and label both sides equally at fault, to ignore the facts of history and the aggressive impulses of an evil empire, to simply call the arms race a giant misunderstanding and thereby remove yourself from the struggle between right and wrong and good and evil."[17]

"Evil empire?" In the bars and cafes of Washington, London, and Paris, where the West's intelligentsia met to discuss the day's events, Reagan's language came under fierce attack. His rhetoric, critics said, went beyond the pale of acceptable discourse. It was undiplomatic, even undignified. Worse, it was counterproductive, for it would raise tensions between Washington and Moscow, threatening peace. Anthony Lewis, the *New York Times* columnist who had praised Carter for his human rights advocacy, called the language "primitive."[18] Rick Hertzberg, a Carter speechwriter, said the speech was "not presidential."[19]

That's not how it looked, however, thousands of miles away in the Soviet gulag, where prisoners learned of Reagan's speech from "an article from [the Soviet-run newspaper] *Pravda* or *Investia* that found its way into the prison." Upon reading about it, Sharansky recalled, "our whole block burst out into a kind of loud celebration." It was, Sharansky explained, "the great brilliant moment."

> It was the brightest, most glorious day. Finally a spade had been called a spade. Finally, Orwell's Newspeak was dead. President Reagan had from that moment made it impossible for anyone in the West to continue closing their eyes to the real nature of the Soviet Union. It was one of the most important, freedom-affirming declarations, and we all instantly knew it. For us, that was the moment that really marked the end for them, and the beginning for us. The lie had been exposed and could never, ever be untold now.[20]

On human rights, Carter and Reagan were mirror images of one another. Carter proclaimed an "absolute" commitment to human rights and applauded the end of America's "inordinate fear of communism." Reagan believed that human rights abuse was most pronounced in the Soviet bloc due to the very nature of communism and that the best human rights policy was one that halted Soviet expansionism, turned back earlier Soviet gains, and weakened the Soviet empire over time.[21]

By the time Reagan assumed office, the Soviet Union had enjoyed several years of geopolitical gains at America's expense. Six countries fell to communism in the mid-1970s, five more by 1979. The Soviets, assisted by Castro's Cuba, sent troops to Angola, Ethiopia, and other nearby countries to bolster communist movements and destabilize U.S.-backed governments.

Moscow deployed more SS-20 missiles, with multiple warheads, that put all NATO capitals within reach. Together with the fall of Iran's Shah and the ensuing hostage crisis, these developments gave the United States the look of both a "paper tiger" and a nation in long-term decline. [22]

Reagan had a straightforward view of the Cold War and the Soviet Union. His goal, he told a friend in 1977: "We win and they lose." [23] A year later, as he prepared to run for president, he visited Berlin. Standing at the Berlin Wall, he said to his advisors, "We have got to find a way to knock this thing down." [24] Once in office, Reagan sought to rewrite more than thirty years of U.S. policy toward the Soviets that was shaped by the doctrine of "containment." To Reagan, containing the Soviets—that is, ensuring that they don't overrun Western Europe—was necessary but not sufficient. In a 1983 directive, he pronounced that a key goal of U.S. policy was "to contain *and over time reverse Soviet expansionism*" (my emphasis). To reach that goal, "The U.S. must rebuild the credibility of its commitment to resist Soviet encroachment on U.S. interests and those of its Allies and friends, and to support effectively those Third World states that are willing to resist Soviet pressures or oppose Soviet initiatives hostile to the United States, or are special targets of Soviet policy." [25]

It amounted to a "Reagan Doctrine," as the president enunciated it in his 1985 State of the Union address: "We must stand by all our democratic allies. And we must not break faith with those who are risking their lives—on every continent, from Afghanistan to Nicaragua—to defy Soviet-supported aggression and secure rights which have been ours from birth." [26]

To be sure, not all efforts of this kind began with Reagan. Carter was the first president to send aid to the mujahideen, who fought Soviet troops after they invaded Afghanistan in late 1979. But Reagan went much further. He provided strong and controversial support for Nicaragua's contras, the rebels (or "freedom fighters," in Reagan's words) who sought to topple the communist Sandinistas who had earlier overthrown Anastasio Somoza. [27] He also provided covert support to democracy movements behind the Iron Curtain, especially in Poland.

In essence, Reagan launched a direct attack on the "Brezhnev Doctrine"—the declaration of Soviet leader Leonid Brezhnev and others that Moscow reserves the right to use force to prevent a socialist country from abandoning socialism. As columnist Charles Krauthammer wrote at the time, "The Brezhnev Doctrine proclaimed in 1968 that the Soviet sphere only expands. The Reagan Doctrine is meant as its antithesis. It declares that the U.S. will work at the periphery to reverse that expansion." [28]

With Reagan, the U.S. effort to promote human rights and reverse Soviet advances where possible involved not just words and weapons. It also included a long-term effort to construct the building blocks of democracy in authoritarian lands. Speaking to Britain's House of Commons in 1982, Reagan proposed a new mechanism "to foster the infrastructure of democracy, the system of a free press, unions, political parties, universities, which allows a people to choose their own way to develop their own culture, to reconcile their own differences through peaceful means." He noted that the bipartisan American Political Foundation was working with the chairs of both U.S. political parties to develop such a mechanism and said that he eagerly awaited its recommendation.[29]

The result: the National Endowment for Democracy (NED), a federally funded, privately operated nonprofit corporation that, to this day, enjoys close ties to both parties and to business and labor leaders.[30] It has four affiliated institutes: the National Democratic Institute for International Affairs (NDI), the International Republican Institute (IRI), the Center for International Private Enterprise (CIPE), and the American Center for International Labor Solidarity. The first two are affiliated with the two parties, the third with the U.S. Chamber of Commerce, and the fourth with the AFL-CIO. NED allots about half of its grant funds each year to the four institutes, with which they promote freedom and democracy, and the other half to hundreds of organizations for discreet projects. Of late, NED has allocated "over 1,200 grants each year to support pro-democracy groups in more than 90 countries in Africa, Asia, Central and Eastern Europe, Eurasia, Latin America and the Caribbean, and the Middle East."[31]

Among NED's recipients was a trade union in Poland named *Solidarność* (Solidarity). It was established in late September 1980, just weeks before American voters swept Reagan into office by an overwhelming margin. At the time, the Soviet Union seemed strong, the United States a bit on its heels. Before long, Solidarity would come to symbolize the fragility of Soviet rule as well as the power of Reagan's multifaceted efforts to weaken Moscow and win the Cold War.

Polish unrest did not begin with Solidarity.[32] Workers protested in 1956 on the streets of Poznan, Poland's fourth largest city, but the government suppressed the demonstrations in brutal fashion, leaving a hundred or so dead. Students and intellectuals sought greater political freedoms in 1968, but the government staged "demonstrations" against them while suppressing their efforts with little trouble. Workers demonstrated in major coastal cities in 1970, and the resulting crackdown left forty-five dead and thousands wounded. Workers revolted again in 1976, this time joined by intellectuals, but the government ended the uprising by arresting hundreds of workers. A year later, after a twenty-three-year-old anti-communist was killed (probably on government orders), students created an underground system of alternative education that was conducted in churches and homes. By the end of 1979, an underground opposition press consisted of more than four hundred publications.

The late 1970s brought another milestone event in the eventual demise of communist rule in Poland and its neighboring states and, with that, the end of the Soviet empire. In the secret offices of the Vatican, church leaders decided that, after the death of Paul VI, they should elevate Karol Jozef Wojtyla to the position of Pope John Paul II. Wojtyla, who became pope in October 1978, was the first non-Italian to serve in that capacity in more than 450 years and the first Pole to become pope.

On June 7, 1982, a day before Reagan addressed Britain's House of Commons, he met with the pope in the Vatican library. So began, as Reagan's first National Security Adviser, Richard Allen, wrote later, "one of the great secret alliances of all time." The two spoke for fifty minutes, most of it dominated by the subjects of Poland, the Soviet Union, and the Soviet bloc in general. While top aides to each man met separately, the leader of the free world and the leader of the Catholic world agreed on a secret plan "to hasten the dissolution of the communist empire." Their main target: Poland.

"Reagan and John Paul II," Carl Bernstein wrote in a fascinating account for *Time* in early 1992, "refused to accept a fundamental political fact of their lifetimes: the division of Europe as mandated at Yalta and the communist dominance of Eastern Europe. A free, noncommunist Poland, they were convinced, would be a dagger to the heart of the Soviet empire; and if Poland became democratic, other East European states would follow."[33] As Reagan put it, "We both felt that a great mistake had been made at Yalta and something should be done. Solidarity was the very weapon for bringing this about, because it was an organization of the laborers of Poland."[34]

By the time Reagan met with the pope, the latter's efforts had been underway for at least three years. In June 1979, he took a historic trip to his native country, telling millions of Poles in Warsaw, "Do not be afraid."[35] With his encouragement, the Polish people increasingly put their desire for freedom and democracy in their own hands. A year after the pope's pilgrimage, and in response to a sinking economy and their growing hardship, workers across the country launched massive strikes. The delegates of thirty-six regional trade unions came together to form Solidarity and choose Lech Walesa, an electrician from the Gdansk shipyards of northern Poland, as its leader. Within weeks after the government recognized the union—the first legal trade union in the Soviet bloc—10 million people, including 80 percent of state employees (many of them Communist Party members), joined.[36] In early January 1980, Solidarity leaders met with the pope in Rome. Two months later, when state police assaulted Solidarity members in Bydgoszdz, workers launched a nation-wide strike, forcing the government to back down by promising an investigation into the incident and allowing the news to reach the international press.[37]

Such governmental acquiescence, however, proved short-lived. Pressed by Moscow, Poland's military leaders imposed martial law in December 1981, arresting five thousand leaders and other Solidarity members in the middle of the night, including Walesa. The following October, the government outlawed Solidarity. The nation's opposition movement was forced underground. It not only survived, however, but thrived. It formed Solidarity Radio and its network of underground publications grew to over five hundred. For the rest of the decade, the government struggled to contain the union and the larger social movement, the latter of which was supported publicly and behind the scenes by Reagan, the pope, U.S. and European labor leaders, the NED, and other institutions.

After Warsaw outlawed Solidarity, Reagan ordered an end to Poland's "most favored nation" trading status, raising tariffs on U.S. imports of Polish manufactured goods. Washington also vetoed Warsaw's application for membership in the International Monetary Fund.[38] Making it clear, however, that his actions were directed against the government, and that his sympathies lay with the Polish people, Reagan also promised to continue providing humanitarian aid through CARE, Catholic Relief Service, and other such organizations.[39] Secretly, Reagan signed a National Security Decision Directive (NSDD 32) that launched a host of economic, diplomatic, and covert efforts to weaken the Soviet hold on Eastern Europe, with a particular focus on Poland.

The CIA and the Catholic Church worked with priests in Poland and with U.S. and European labor leaders to smuggle money and tons of equipment to Poland's underground—fax machines, printing presses, telephones, shortwave radios, cameras, copiers, computers, word processors, and the like. The Polish people enjoyed access to an ever-growing underground supply of books, magazines, comic books, and documentaries that challenged the legitimacy of communist rule. Washington and the Vatican provided strategic advice to Walesa and other Solidarity leaders, transmitting it the same way that they provided the equipment. They also shared intelligence and plotted strategy with one another, with Reagan and the pope chatting occasionally by phone.[40]

Poland's government relented a bit in the months soon after the crackdown, freeing Walesa and other Solidarity leaders and ending martial law. But not until the late 1980s, after Soviet leader Mikhail Gorbachev gave further momentum to liberalization efforts across the Soviet empire with his political and economic reforms, did Warsaw fully reverse itself. By 1988, Poland's economy had sunk further, evoking another wave of strikes. The government agreed to negotiate with Solidarity, and a year later it legalized the union once more and allowed it to field candidates for upcoming national elections.

Solidarity won virtually every contest for the legislature (the Sejm) for which it sponsored a candidate, and the Sejm chose a Solidarity representative as prime minister—"the first non-communist prime minister in Poland since 1945 and the first anywhere in Eastern Europe for 40 years."[41] A year later, Walesa became Poland's first president ever elected by popular vote. The United States recognized the changes that were occurring and responded accordingly, with Reagan lifting sanctions in 1987 and his successor, George H. W. Bush, working with Congress to provide economic aid for the new government in Warsaw.

By November 1989, when Walesa visited Washington and addressed a joint session of Congress, the Cold War was fast ending. Moscow retreated, its Eastern European satellites went their own way, the Berlin Wall came down, and the Soviet Union split into Russia and a host of newly independent states.

The question was, why did it happen?

To be sure, Soviet-led communism made no sense from the start. Its government-run economy could never provide basic goods and services for its people, and a huge share of its output went for its military, further shortchanging domestic needs. Its political system provided neither freedom nor democracy, causing public discontent to fester and, at times, boil over into protests and strikes that highlighted the instability of the Soviet bloc. Nevertheless, the Cold War was, in fact, a war—of ideas, of economics, and of social organization, with U.S. troops and weapons positioned to "contain" Moscow's expansionist impulses. The Soviet empire did not simply disintegrate. The United States played a big role in its collapse. We fought a war—and won.

At its most basic level, victory was a testament to nearly a half-century of U.S. resolve and consensus, among its leaders and people, that freedom was worth defending against a potential onslaught by Soviet-led communism. The future that Kennedy envisioned at the Berlin Wall, of "this city . . . joined as one" and of "this country, and this great Continent of Europe, in a peaceful and hopeful globe," had come to pass. U.S. victory in the Cold War was also a huge victory for U.S. human rights promotion. The United States had spent many dollars and much energy to defend freedom and democracy across the globe, and the Soviet collapse vindicated that commitment.

America's victory also demonstrated the power of words and action, of moral suasion and economic pressure. While U.S. leaders drew clear distinctions between the free and communist worlds, building ties with oppressed populations behind the Iron Curtain and putting Moscow on the defensive, they also took more tangible steps to confront the Soviet empire. The Jackson-Vanik amendment made Moscow's behavior toward its people a central issue of U.S. foreign policy. The Helsinki Accords of 1975 proved an unexpectedly important tool of empowerment for people within the Soviet empire. The public words and private actions of Reagan and John Paul II stirred the pot further, providing important moral and tangible support for the activists, unionists, and others who took matters into their own hands and deposed longstanding autocrats. Tens of millions of once-enslaved people were now free and, by promoting human rights, the United States could claim a large share of the credit.

THE SEARCH FOR ORDER

"I have seen the birth of communism and the death of communism,"[42] Reagan said in a moment of triumph. Reagan could take unfettered satisfaction in what he had witnessed, for he did not have to steer U.S. policy through the immediate post–Cold War period. That task fell to his successor who, having served as Reagan's vice president, nevertheless had a profoundly different take on foreign policy. After four years of Carter's mushy idealism and eight years of Reagan's fierce anti-communism, Bush launched a new period of realism. Predictably, he downplayed human rights, leaving values-driven conservatives and liberals alike dissatisfied with the tilt of U.S. foreign policy.

Early in Bush's tenure, the world changed at a breath-taking pace. Bush took office in January 1989. That month, the Soviets withdrew from Afghanistan. In June, Poland became independent. In September, Hungary followed. In November, East Germany declared that the Berlin Wall was open for passage, and almost immediately East Germans gathered to dismantle it with hammers and picks. In December, communist governments fell in Czechoslovakia, Bulgaria, and Romania. In January 1990, in his State of the Union address, Bush expressed delight:

> A year ago in Poland, Lech Walesa declared that he was ready to open a dialogue with the Communist rulers of that country. And today, with the future of a free Poland in their own hands, members of Solidarity lead the Polish Government. And a year ago, freedom's playwright, Vaclav Havel, languished as a prisoner in Prague. And today it's Vaclav Havel, president of Czechoslovakia. And one year ago, Erich Honecker of East Germany claimed history as his guide. And he predicted the Berlin Wall would last another hundred years. And today, less than one year later, it's the wall that's history. Remarkable events, remarkable events, events that fulfill the long-held hopes of the American people. Events that validate the longstanding goals of American policy, a policy based on a single shining principle: the cause of freedom.[43]

Change brings challenge, however. Like any realist, Bush prized stability. In that sense, the Cold War had proved convenient. Yes, it carried the risk of catastrophe, as highlighted by the Cuban Missile Crisis and the constant threat of a U.S.-Soviet confrontation over Berlin. But it also brought stability—two superpowers facing one another, each checking the global ambitions of the other, and much of the world lined up behind one or the other. The end of the Cold War, while rewarding U.S. resolve, begged two questions: What would come next? And would it be as stable as what had come before?

In an ode to stability, realist John J. Mearsheimer wrote in the *Atlantic Monthly* in August 1990:

> Peace: it's wonderful. I like it as much as the next man, and have no wish to be willfully gloomy at a moment when optimism about the future shape of the world abounds. Nevertheless my thesis in this essay is that we are likely soon to regret the passing of the Cold War. To be sure, no one will miss such by-products of the Cold War as the Korean and Vietnam conflicts. No one will want to replay the U-2 affair, the Cuban missile crisis, or the building of the Berlin Wall. And no one will want to revisit the domestic Cold War, with its purges and loyalty oaths, its xenophobia and stifling of dissent. We will not wake up one day to discover fresh wisdom in the collected fulminations of John Foster Dulles. We may, however, wake up one day lamenting the loss of the order that the Cold War gave to the anarchy of international relations. For untamed anarchy is what Europe knew in the forty-five years of this century before the Cold War, and untamed anarchy—Hobbes's war of all against all—is a prime cause of armed conflict. Those who think that armed conflicts among the European states are now out of the question, that the two world wars burned all the war out of Europe, are projecting unwarranted optimism onto the future. The theories of peace that implicitly undergird this optimism are notably shallow constructs. They stand up to neither logical nor historical analysis. You would not want to bet the farm on their prophetic accuracy.[44]

"The point is clear," Mearsheimer went on.

> Europe is reverting to a state system that created powerful incentives for aggression in the past. If you believe (as the Realist school of international-relations theory, to which I belong, believes) that the prospects for international peace are not markedly influenced by the domestic political character of states—that it is the character of the state system, not the character of the individual units composing it, that drives states toward war—then it is difficult to share in the widespread elation of the moment about the future of Europe. Last year was repeatedly compared to 1789, the year the French Revolution began, as the Year of Freedom, and so it was. Forgotten in the general exaltation was that the hope-filled events of 1789 signaled the start of an era of war and conquest.[45]

Bush may not have "missed" the Cold War, but the instability of its aftermath surely gave him pause. As the Berlin Wall fell and Eastern Europeans replaced authoritarianism with democracy, Bush rebuffed calls by leading

Democrats, including Senate Majority Leader George Mitchell and House Majority Leader Richard Gephardt, and even from some of his advisors to more openly gloat about U.S. victory in the Cold War—perhaps by visiting the now-open Berlin Wall. He did not want to create more problems for Soviet leader Mikhail Gorbachev, who was trying to manage the tumultuous change within the Soviet empire while keeping the Soviet Union together. "I will not be dancing on the wall," he told an appreciative Gorbachev privately.[46]

When Bush addressed the Supreme Soviet of the Ukraine in August 1991, he dampened hopes of U.S. support for Ukrainian independence from Moscow, declaring that "Americans will not support those who seek independence in order to replace a far-off tyranny with a local despotism. They will not aid those who promote a suicidal nationalism based upon ethnic hatred."[47] The acerbic *New York Times* columnist, William Safire, memorably dubbed the speech "Chicken Kiev."[48]

Bush sought stability elsewhere as well. When China's government ordered its troops to end the Tiananmen Square democracy protests in June 1989, slaughtering hundreds with tanks and bullets, Bush condemned the action in markedly restrained language, imposed only limited and temporary penalties on Beijing, and opposed congressional efforts to go further. A month later, he sent National Security Advisor Brent Scowcroft to Beijing to prevent any rupture in U.S.-China relations.[49] He sent him again in December, at which point Scowcroft, in his toast to China's leaders, acknowledged "profound areas of disagreements" that included "the events at Tiananmen" but also stated: "We . . . come today to bring new impetus and vigor into our bilateral relationship and seek new areas of agreement—economic, political, and strategic. And we come to reduce the negative influence of irritants in the relationship."[50]

What would follow the Cold War? Bush sought to provide an answer. Termed the "New World Order," it arose partly in response to an act of "naked aggression" that, Bush believed, tested the global community in the post–Cold War period. Iraq's brutal dictator, Saddam Hussein, invaded Kuwait in August 1990, seizing its oil fields and positioning Iraq to threaten the larger oil fields of Saudi Arabia and, in turn, wreak havoc with oil supplies to the West. "This will not stand, this aggression against Kuwait," Bush declared.[51]

In the New World Order, the United States would call the shots as the world's unchallenged power, but it would cooperate with other leading powers to enforce the rule of law and keep the peace (akin to what FDR had envisioned for the United Nations once the allies had won World War II). The broad coalition of nations that Bush assembled to endorse a U.S.-led effort to forcefully remove Saddam from Kuwait was the first act in this new play. In late January 1991, two weeks after the coalition launched a massive attack on Saddam's forces from the air, Bush declared, "We will succeed in the Gulf. And when we do, the world community will have sent an enduring warning to any dictator or despot, present or future, who contemplates out-law aggression. The world can, therefore, seize this opportunity to fulfill the long-held promise of a new world order, where brutality will go unrewarded and aggression will meet collective resistance."[52]

In late February, the coalition sought to deliver the final blow by attack-ing Saddam's weakened forces on the ground. Within days, the Iraqi leader agreed to withdraw from Kuwait. Mission accomplished. Or was it? Before long, the question arose in conservative circles: Should the United States stop there, with Saddam still in power? Bush thought so. He had assembled his coalition, and sought U.S. public support, based on one goal: to reverse Iraq's invasion of Kuwait. He rebuffed calls to go further, to march to Bagh-dad and remove Saddam, for fear of losing support at home and abroad.

But, as with the Hungarian uprising of 1956, U.S. signals were not quite as clear as the president suggested. In 1956, as we saw in chapter 2, the broadcasts of Radio Free Europe had suggested that Hungarians should maintain their uprising against their communist government because the United States almost certainly would assist them militarily. The people did so, Washington sat back for fears of inciting World War III, Moscow sup-pressed the uprising from the air and on the ground, and many Hungarians remained embittered toward the United States for decades to come. In 1991, Bush sent somewhat more nebulous signals about future U.S. action, but the results were eerily similar.

In February, a month after the U.S.-led coalition launched its attack, Bush visited a Raytheon missile systems plant in Andover, Massachusetts, to thank its employees for building the Patriot missile defense system that was de-stroying Saddam's Scud missiles. After reviewing his demands—Iraq's with-drawal from Kuwait, full implementation of all UN Security Council resolu-tions, and the return of Kuwait's leaders—Bush said:

> Compliance with the resolutions will instantly stop the bloodshed. And there's another way for the bloodshed to stop, and that is for the Iraqi military and the Iraqi people to take matters into their own hands and force Saddam Hussein, the dictator, to step aside and then comply with the United Nations resolutions and rejoin the family of peace-loving nations. We have no argument with the people of Iraq. Our differences are with that brutal dictator in Baghdad.[53]

Heeding his call were two parties that had long suffered under Saddam's rule—Shi'ites in southern Iraq and Kurds in the north. They both launched insurrections on March 1, a day after Bush ended U.S. combat operations. In response, Saddam ordered his forces to suppress the uprisings, which they did in brutal fashion. Washington rebuffed Shi'ite and Kurdish requests for help. Worse, Washington had previously agreed (in its cease-fire deal with Baghdad) to let Iraq's military continue flying its helicopters. That enabled Saddam to attack the rebels both from the air and the ground.

Bush's national security advisor, Brent Scowcroft, was and remains one of America's leading realists. At a 2011 conference, "The Gulf War: Twenty Years Later," he explained in classic realist terms why, in retrospect, he would not do things "much differently" if he had the chance: "We were trying to put this in the context of a world emerging from the Cold War. And one of the things we wanted to do was establish a sort of framework for how this world ought to operate. And therefore, we saw ourselves not just as the United States flexing its muscles in dealing with a bad guy, but as a representative of the world community dealing with a case of unprovoked aggression, or naked aggression."[54]

"Strategically, however," Scowcroft went on,

> we were very much aware that U.S. policy since the British essentially turned over security interests in the region to us had been, since the fall of the Shah [of Iran], to balance the two largest military forces, Iran and Iraq, off against each other. . . . We did not want Iraq split into its constituent parts. And to go on to Baghdad, take down the regime and so on, would also have destroyed that balance. . . . We didn't like the Iranians any more than we did Saddam. That was not the point. It was how can we maintain a balance in the region without massive U.S. forces there. And that was easiest to be done by Iran and Iraq offsetting each other.[55]

Paul Wolfowitz, known in later years as one of Washington's leading neoconservatives, was serving in 1991 as undersecretary of defense for policy. At the 2011 conference, he offered a strikingly different view:

> I do think that it was a tragic mistake with real strategic consequences that we failed to support those uprisings when they started. I would have—I agreed with the view that we should not risk American lives now on something that goes beyond our basic objectives. But we had pilots flying overhead watching helicopters slaughter Iraqis. We had our divisions on the south side of the Euphrates watching the Republican Guards go south to slaughter Iraqis. That was a second highway of death, and I think it should not have been permitted.[56]

"The Shia in Iraq to this day remember what happened, and very unfairly they blame the Saudis," Wolfowitz continued. "They think the Saudis were the people who told us to stop, and that's not the case. I was in Saudi Arabia with Secretary [of State James] Baker on his first trip after the war, and it was remarkable to hear Prince Bandar and Prince Saud al-Faisal, the foreign minister, saying, 'Saddam is like a wounded snake. Leaving him in power is very dangerous. You need to support these rebellions.'"[57]

Scowcroft and Wolfowitz represent the ends of the foreign policy spectrum—one a classic realist, the other a human rights–focused idealist. Another important player in the Gulf War drama was Secretary of State Baker (referenced above). A realist, he was later interviewed about the Gulf War and, not surprisingly, largely echoed Scowcroft's justifications for not extending the U.S. military involvement. Nevertheless, he bridged the gap a bit between Scowcroft and Wolfowitz, agreeing that the Bush team erred in letting Saddam's military continue to fly its helicopters. "That," he said, "was a mistake on our part."[58]

Before long, the New World Order looked much like the old. Autocrats abused their people at home and sought conquest abroad. The United States had limited resources or appetite to respond to every provocation. Bush's hopes that his era's "Great Powers" would consort to keep the peace prove illusory. Washington, as usual, would pick its spots on its own, weighing its strategic interests as well as its values, its goals for both the short and long term. For Bush and his successor, key tests would come in the poor African nation of Somalia and in the turbulent Balkans in Europe.

DIFFERENT DOCTRINES, SHARED PROBLEMS

"I am going to focus like a laser beam on this economy," Bill Clinton told ABC's Ted Koppel a day after winning the presidency in 1992, "and foreign policy will come into play in part as it affects the economy."[59]

Clinton rode a weak economy to victory. During his White House run, a sign at campaign headquarters in Little Rock, Arkansas reminded staff of where to focus their efforts: "It's the economy, stupid." Bush had looked unbeatable a year earlier after his masterful performance in building the global coalition that ousted Iraq from Kuwait. Mario Cuomo and other leading Democrats chose not to run for president, and some Democratic insiders joked darkly about not even nominating a candidate. The savvy Clinton, however, detected Bush's vulnerability in an economy that was creating few jobs and in the many families across America that were struggling to get by.

Bush had taken a traditional approach to the job. There was domestic policy and there was foreign policy. The former involved such issues as the economy, health care, and education. The latter involved such issues as war and peace, security and diplomacy, global stability and bilateral deal-making. Clinton brought domestic and foreign policy together as never before. The economy was central to his concerns, whether he was seeking to raise living standards at home or to improve America's position abroad. He created a National Economic Council, modeled on the National Security Council and marking the elevation of economics to the top of his agenda. That Clinton's economic policy was working by the mid-1990s in ways that Bush could only envy—with growth surging, jobs booming, and living standards rising—seemed to validate his efforts.

The dramatic change in perspective drove an equally dramatic change in strategic direction. Bush's "New World Order" focused on the bread and butter of foreign policymaking. When rogue actors caused conflict, the United States would work with other leading nations to confront them and restore peace. Clinton, by contrast, enunciated a broader, more economically driven doctrine of "democratic enlargement," which he pronounced in a late 1993 address at the United Nations and fleshed out in subsequent strategic documents. To promote peace and prosperity at home and abroad, the United States would grow the global economy and expand the community of free-market democracies. Successes included NATO's enlargement with the addition of Poland, Hungary, and the Czech Republic, and a raft of global, regional, and bilateral trade agreements—including a new General Agreement on Tariffs and Trade (GATT), the North American Free Trade Agreement (NAFTA), the creation of the World Trade Organization (WTO), and permanent normal trade relations (PNTR) with China.

"Democratic enlargement" tapped the intellectual foundation of U.S. human rights promotion: that more freedom and democracy means more peace and prosperity, and that freedom and democracy are geographically contagious. "Our national security strategy is based on enlarging the community of market democracies while deterring and containing a range of threats to our nation, our allies and our interests," the White House wrote in "A National Security Strategy of Engagement and Enlargement" in early 1995. "The more that democracy and political and economic liberalization take hold in the world, particularly in countries of geostrategic importance to us, the safer our nation is likely to be and the more our people are likely to prosper." The three key parts of engagement and enlargement were "our efforts to enhance our security by maintaining a strong defense capability and promoting cooperative security measures; our work to open foreign markets and spur global economic growth; and our promotion of democracy abroad."[60]

Clinton's eco-centric outlook mirrored the eco-driven optimism that increasingly infused policymaking circles at the time.[61] As the economy surged, with growth rates that exceeded most forecasts, some experts began to suggest that the economy had evolved into something new, something immune from the normal cycles of growth and recession, something that held the prospect of continuous growth. Meanwhile, foreign policy experts noted not just the growing number of free and democratic nations,[62] but also the growing global consensus that the future belonged to U.S.-style freedom and democracy. "What we may be witnessing," Francis Fukuyama wrote in "The End of History?" a landmark article for the *National Interest* that he later expanded into a book, "is not just the end of the Cold War, or the passing of a particular period of post-war history, but the end of history as such: that is, the end point of mankind's ideological evolution and the universalization of Western liberal democracy as the final form of human government."[63]

History, however, pushed back. It advanced in all-too-familiar ways in the 1990s under both Bush and Clinton, leaving horror in its wake and complicating the doctrinal assumptions of these two U.S. presidents. In Somalia on the east coast of Africa and in the Balkans in the heart of Europe, millions of people were facing the horror of indiscriminate killing, torture, starvation, forced migration, and other human rights abuses. Bush and Clinton both deployed U.S. power to ease the suffering, making clear just how central human rights promotion had become to U.S. foreign policy.

As the Bush administration was ending, Somalia was descending into humanitarian horror. Rebel forces that had driven strongman Mohamed Siad Barre from power were now battling one another to replace him. By early 1992, half of the country's six million people were severely malnourished; hundreds of thousands had already died of starvation and thousands more were dying each day; tens of thousands had been killed by rebel forces; half a million had fled; and most of the country's livestock had died.[64] For most of 1992, Bush resisted calls to send U.S. troops on a humanitarian mission to ensure that food reached the starving. He and his advisors did not view Somalia as central to U.S. national interests, and U.S. military leaders feared that the troops could neither distribute food effectively nor protect themselves in the chaos.

Bush, however, shifted course in two stages. In August, he dispatched Air Force C-130s to help provide famine relief. Then, in December, he sent more than 25,000 U.S. troops as part of a United Nations international task force (UNITAF) for the same purpose. Bush's reversal arose at least partly from public pressure. Approaching Election Day, the president was under attack for letting humanitarian disaster continue unabated in Somalia and in the Balkans (discussed below). As Scowcroft recalled later, "We did not want to portray the Administration as wholly flint-hearted realpolitik, and an airlift in Somalia was a lot cheaper [than intervention in Bosnia] to demonstrate that we had a heart."[65]

As Nixon and Ford discovered in the mid-1970s, a U.S. foreign policy that aspires to little more than the national interest can leave many Americans dissatisfied. With an eye on public opinion, Joint Chiefs of Staff Chairman Colin Powell named the mission Operation Restore Hope. "From what we saw of the public commentary and the political debates prior to the decision," Scowcroft went on, "we knew everyone in Washington supported this one."[66]

Clinton, who took office in January 1993, continued the mission until May, when he declared it a success and pulled most U.S. troops out. With UN forces under fire later that year, however, Clinton "sent in a force of

Rangers and Special Forces units to capture the brutal warlord Mohammad Farrah Aidid and restore order."[67] In early October, in what became known as the First Battle of Mogadishu, rebels shot down two U.S. Blackhawk helicopters, killed eighteen U.S. soldiers, and later paraded the bodies of some of them through the streets of Mogadishu, angering Americans and embarrassing Clinton. Defense Secretary Les Aspin resigned, admitting error in rejecting the military's request for more armor, and Clinton soon abandoned the mission. The events in Somalia contributed to Clinton's reticence to respond forcefully a year later to a humanitarian horror in Rwanda, where the United States did nothing as Hutu soldiers and citizens slaughtered eight hundred thousand Tutsis.[68]

Bush and Clinton reversed roles in another horror show around the same time. By the early 1990s, the ethnic hatreds that Yugoslavian strongman Josip Broz Tito had contained until his death in 1980 bubbled over and Yugoslavia descended into a series of conflicts among its six republics. By mid-1992, the Serbian forces of Slobodan Milosevic were engaging in a brutal campaign of ethnic cleansing against Muslims in Bosnia, killing indiscriminately, driving 2.5 million people from their homes, and establishing concentration camps where skeletal figures looked out from behind barbed wire. In September, the CIA warned that 250,000 Bosnian Muslims might die that winter from starvation and exposure. Administration realists, however, did not believe that vital U.S. interests were at stake—"We don't have a dog in that fight," Secretary of State Baker had memorably said—and military leaders worried about the fate of U.S. troops in such a chaotic environment. Unlike Somalia, Bush would not change course, leaving the festering problem to his successor.[69]

Under Clinton, who had chastised Bush for inaction in the Balkans during his 1992 run for president, the horror continued. After the United Nations created peacekeeping safe havens in several Bosnian cities in 1993, Serb forces attacked them. Two years later, the Serbs attacked a UN safe haven in Srebrenica, overwhelmed the six hundred Dutch troops on hand, and then slaughtered seven thousand Muslims. Within weeks, Serbs overtook a safe haven in Zepa. The U.S.-led West finally responded, with NATO launching 750 air strikes on Serbian targets. That fall, Assistant Secretary of State Richard Holbrooke engineered a peace treaty known as the Dayton Accords. It allocated land among Serbs, Croats, and Muslims and created an international Implementation Force (IFOR), for which the United States provided twenty thousand troops, to maintain peace and investigate human rights violations.

Then, in 1999, the United States joined with NATO to end another round of ethnic cleansing by Milosevic's Serbian forces, this time against Albanians in Kosovo. The Serbs had murdered thousands and created refugees out of hundreds of thousands. The United States and its allies took to the air, bombing Serbian troops and forcing their withdrawal from the region. Western nations contributed troops for a peacekeeping mission in Kosovo. Milosevic was later arrested and turned over to the United Nations International Criminal Tribunal in The Hague, which had been building a case against him for ethnic cleansing since 1996. He died of a heart attack while awaiting the verdict from his trial.[70]

Bush and Clinton were very different men, and their presidencies progressed in very different ways. Bush left office after one term, the victim of a weak economy that created few jobs. Clinton served for two, the beneficiary of a roaring economy that created jobs at a record pace and raised living standards at all income levels. Bush was a foreign policy aficionado, as witnessed by his performance in the months after Iraq invaded Kuwait. Clinton was a foreign policy novice whose early months were marked by missteps and uncertainty. On their separate watches, however, each felt compelled to respond to humanitarian horror thousands of miles from home. That they did highlights the central role that human rights promotion had come to assume in U.S. foreign policy as well as the expectations that presidents face when such horror surfaces.

CONCLUSION

Could the United States make a difference on the human rights front? The quarter-century that began with Carter and ended with Clinton left no doubt. Decades of U.S. "containment" and targeted operations to exploit Soviet vulnerabilities helped catapult the United States to victory in the Cold War, freeing tens of millions of people from political oppression and geographic isolation. U.S. military power also helped to bring relief to some of the millions of people in Europe and Africa who were suffering particularly egregious abuses of human rights.

The Soviet collapse, later combined with a roaring Western economy, evoked an understandable euphoria in Western circles. The United States had not just won a long and bitter struggle with an implacable enemy. It had offered a roadmap to peace and prosperity in a post–Cold War world. History, we were told, was over. The way forward was with U.S.-led democracy and free markets. The more that nations adopted the U.S. approach, the more peaceful and prosperous the world would be. The more that peace and prosperity spread, the more that human rights would advance.

History would prove stubborn, however, rearing its ugly head on a sunny, cloudless day in September 2001.

NOTES

1. Daniel Patrick Moynihan, "The Politics of Human Rights," *Commentary* (August 1977).

2. Jimmy Carter, Inaugural Address, January 20, 1977.

3. Jimmy Carter, Commencement Address at Notre Dame University, May 22, 1977.

4. Moynihan, "Human Rights."

5. Friedbert Pfluger, "Human Rights Unbound: Carter's Human Rights Policy Reassessed," *Presidential Studies Quarterly*, vol. 19, no. 4 (Fall 1989): 706–10.

6. Sandy Vogelgesang, "Diplomacy of Human Rights," *International Studies Quarterly*, vol. 23, no. 2 (June 1979): 223–24; Mark L. Schneider, "Human Rights Policy under the Carter Administration," *Law and Contemporary Problems*, vol. 43, no. 2 (Spring 1979): 262–63.

7. Jerome J. Shestack, "Human Rights, the National Interest, and U.S. Foreign Policy," *Annals of the American Academy of Political and Social Sciences*, vol. 506 (November 1989): 23. In an essay for *Foreign Affairs* in 1978, historian Arthur M. Schlesinger Jr. described Carter's inconsistency this way: "Washington was fearless in denouncing human rights abuses in countries like Cambodia, Paraguay and Uganda, where the United States had negligible strategic and economic interests; a good deal less fearless toward South Korea, Saudi Arabia, Yugoslavia and most of black Africa; increasingly circumspect about the Soviet Union; totally silent about China." See Schlesinger, "Human Rights and the American Tradition," *Foreign Affairs*, vol. 57, no. 3 (1978).

8. Michael Stohl, David Carleton, and Steven E. Johnson, "Human Rights and U.S. Foreign Assistance from Nixon to Carter," *Journal of Peace Research*, vol. 21, no. 3 (1984): 223.

9. Stephen Cohen, "Conditioning U.S. Security Assistance on Human Rights Practices," *American Journal of International Law*, vol. 76, no. 2 (April 1982): 264, as cited in Stohl, Carleton, and Johnson, "Human Rights," 223.

10. Public Broadcasting Service, "The Iranian Hostage Crisis," www.pbs.org/wgbh/americanexperience/features/general-article/carter-hostage-crisis.

11. Jeane J. Kirkpatrick, "Dictatorships and Double Standards," *Commentary* (November 1979).

12. Administration officials themselves worried about that perception. National Security Advisor Zbigniew Brzezinski later wrote in his memoirs that "our human-rights policy was in danger of becoming one-sidedly anti-rightist." Cited in Clair Apodaca, *Understanding U.S. Human Rights Policy* (New York: Routledge, 2006), 58.

13. Kirkpatrick, "Dictatorships."

14. Kirkpatrick, "Dictatorships."

15. Doug MacEachin and Janne E. Nolan, co-chairs, Discourse, Dissent, and Strategic Surprise: Formulating American Security in an Age of Uncertainty, Institute for the Study of Diplomacy, Edmund A. Walsh School of Foreign Service, Georgetown University, "The Soviet Invasion of Afghanistan in 1979: Failure of Intelligence or of the Policy Process?" Working Group Report No. 111, September 26, 2005; Pfluger, "Human Rights," 707–8; and Jimmy Carter, Interview with ABC's *World News Tonight*, January 19, 1980, as quoted in Jerl A. Rosati, "Jimmy Carter, A Man Before His Time? The Emergence and Collapse of the First Post–Cold War Presidency," *Presidential Studies Quarterly*, vol. 23, no. 3 (Summer 1993): 472.

16. "The View from the Gulag: An Interview with Natan Sharansky," *Weekly Standard*, June 21, 2004.

17. Ronald Reagan, Address to the National Association of Evangelicals, Orlando, Florida, March 8, 1983.

18. Anthony Lewis, "Onward, Christian Soldiers," *New York Times*, March 10, 1983.

19. Juan Williams, "Writers of Speeches for President Claim Force Is with Him," *Washington Post*, March 19, 1983.

20. "The View," *Weekly Standard*.

21. As Reagan's secretary of state, Alexander Haig, said in a March 31, 1981, speech to the Trilateral Commission, "The Soviet Union and its allies—countries that reject our concepts of human rights—continue to enlarge their military power and seem increasingly inclined to use their arms to advance their cause. Unlike the Soviets, we are not going to deprive peoples of their dignity and choice. Nonetheless, we are not prepared to see the world remade by others hostile to our deepest convictions, convictions held by civilized societies everywhere. Our resistance to this aggression and our assistance to its victims constitutes a defense of human rights that is at the very basis of our foreign policy and our national interest." Cited in *New York Times*, "Excerpts from Haig's Speech on Human Rights and Foreign Policy," April 21, 1981.

22. Joan A. Soares, "Strategy, Ideology, and Human Rights: Jimmy Carter Confronts the Left in Central America, 1979–1981," *Journal of Cold War Studies*, vol. 8, no. 4 (Fall 2006): 58–63.

23. Richard V. Allen, "The Man Who Won the Cold War," *Hoover Digest*, January 30, 2000, www.hoover.org/publications/hoover-digest/article/7398.

24. Allen, "The Man." Reagan's private remark presaged his far more public challenge to Soviet leader Mikhail Gorbachev nearly a decade later as he again stood at the Wall: "Mr. Gorbachev, tear down this wall!"

25. Office of the Historian, U.S. Department of State, "Milestones: 1981–1989: Reagan Doctrine, 1985," http://history.state.gov/milestones/1981-1989/ReaganDoctrine.

26. Ronald Reagan, State of the Union Address, February 6, 1985.

27. The effort badly tarnished Reagan in his second term when, after Congress enacted the Boland Amendment to prohibit more federal funds for the contras, the administration engaged in what became known as the Iran-Contra affair—a secret plot to bypass the congressional restrictions by selling weapons to Iran and funneling some of the proceeds to the contras.

28. Charles Krauthammer, "Essay: The Reagan Doctrine," *Time*, April 1, 1985.

29. Ronald Reagan, Address to the House of Commons, London, June 8, 1982.

30. Key lawmakers had been pushing for such an institution for years. Representative Dante Fascell, a Florida Democrat and later chairman of the House Foreign Affairs Committee, proposed legislation to create an Institute of International Affairs in 1967, and he and Representative Donald Fraser, a Minnesota Democrat, proposed a QUANGO (quasi-autonomous, nongovernmental organization) in 1978. David Lowe, "Idea to Reality: NED at 25," National Endowment for Democracy, www.ned.org/about/history.

31. International Human Rights Funders Group, "National Endowment for Democracy," www.ihrfg.org/funder-directory/national-endowment-democracy-ned.

32. Maciej Bartkowski, "Poland's Solidarity Movement (1980–1989)," International Center on Nonviolent Conflict, www.nonviolent-conflict.org/index.php/movements-and-campaigns/movements-and-campaigns-summaries?sobi2Task=sobi2Details&catid=27&sobi2Id=8.

33. Carl Bernstein, "The Holy Alliance: Ronald Reagan and John Paul II," *Time*, February 24, 1992.

34. Bernstein, "Holy Alliance."

35. Stefan Chwin, "Poland's Holy Father," *New York Times*, April 5, 2005.

36. Bartkowski, "Poland's Solidarity Movement"; Maciej Bartkowski, "The Cold War Files: The Solidarity Movement of Poland," Woodrow Wilson International Center for Scholars.

37. Gdansk-Life.com, "The Story of the Solidarity Movement," www.gdansk-life.com/poland/solidarity.

38. Gdansk-Life.com, "Solidarity Movement"; U.S. Library of Congress, "The United States and Poland Country Study," http://countrystudies.us/poland/92.htm.

39. Ronald Reagan, Address to the Nation, October 9, 1982.

40. Bernstein, "Holy Alliance."

41. Gdansk-Life.com, "Solidarity Movement."

42. Ronald Reagan, Address to the Republican National Convention, August 17, 1992.

43. George H. W. Bush, State of the Union Address, January 31, 1990.

44. John J. Mearsheimer, "Why We Will Soon Miss the Cold War," *Atlantic Monthly*, August 1990.

45. Mearsheimer, "Why We Will Soon."

46. Public Broadcasting Service, "George H. W. Bush: A New World Order," The American Experience, www.pbs.org/wgbh/amex/presidents/video/ghw_bush_12.html#v264.

47. George H. W. Bush, Address to the Supreme Soviet of Ukraine, August 1, 1991.

48. William Safire, "Putin's 'Chicken Kiev,'" *New York Times*, December 6, 2004.

49. Apodaca, *Understanding*, 122–23; Miller Center, "George H. W. Bush: Foreign Affairs," http://millercenter.org/president/bush/essays/biography/5.

50. Brent Scowcroft, "Toast by the Honorable Brent Scowcroft, Assistant to the President for National Security Affairs, Beijing, December 9, 1989," *New York Review of Books*, June 23, 2011.

51. Michael Howard, "The Prudence Thing: George Bush's Class Act," *Foreign Affairs* (November/December 1998): 133.

52. George H. W. Bush, State of the Union Address, January 29, 1991.

53. George H. W. Bush, Remarks to Raytheon Missile Systems Plant Employees in Andover, Massachusetts, February 15, 1991.

54. Council on Foreign Relations, "The Gulf War: Twenty Years Later," February 15, 2011, www.cfr.org/middle-east/gulf-war-twenty-years-later/p24150.

55. Council on Foreign Relations, "Gulf War."

56. Council on Foreign Relations, "Gulf War."

57. Council on Foreign Relations, "Gulf War."

58. Public Broadcasting Service, "Gunning for Saddam: Interview, James Baker," www.pbs.org/wgbh/pages/frontline/shows/gunning/interviews/baker.html.

59. Don Oberdorfer, "Clinton Prepares to Take on World—He's Becoming a Student of Foreign Policy," *Seattle Times*, November 7, 1992.

60. White House, "A National Security Strategy of Engagement and Enlargement," February 1995, 2–3.

61. "The age of geopolitics has given way to an age of what might be called geo-economics," Martin Walker wrote in the *New Yorker* in late 1996. "The new virility symbols are exports and productivity and growth rate and the great international encounters are the trade pacts of the economic superpowers." Cited in Douglas Brinkley, "Democratic Enlargement: The Clinton Doctrine," *Foreign Policy* (Spring 1997).

62. The number of countries that Freedom House listed as "free" rose from sixty-one at the end of the 1980s to eighty-eight a decade later, or from 37 percent to 46 percent of all countries on earth. "Freedom in the World Country Ratings," www.freedomhouse.org/images/File/fiw/historical/CountryStatusRatingsOverview1973-2011.pdf.

63. Francis Fukuyama, "The End of History?" *National Interest* (Summer 1989).

64. George B. N. Ayittey, "The Somali Crisis: Time for an African Solution," Cato Institute, Policy Analysis No. 205, March 28, 1994; Jon Western, "Sources of Humanitarian Intervention: Beliefs, Information, and Advocacy in the U.S. Decisions on Somalia and Bosnia," *International Security*, vol. 27, no. 1 (July/August 1999).

65. Western, "Sources of Humanitarian Intervention."

66. Western, "Sources of Humanitarian Intervention."

67. "Clinton's Black Hawk Down History—On Somalia, the Ex-President is as Mendacious as Ever," *Wall Street Journal*, August 6, 2002.

68. Mark Bowden, "A Defining Battle," *Philadelphia Inquirer*, November 16, 1997, http://inquirer.philly.com/packages/somalia/nov16/rang16.asp; Miller Center, "Bill Clinton: Foreign Affairs," http://millercenter.org/president/clinton/essays/biography/5; and Samantha Power, "Bystanders to Genocide: Why the United States Let the Rwandan Tragedy Happen, *Atlantic Monthly*, September 2001.

69. Western, "Sources of Humanitarian Intervention," and J. F. O. McAllister, "Atrocity and Outrage," *Time*, August 17, 1992.

70. Miller Center, "Bill Clinton: Foreign Affairs"; Natalie Pierce, "The Clinton Years: Assessing Success in the Bosnian Genocide Intervention," *Global Tides*, http://global-tides.pepperdine.edu/clinton-years.pdf.

Chapter Five

Terror and Its Aftermath: From Bush to Obama

The terrorist attacks of September 11 prompted a new phase of U.S. foreign policy, one in which the nation's military and diplomatic efforts focused largely on winning a new "war on terror." A nation that, for a decade after the Cold War, basked in hopes that U.S.-led freedom and democracy would inevitably advance around the world, nourishing peace and prosperity, now found itself forced to learn about and respond to the challenge of radical Islam. The United States went to war in Afghanistan and Iraq and mounted a major effort to better protect its homeland.

The first two presidents of the post–September 11 period took markedly different approaches to the threat—and to the role that human rights promotion would play in addressing it. George W. Bush enunciated a "Bush Doctrine" that included a "freedom agenda" through which the United States would push forcefully to advance freedom and democracy as an antidote to terror. With freedom and democracy, restive populations in the Middle East, North Africa, and elsewhere presumably would neither seek meaning in radical ideologies nor be tempted by terrorism. By contrast, Barack Obama eschewed talk of crusades for freedom and democracy and sought instead to improve U.S. relations with its adversaries in order to reduce terrorist threats.

The Bush-Obama years illustrated the promise and peril of human rights promotion—and the benefits and drawbacks of elevating or downplaying the effort. With his powerful rhetoric, Bush inspired democratic activists to action in multiple countries. But when he and his team failed to do the hard work of nourishing freedom and democracy for the long term, they helped position terrorist groups to seize power in key parts of the Middle East. Then, perhaps chastened by those results, Bush failed to maintain his rhetorical push for human rights, providing a symbolic green light for autocrats to reassert their control. Obama, a self-described "realist," spoke eloquently about human rights on several occasions but operated pragmatically, putting human rights promotion on the back burner in the interest of power politics. He gave little public support to democracy-seeking activists in China, Russia, and other authoritarian nations and, seeking better ties with Tehran, he largely let pass a monumental opportunity to help the Iranian people topple their terror-sponsoring, nuclear weapons-seeking, and rights-abusing regime.

A WORLD TRANSFORMED

It was early September 2001 and Washington was chugging along with a typical set of preoccupations. President Vincente Fox was visiting from Mexico and President Bush was talking about immigration reform. Bush had pushed a huge tax cut through Congress earlier in the year, and the two branches were now locked in combat over the spending bills that would fund the government. First Lady Laura Bush launched her annual National Book Festival with a black-tie dinner on Friday, September 7, at the Library of Congress, a breakfast at the White House the next morning, and a festival that weekend along Washington's National Mall.

Bush had won the presidency in a most unusual way, and the bitterness among Democrats cast a shadow over inter-party relations for his entire tenure. His contest with Al Gore in 2000 had ended in a virtual dead heat, with the votes so close that Gore called Bush on election night to congratulate him on winning, then called again to take it back when more vote counts poured in from Florida. After Bush won Florida by a razor-thin margin, the state launched a recount. The final tally would determine who would become president, so activists from both parties flew down from Washington to work the courts, shape media coverage, and prevent the other side from stealing victory. The Supreme Court eventually stepped in, stopped the recount, and awarded the win to Bush.

That Bush found himself the subject of bitter partisanship was ironic. In 1994, he had unseated Texas Governor Ann Richards in a national Republican wave and won a sweeping reelection in 1998, becoming his state's first governor to win a second straight four-year term and raising coast-to-coast expectations among Republicans that he was the man to regain the presidency for them. In Austin, he governed from the center and touted his close ties to Democrats, most notably Lieutenant Governor Bob Bullock, who had endorsed his reelection. Accepting the presidential nomination at the 2000 Republican National Convention in Philadelphia, he told a nation-wide audience, "I don't have enemies to fight. And I have no stake in the bitter arguments of the last few years. I want to change the tone of Washington to one of civility and respect."[1] On the campaign trail, he described himself often as "a uniter, not a divider."

On foreign policy, Bush promised to steer a global leadership that was "humble," not "arrogant." Though he would use force to defend U.S. interests, he offered a limited set of conditions: "[T]he cause must be just, the goal must be clear, and the victory must be overwhelming."[2] He promised to "stand by Israel" while reaching out to "moderate" Arab states like Egypt, Saudi Arabia, Jordan, and Kuwait. He reaffirmed the longstanding Republican push to develop a missile defense system to protect the United States and its allies from nuclear weapons-seeking states like Iraq and Iran. He supported NATO's bombing of Serbia in the 1990s to bring Slobodan Milosevic to justice and criticized President Clinton only for ruling out the use of ground troops. But he also praised Clinton for not intervening in Rwanda despite the horrific genocide there, explaining that, unlike Serbia, Rwanda was not in America's strategic interest. Bush sharply criticized the notion that America's military should engage in "nation building," saying, "[O]ur military is meant to fight and win war . . . and when it gets overextended, morale drops."[3] Thus, he chastised Clinton for sending troops to Haiti in 1994 to restore to power Jean-Bertrand Aristides, the democratically elected president who was ousted in a coup. Though he promised to encourage the advance of freedom and democracy, he advised other nations to follow their own paths to get there. "I just don't think it's the role of the United States to walk into a country and say, we do it this way, so should you."[4]

On September 10, Bush's secretary of defense, Donald H. Rumsfeld, was talking about America's national security. In fact, in a speech at the Pentagon, he sought to focus the attention of his Department of Defense (DoD) staff on "a serious threat to the security of the United States of America."

This adversary is one of the world's last bastions of central planning. It governs by dictating five-year plans. From a single capital, it attempts to impose its demands across time zones, continents, oceans and beyond. With brutal consistency, it stifles free thought and crushes new ideas. It disrupts the defense of the United States and places the lives of men and women in uniform at risk. Perhaps this adversary sounds like the former Soviet Union, but that enemy is gone: our foes are more subtle and implacable today. You may think I'm describing one of the last decrepit dictators of the world. But their day, too, is almost past, and they cannot match the strength and size of this adversary. This adversary's closer to home. It's the Pentagon bureaucracy. Not the people, but the processes. Not the civilians, but the systems. Not the men and women in uniform, but the uniformity of thought and action that we too often impose on them.[5]

DoD had too much overhead, too much bureaucracy, too many layers, and too much infrastructure. It could not account for a whopping $2.3 trillion in "transactions." It could not share information within the department because its computer systems were incompatible with one another. It needed to "slash duplication and encourage cooperation," "support information sharing" and "speed decision-making," reduce staff and rely on "commercial outsourcing" for some functions," "streamline the acquisition process and spur innovation," and improve the health care and housing of its war-fighters.

With America at peace, Rumsfeld could devote a huge chunk of his time and energy to the challenge of modernizing a vast bureaucracy of more than two million men and women, most of them in uniform.

Then came the news.

It was Tuesday, September 11, 2001, 8:46 a.m., EST. At the southern tip of Manhattan, a Boeing 767 that had taken off from Boston en route to Los Angeles crashed into an upper floor of the World Trade Center's north tower—a majestic symbol of America's financial prowess in the heart of New York's financial district. Seventeen minutes later, another Boeing 767 on the Boston-to-Los Angeles route tore through the south tower, removing any doubt that the United States was under attack. New Yorkers looked up in horror as flames flew, smoke blanketed the sky, and men and women trapped by fire jumped to their deaths. At about 9:40 a.m. in suburban Washington, a Boeing 757 that had taken off from Dulles International Airport en route to LA struck the Pentagon—a massive symbol of America's military prowess. Meanwhile, another hijacked Boeing 757 on a Newark-to-San Francisco flight was probably headed to the White House or Capitol—each a symbol of America's democratic prowess. On that flight, passengers who learned of the havoc in New York and Washington from cell phone conversations with loved ones decided to confront their hijackers rather than allow for more death and destruction. After an on-board struggle, the plane crashed in a field in Shanksville, Pennsylvania, southeast of Pittsburgh.

This well-coordinated plot by nineteen terrorists with knives and box cutters, which was hatched from caves half a world away, was the deadliest attack on U.S. soil in the nation's history, killing nearly three thousand people in New York, Washington, and Pennsylvania. It awoke the United States to a threat that had festered for years in the turbulent Middle East, North Africa, and Central Asia: radical Islamist ideology and the terrorism that it fosters. It made a household name of the perpetrators—Osama bin Laden and his organization, al Qaeda—but the threat extended far beyond one person or one organization.

America's adversary was a web of terrorist groups and the radical governments that gave them not only safe havens from which to operate but also money, weapons, training, and logistical support. This web of groups and governments was fueled by a radical ideology whose theological roots date back more than fourteen centuries. It is fiercely anti-modern and anti-Western, anti-Jewish and anti-Christian.

On foreign policy, the events of September 11 changed . . . well . . . everything. The United States was attacked and, of course, it would respond. That was the least—or, more correctly, the least controversial—of things to come. Terrorism represented a new kind of foreign policy challenge, and it demanded a new kind of response. That response marked the third major phase of U.S. foreign policy since World War II.

For the first half-century of the postwar period, U.S. foreign policy revolved around efforts to "contain" the Soviet Union and win the Cold War. In the 1990s, Presidents George H. W. Bush and Clinton each sought to craft a vision for a hopeful world in which the United States reigned supreme, its military unchallenged and its economy showcasing the benefits of free-market capitalism. With September 11, America came to realize that it faced a new challenge that demanded a new vision.[6]

The terrorists had launched a war on not just the United States but also freedom itself, presenting as stark a challenge to U.S. values as communism during the Cold War.

THE NEW CHALLENGE

"Why do they hate us?"

It was the question that dominated public discourse across the United States in the days after September 11. Why, more precisely, were nineteen men moved to hijack airplanes and fly them into some of America's most symbolic structures, taking their own lives and killing thousands of innocent people in the process?

Among experts, the answers divided along two basic lines. One group suggested that the United States brought the attacks upon itself with its aggressive and imperialistic foreign policy across the Greater Middle East over several decades. That policy, these experts said, tilted too much toward Israel, meddled too much in Arab affairs, and revolved too much around America's dependence on Middle East oil.

To be sure, U.S. foreign policy had not been perfect. It had been overly aggressive on some occasions, imperialistic on others. But, as a second group of experts argued, the attacks were less the result of U.S. foreign policy than a natural outgrowth of the radical, anti-Western ideology that fueled the terrorist network. Put simply, the attack was less about what America had done and more about who we are, what we believe, what values we cherish, and how we view government and society.

In her 2006 book, *Knowing the Enemy*, Johns Hopkins University scholar Mary Habeck puts it well: "[T]he nineteen men who attacked the United States and the many other groups who continue to work for its destruction—including al-Qaida [*sic*]—are part of a radical faction of the multifaceted Islamist belief system. This faction—generally called 'jihadi' or 'jihadist'—has very specific views about how to revive Islam, how to return Muslims to political power, and what needs to be done about its enemies, including the United States."[7]

To the jihadists, Islam is everything. And in elevating their orthodox interpretation of Islam to this exalted, all-encompassing position, the jihadists reject the most cherished of Western values. They recognize no separation of church and state; in essence, religion is the state. They reject Western notions of personal freedom; people are "free" only to follow the dictates of Islam, and all Muslims must confront those who do not. They reject democracy because people should have no power to decide how they will be governed; Islam provides the answer. They reject equality between the sexes; men rule over women, the latter of whom have no power to pursue independent lives.

Jihadism has roots in both branches of Islam—the Sunni, to which most Muslims belong, and the Shia.[8] Their rivalry "goes back to the early days of Islam and the succession crisis that followed the Prophet Mohammed's death in 632 C.E."[9] Today, Sunni states (led by Saudi Arabia) and Shia states (led by Iran) eye each other warily and compete for regional dominance. Sunnis dominated the region for decades until the Iranian Revolution of 1979, which brought a radical Shia theocracy to power.

Nevertheless, jihadists of both strains often enter "marriages of convenience" with one another to pursue their shared agenda of weakening the United States, its European allies, and Israel. Shia Iran funds the Palestinian terrorist group Hamas, which is an offshoot of the Sunni Muslim Brotherhood. Iran has worked with al Qaeda, a Sunni group. Hezbollah, the Lebanese Shia militia, works closely with Hamas and other terrorist groups to pursue their shared commitment to destroy Israel.

The events of September 11 sent shock waves through the nation, leaving it reeling. On that day in New York, flames engulfing the Twin Towers were visible from miles away. In Washington, where the Pentagon was ablaze, Bush staffers were ordered to run from the White House out of fears that a plane was headed their way. In the ensuing days, Americans sat glued to their TV sets, watching tapes of the attacks unfold time after time and listening to experts decipher their meaning. With no one sure when another attack might come, and from where, the National Guard patrolled the streets of Washington while F-16 fighter jets protected the east coast from the sky.

The nation, however, had no good excuse for its shock. America's enemies had openly warned that they were coming, and they had mounted evermore brazen attacks on U.S. interests abroad over the previous two decades.

On the Sunni side, the warnings from al Qaeda dated back more than a decade. In its February 23, 1998, "Declaration of War against Americans," published in the Arabic newspaper *Al-Quds Al-Arabi*, the organization wrote,

> The ruling to kill the Americans and their allies—civilians and military—is an individual obligation incumbent upon every Muslim who can do it and in any country. . . . By Allah's leave we call upon every Muslim who believes in Allah and wishes to be rewarded to comply with Allah's order to kill the Americans and seize their money wherever and whenever they find them. We also call on Muslim *ulema* [scholars], leaders, youths, and soldiers to launch the raid on the Devil's army—the Americans—and whoever allies with them from the supporters of Satan, and to rout those behind them so that they may learn [a lesson]. [10]

In August 1998, al Qaeda bombed U.S. embassies in Nairobi, Kenya, and Dar es Salaam, Tanzania, killing more than two hundred people and injuring five thousand. In late 1999 and early 2000, it planned to attack U.S. and Israeli tourists who were visiting Jordan for millennium celebrations and to attack Los Angeles International Airport, but Jordanian and U.S. authorities thwarted their plots. In early 2000, it tried to attack the USS *The Sullivans*, which was stationed in the port city of Aden, Yemen, but its boat of explosives sank. Later in 2000, al Qaeda bombed the USS *Cole* while it refueled in Aden, killing seventeen U.S. sailors, injuring thirty, and blowing a huge hole in the Navy destroyer.

On the Shia side, the threat was headquartered in Tehran, where a radical regime had been waging war with the United States ever since it assumed power in 1979. It was aggressive, expansionist, and rabidly anti-American. Iran was responsible (directly or through surrogates) for hundreds of U.S. deaths, either on battlefields in Iraq and Afghanistan or elsewhere through its terrorist network. As the world's most aggressive state sponsor of terrorism, it provided significant funding, training, and weapons to such groups as Hezbollah, Hamas, Palestinian Islamic Jihad, the al-Aqsa Martyrs Brigade, and the Popular Front for the Liberation of Palestine-General Command. Tehran worked closely with the Syrian government of Bashar al-Assad on terrorism and other joint interests.

Hezbollah was behind the 1983 suicide bombing of the U.S. embassy in Beirut, Lebanon, which killed more than 60 people; the 1983 truck bombing of the U.S. Marine barracks in Beirut, which killed 241 U.S. Marines and other service members; and likely the 1996 bombing of Khobar Towers in Dharan, Saudi Arabia, which killed 19 U.S. servicemen. In Iraq, Iran provided Shia militias and insurgents with armor-piercing munitions, "explosively formed penetrators," surface-to-air missiles, and other sophisticated weaponry to use against U.S. forces. In Afghanistan, it shipped explosive devices to insurgents for the same purpose.

The combustible mix of radical ideology, radical governments, and radical terrorist groups has fueled a scholarly debate over the nature of Islam and its connection to terrorism. One school argues that Islam is, at its core, anti-modern, anti-Western, and anti-democratic (per the writings of Ayaan Hirsi Ali,[11] Wafa Sultan,[12] and Brigitte Gabriel[13]), while another argues that Islam is amenable to Western values but has been hijacked by the radical forces of jihadism (per the writings of Irshad Manji,[14] Zainab Al-Suwaij,[15] and Zuhdi Jasser[16]). That debate has spurred an equally intense exchange of views about how to confront the challenge—from using military force against terrorists and terror-sponsoring governments to waging a war of ideas against jihadists; from pressuring radical governments publicly to engaging them privately; from maintaining U.S. forces across the Middle East to reducing the U.S. footprint; from standing firmly with Israel to taking a more "balanced" approach to the Arab-Israeli conflict.

Tutored by different scholars, our two post–September 11 presidents approached the challenge in different ways.

BUSH'S TRANSFORMATION

"Great harm has been done to us," President Bush told a joint session of Congress nine days after September 11.

> We have suffered great loss. And in our grief and anger we have found our mission and our moment. Freedom and fear are at war. The advance of human freedom—the great achievement of our time, and the great hope of every time—now depends on us. Our nation—this generation—will lift a dark threat of violence from our people and our future. We will rally the world to this cause by our efforts, by our courage. We will not tire, we will not falter, and we will not fail.[17]

In his call to arms, his Churchillian reassurance of ultimate victory, Bush equated the new threat to freedom with America's most serious security challenges of yesteryear. He echoed the language of FDR, Truman, Kennedy, and Reagan because he believed that the challenge of terrorism was similar in scope with what his predecessors had faced during World War II and the Cold War.

After describing a global network of terrorist groups that operates in more than sixty countries, that seeks to impose its strict interpretation of Islam on lands both near and far, that works to topple governments across the Middle East and destroy Israel, and that plots to kill Christians and Jews, he said,

> We are not deceived by their pretenses to piety. We have seen their kind before. They are the heirs of all the murderous ideologies of the 20th century. By sacrificing human life to serve their radical visions—by abandoning every value except the will to power—they follow in the path of fascism, Nazism, and totalitarianism. And they will follow that path all the way, to where it ends: in history's unmarked grave of discarded lies.[18]

That night, Bush announced a global "war on terror." Then, in a year-long effort that culminated in "The National Security Strategy of the United States of America,"[19] he crafted what became known as the "Bush Doctrine." It defined the terrorist challenge broadly, set new conditions for U.S. military action, and included a "freedom agenda" to advance human rights as an antidote to extremism and terror.

Experts continue to define the doctrine differently, but it includes at least the following three elements.

First, the United States would treat terror-sponsoring states no differently than the terrorists themselves.

Addressing the nation on the evening of September 11, Bush vowed to "make no distinction between the terrorists who committed these acts and those who harbor them."[20] In his September 20 address to Congress, he explained more broadly, "We will pursue nations that provide aid or safe haven to terrorism. Every nation, in every region, now has a decision to make. Either you are with us, or you are with the terrorists. From this day forward, any nation that continues to harbor or support terrorism will be regarded by the United States as a hostile regime."[21]

Second, the United States would act preemptively to confront mounting threats, rather than merely respond to attack.

The United States faced a growing, and profoundly frightening, threat— that terrorists or terror-sponsoring states might develop or acquire weapons of mass destruction, enabling them to wreak a far greater havoc than what occurred in New York and Washington on September 11 or in Beirut in 1983, Dharan in 1996, or Nairobi or Dar es Salaam in 1998. Though Bush would not seek a military confrontation, he also would not stand idly by as dangers mounted. If need be, he would take preemptive action to address them.

"We cannot defend America and our friends by hoping for the best," Bush said in a high-profile address at West Point on June 1, 2002.

We cannot put our faith in the word of tyrants, who solemnly sign non-proliferation treaties and then systemically break them. If we wait for threats to fully materialize, we will have waited too long. . . . Our security will require transforming the military you will lead—a military that must be ready to strike at a moment's notice in any dark corner of the world. And our security will require all Americans to be forward-looking and resolute, to be ready for preemptive action when necessary to defend our liberty and to defend our lives.[22]

Third, the United States would reduce the threat of terrorism, and the appeal of radical ideologies that fuel terrorism, by advancing freedom and democracy across the Middle East and elsewhere.

With freedom and democracy, the people of once-oppressed nations would have more opportunity to pursue their dreams and less temptation to extremism and violence. As with Truman and the Marshall Plan, Kennedy and a revamped foreign aid program, and Reagan and his efforts to weaken the Soviet empire, so with Bush and his "freedom agenda": the advance of human rights was both a moral duty and a national imperative.

"We have seen our vulnerability—and we have seen its deepest source," Bush said in promoting his "freedom agenda" during his second inaugural address in January 2005:

For as long as whole regions of the world simmer in resentment and tyranny—prone to ideologies that feed hatred and excuse murder—violence will gather, and multiply in destructive power, and cross the most defended borders, and raise a mortal threat. There is only one force of history that can break the reign of hatred and resentment, and expose the pretensions of tyrants, and reward the hopes of the decent and tolerant, and that is the force of human freedom. . . .
So it is the policy of the United States to seek and support the growth of democratic movements and institutions in every nation and culture, with the ultimate goal of ending tyranny in our world.[23]

Six months later to the day, Secretary of State Condoleezza Rice visited Cairo—the capital of what has long been considered the leading Arab state—to push the envelope of U.S. foreign policy even further.

For decades, the United States had pursued the same basic strategy in the Middle East. Heavily dependent on the oil-exporting states to power its economy, and determined to protect its closest ally in the region (Israel), Washington sought regional stability by backing autocrats in Egypt, Saudi Arabia, Jordan, and elsewhere. Washington armed and defended their governments and, for the most part, they kept the oil flowing to the United States and controlled the anti-American forces within their societies. This bargain between the United States and its autocratic allies in the Middle East was a prime example of foreign policy realism—and every postwar president supported it.

But, as September 11 demonstrated, this bargain could not fulfill its promise forever. As Rice explained, it was time for a change. "For 60 years," she said, "my country, the United States, pursued stability at the expense of democracy in this region here in the Middle East—and we achieved neither. Now, we are taking a different course. We are supporting the democratic aspirations of all people."[24]

This was no passive activity. Rather than merely "support" democratic aspirations, Bush tried to force-feed democracy onto a region that had known precious little over its long history. He led an international "coalition of the willing" into Iraq in early 2003, toppling Saddam Hussein in less than a month. He used the opportunity of Hezbollah's war with Israel in 2006 to pressure Syria to end its hegemony over Lebanon and allow for democracy in that troubled land. And he pushed for Palestinian elections as a way to jump-start freedom and democracy in the West Bank and Gaza.

Bush's push for freedom and democracy was inspiring, but it was risky as well—as its aftermath made clear.

DEVILS IN THE DETAILS

Do the words of a U.S. president matter around the world? Consider the events of the early Bush years.

In Washington, Bush was issuing some of the most stirring calls for freedom and democracy of any president in history.

At the American Enterprise Institute in February 2003, just weeks before the U.S.-led invasion of Iraq, he said, "We go forward with confidence, because we trust in the power of human freedom to change lives and nations. By the resolve and purpose of America, and of our friends and allies, we will make this an age of progress and liberty. Free people will set the course of history, and free people will keep the peace of the world."[25]

Aboard the USS *Abraham Lincoln* on May 1 of that year, a few weeks after coalition forces deposed Saddam Hussein, he said:

> Our commitment to liberty is America's tradition—declared at our founding; affirmed in Franklin Roosevelt's Four Freedoms; asserted in the Truman Doctrine and in Ronald Reagan's challenge to an evil empire. We are committed to freedom in Afghanistan, in Iraq, and in a peaceful Palestine. The advance of freedom is the surest strategy to undermine the appeal of terror in the world. Where freedom takes hold, hatred gives way to hope. When freedom takes hold, men and women turn to the peaceful pursuit of a better life. American values and American interests lead in the same direction: We stand for human liberty.[26]

At the twentieth anniversary celebration of the National Endowment for Democracy six months later, he declared:

> The advance of freedom is the calling of our time; it is the calling of our country. From the Fourteen Points to the Four Freedoms, to the Speech at Westminster, America has put our power at the service of principle. We believe that liberty is the design of nature; we believe that liberty is the direction of history. We believe that human fulfillment and excellence come in the responsible exercise of liberty. And we believe that freedom—the freedom we prize—is not for us alone. It is the right and the capacity of all mankind. [27]

Bush's words inspired activists and put autocrats on the defensive. Tens of thousands of people took to the streets, defying the warnings of autocratic governments. Those governments, in turn, extended some limited rights to their people, hoping to defuse the protests and curry favor with Washington.

In 2003, a "Rose Revolution" in the former Soviet Republic of Georgia ousted its corrupt president, Eduard Shevardnadze. A year later, an "Orange Revolution" in Ukraine prevented Viktor Yanukovych, anointed successor to the corrupt President Leonid Kuchma, from taking office. In 2005, the "Cedar Revolution" erupted in Lebanon after the assassination of Prime Minister Rafik Hariri. Amid widespread suspicions that Syria had engineered Hariri's murder, the Lebanese people demanded an end to Syria's longstanding political and military domination of their nation. Also that year, Egyptian leader Hosni Mubarak loosened his grip temporarily, allowing democratic activist Ayman Nour to run for president (before jailing him later). In 2006, Palestinians voted in parliamentary elections. Throughout those years, autocrats in Morocco, Jordan, the United Arab Emirates, Kuwait, and Saudi Arabia also introduced modest democratic reforms. [28]

A president spoke, the world took notice, and efforts to advance freedom and democracy ensued. (Bush admittedly did not create democratic movements on his own, but he gave those in place an important push forward). But, as Bush would learn to his dismay, it takes more than words to advance real freedom and build real democracy. It takes hard work.

Experts have long debated how to build free and democratic societies for the long term. Is prosperity a prerequisite for democracy? Must the architecture of democracy (the rule of law, opposition parties, a free and independent media, and so on) precede elections, or can elections come first? No one formula applies in every case, for the world is a mix of different peoples of different cultures. Nevertheless, certain factors can prove more effective than others in planting the seeds of freedom and democracy. When, in 2005, Freedom House studied sixty-seven countries that made the transition from authoritarianism to democracy over the previous thirty-three years, it found that "people power" movements of nonviolent civic forces tend to bring decisive change; "top-down" transitions led by elites tend *not* to bring such change; "strong and cohesive civic coalitions" can play a big role in nourishing freedom; and prospects for freedom improve when opposition forces do not resort to violence.[29]

Whatever the right formula, history shows that crafting a political system that protects freedom and sustains democracy, and institutionalizing and strengthening it for the long term, is hard work. That's why nations sometimes advance to freedom and democracy and then revert back to autocracy. That's why the United States took twelve years, from its Declaration of Independence in 1776 to ratification of its Constitution in 1788, to have a functional government—and why it took many years more to free the slaves, ensure political rights for blacks, and give women the vote. The desire for freedom and dignity may "beat in every heart," in the words of President Obama,[30] but that doesn't mean that, when suddenly free after years of oppression, a people in Asia, Africa, or Latin America will know how to build a democracy or guarantee human rights.

Bush and his team were not ready for the hard work. They had no plan to prevent chaos in Iraq after Saddam's demise; they were left unprepared when Palestinian elections gave power to the terrorist group Hamas; and they had no answer when the terrorist group Hezbollah climbed the political ladder in Lebanon.

In Iraq, U.S. leaders had given little thought to what would happen on the day after victory, with Saddam gone and the Iraqi people leaderless.[31] Their failure to craft and execute a long-term plan for democratic transformation left the country largely directionless. An interim government managed to develop a process for elections, and the Iraqi people weathered threats from terrorist groups by voting in extraordinary numbers in early 2005, proudly displaying their purple, ink-stained index fingers.

"Some danced or distributed chocolates, some wept with joy, others grimly pressed forward as if their lives literally depended on it," the *Washington Post* wrote in a celebratory editorial. "A 32-year-old man who lost his leg in a suicide bombing arrived at the polls in Baghdad and told a Reuters reporter, 'I would have crawled here if I had to.'"[32]

But even in the aftermath of elections, the country remained riven by sectarian violence, with Sunnis and Shias battling to control Iraq's future. Bush sent a "surge" of more than twenty thousand additional troops to quell the violence but, as his presidency ended and Obama's began, violence continued to plague the country.

In the Palestinian territories, for which Bush had pushed for elections, voters surprised virtually everyone in early 2006 by giving Hamas a majority of seats in their parliament. Whether Palestinians were expressing support for Hamas' vow to destroy Israel, rejecting a corrupt and incompetent Fatah Party that ruled the Palestinian Authority, or both, was unclear. But Hamas was no freedom-loving entity, its leaders no heirs to Jefferson and Madison.

A year later, Hamas seized control of Gaza in a violent coup and proceeded to rule the narrow strip along the Mediterranean Sea with an iron fist while launching thousands of rockets into southern Israel. That, in turn, subjected the Palestinians of Gaza to a full-fledged Israeli military response in late 2008.

In Lebanon, Hezbollah maintained its war with Israel along Lebanon's southern border while participating in electoral politics. Around early 2011, the group withdrew its support for the government of Prime Minister Saad Hariri over the latter's refusal to denounce a UN-backed tribunal that was expected to implicate Hezbollah in the 2005 murder of Hariri's father, Rafik. By mid-year, Hezbollah had engineered the selection of its candidate, Najib Mikati, as the country's next prime minister, and Mikati selected a cabinet in which Hezbollah and its allies held most of the seats. All of that gave Hezbollah effective control of Lebanon's government and thus more freedom to maintain its war with Israel, strengthen Lebanon's ties to Tehran and Damascus, and quash any advance of freedom and democracy in Lebanon that would threaten its position.[33]

As his presidency wound down, and perhaps chastened by such developments, Bush eased his push for freedom and democracy in the region. America's autocratic allies in Egypt, Saudi Arabia, and elsewhere had long argued that democracy would empower radical Islamists who would rule not as U.S. allies but instead as enemies who would threaten U.S. interests. Developments in the Palestinian territories and Lebanon seemed to validate their predictions. Bush's apparent change of heart empowered the autocrats who had provided some measure of democracy just a few years earlier to retighten their grip on power. Mubarak jailed Nour, while newly elected governments outside the region proved unwilling to build the foundation of long-lasting democratic rule. Across the world, the advance of freedom and democracy stalled in the last years of Bush's presidency.[34]

The strife and disorder of Iraq, Lebanon, and the Palestinian territories also spurred a public backlash against human rights promotion within the United States. There, public support for human rights promotion fell significantly from the heady days of Bush's early years in office. Whereas 70 percent of Americans agreed in a 2002 Pew Global Attitudes Survey that the United States "should be promoting democracy around the world," a mere 23 percent agreed in 2007 that the nation "can effectively help other countries become democratic." Congress cut several democracy promotion programs.[35]

Barack Obama had different ideas. Rather than force change on stagnant regions, he sought to improve relations with America's fiercest adversaries. The implications for U.S. human rights promotion were profound.

OBAMA'S "ENGAGEMENT"

Each presidential campaign has its own ebb and flow, its own particular issues of contention between candidates. Each is shaped by the conditions of the day—a growing or shrinking economy, rising or stagnant living standards, calm or turbulent race relations, peace or war. At their most basic level, however, all campaigns are shaped by one overriding issue: continuity or change. The nation, having judged its incumbent president, decides whether it wants more of the same or a new style and direction. Eisenhower, Nixon, Reagan, and Clinton won the public's confidence, each earning a second term. But an honesty-toting Carter followed a Watergate-tainted Ford; a Reagan promising renewed U.S. global leadership followed a Carter beset by global setbacks; and a Clinton focused on the economy followed a George H. W. Bush who presided over economic uncertainty.

George W. Bush had won reelection, but during his second term, Americans grew weary of his bluster, his my-way-or-the-highway views, and his managerial incompetence. On the domestic front, the government's atrocious response to Hurricane Katrina left the public outraged. On the foreign front, many Americans thought the United States had grown isolated, with more enemies than friends, with strained relations with its allies in Europe and elsewhere. They longed for a president who would tone down the rhetoric, favor cooperation over confrontation, and govern effectively.

Up stepped Obama, the anti-Bush. Rather than an upper-crust product of political dynasty, he was the offspring of a mixed-race marriage who was born in Hawaii, lived in Indonesia as a boy, and was raised by his grandparents. Rather than a tongue-tied Texan, he was a man of soaring rhetoric who could inspire hope for monumental progress. Rather than a yes-or-no decision-maker, he was a man of nuance, a former University of Chicago law professor who appreciated the complexity of issues.

On foreign policy, the new anti-Bush was a fan of . . . the old Bush. Asked during his 2008 campaign about his approach to foreign policy, he spoke approvingly of the "realistic" approach of George H. W. Bush. "The truth is," he said during a campaign stop in Pennsylvania, "that my foreign policy is actually a return to the traditional bipartisan realistic policy of George Bush's father, of John F. Kennedy, or, in some ways, Ronald Reagan."[36] (Whether Kennedy and Reagan were "realists" is another matter.) During the campaign, Obama sought advice from Zbigniew Brzezinski, President Carter's national security advisor and perhaps the Democratic Party's leading realist, who traveled with him and introduced him at a September 2007 event. Nor did Obama disappoint the realists once he took office. Four months into his presidency, Richard Haass, president of the Council on

Foreign Relations and a leading realist himself, gushed, "the foreign policy of the Obama Administration resembles nothing so much as the foreign policy of Bush 41."[37]

To be sure, Obama put his rhetorical skills behind the cause of human rights at key moments. In his inaugural address, in words that echoed Kennedy's vow to "pay any price" and "bear any burden" to defend liberty, and to assist others who seek freedom and prosperity, Obama said:

> Our Founding Fathers, faced with perils that we can scarcely imagine, drafted a charter to assure the rule of law and the rights of man—a charter expanded by the blood of generations. Those ideals still light the world, and we will not give them up for expedience's sake. And so, to all the other peoples and governments who are watching today, from the grandest capitals to the small village where my father was born: know that America is a friend of each nation, and every man, woman and child who seeks a future of peace and dignity. And we are ready to lead once more. . . . To the people of poor nations, we pledge to work alongside you to make your farms flourish and let clean waters flow; to nourish starved bodies and feed hungry minds. And to those nations like ours that enjoy relative plenty, we say we can no longer afford indifference to the suffering outside our borders, nor can we consume the world's resources without regard to effect. For the world has changed, and we must change with it.[38]

In his address to the Muslim world from Cairo in June 2009, in words with which Truman, Kennedy, and Reagan would have been comfortable, he stated:

> I do have an unyielding belief that all people yearn for certain things: the ability to speak your mind and have a say in how you are governed; confidence in the rule of law and the equal administration of justice; government that is transparent and doesn't steal from the people; the freedom to live as you choose. Those are not just American ideas, they are human rights, and that is why we will support them everywhere.[39]

In accepting his Nobel Peace Prize in Oslo that December, he espoused the American view that the spread of human rights advances the cause of peace, and he pledged to stand with those on the front lines of battle:

> I believe that peace is unstable where citizens are denied the right to speak freely or worship as they please, choose their own leaders or assemble without fear. Pent-up grievances fester, and the suppression of tribal and religious identity can lead to violence. We also know that the opposite is true. Only when Europe became free did it finally find peace. America has never fought a war against a democracy, and our closest friends are governments that protect the rights of their citizens. No matter how callously defined, neither America's interests—nor the world's—are served by the denial of human aspirations.[40]

Obama and his team dismissed the notion that they would have to choose between America's security interests and its ideals, calling it a "false choice."[41] Speaking at the 45th Munich Conference on Security Policy in early February 2009, Vice President Biden said, "America will vigorously defend our security and our values, and in doing so we believe we'll all be more secure."[42] That, he said, is why Obama promised to end the torture of prisoners from America's "war on terror" and to close the controversial detention center at Guantanamo Bay, Cuba.[43]

Fine. As a practical matter, however, Obama would have to make such choices on occasion because every president must do so. Faced with a particular foreign policy challenge, every president must balance short- and long-term goals, differing interests and competing priorities. Human rights promotion is but one task of foreign policy. Every president decides where it ranks. When it conflicts with other tasks, every president chooses among them.

Obama chose. On grand stages, as we have seen, he echoed the words of Truman, Kennedy, and Reagan to advance the cause of human rights. In his day-to-day statecraft, however, he mostly sacrificed the cause to the exigencies of power politics and the dictates of realism. Obama was a rhetorical idealist but an operational realist.

Benjamin Rhodes, one of Obama's deputy national security advisors, told the *New Yorker*'s Ryan Lizza in early 2011:

> The project of the first two years has been to effectively deal with the legacy issues that we inherited, particularly the Iraq war, the Afghan war, and the war against al Qaeda, while rebalancing our resources and our posture in the world. If you boil it all down to a bumper sticker, it's "Wind down these two wars, reestablish American standing and leadership in the world, and focus on a broader set of priorities, from Asia and the global economy to a nuclear-nonproliferation regime."[44]

That "project," Lizza noted, "did not include a call to promote democracy or protect human rights."[45]

And so it went.

When, in 2009, Obama and Secretary of State Hillary Clinton visited China, the rising Asian power on which Washington was increasingly dependent to finance its budget deficits, they both avoided public complaints about Beijing's human rights record. Before her trip in February, Clinton said, "We have to continue to press them [on human rights] but our pressing on those issues can't interfere with the global economic crisis, the global climate crisis, and the security crises."[46] Asked two months later while traveling in Latin America whether she would seek better relations with hostile leaders like Venezuela's Hugo Chavez, she said, "Let's put ideology aside; that is so yesterday."[47] When the Dalai Lama, a global icon and the leading human rights thorn in China's side, visited Washington in October, Obama refused to meet with him, apparently to avoid tensions with Beijing before Obama's trip to China a month later.[48] Critics compared the snub to President Ford's refusal in 1975 to meet with Aleksandr Solzhenitsyn, the Nobel Prize–winning Soviet dissident, for fear of upsetting Soviet leader Leonid Brezhnev.

Elsewhere, Obama sought to "hit the re-set button" with Russia, with which U.S. relations had grown increasingly strained during the Bush years due to Washington's complaints about Moscow's retreat on human rights. The administration called for greater engagement with human rights–abusing regimes in Sudan and Burma. Obama's National Security Council down-graded the role of its democracy specialists, and the administration cut funding for independent civil society groups that promote democracy in Egypt and ended it for the Iran-related activities of the Iran Human Rights Documentation Center, International Republican Institute, and Freedom House.[49]

While seeking to improve bilateral relations with adversaries, Obama reached out to the global community writ large. Seeking redemption for America's purported sins, he drew raised eyebrows in some quarters by criticizing U.S. policies while speaking on foreign soil. In Strasbourg, France, in April 2009, he complained that "there have been times where America has shown arrogance and been dismissive, even derisive" toward its European allies.[50] In Cairo in June, he argued that U.S. anti-terror regulations related to charitable giving "have made it harder for Muslims to fulfill their religious obligation" to give to charity, and he acknowledged that the United States helped to engineer the 1953 coup that toppled Iranian Prime Minister Mohammad Mosaddeq, replacing him with the Shah.[51] Asked by a reporter in Strasbourg whether he believes in "American exceptionalism," he replied in a striking bow to nonjudgmentalism, "I believe in American exceptionalism, just as I suspect that the Brits believe in British exceptionalism and the Greeks believe in Greek exceptionalism."[52]

At the United Nations, Obama ordered the United States to join the laughably misnamed Human Rights Council—dominated by some of the world's worst human rights abusers and focused obsessively on Israel—in an effort, his aides said, to improve it from the inside. Obama even considered (before eventually rejecting) U.S. participation in the Durban II conference, a follow-up to the notorious 2001 United Nations gathering in Durban, South Africa, that deteriorated into such an orgy of anti-Semitism and anti-Americanism that Secretary of State Colin Powell ordered the U.S. delegation to leave.

Obama called his approach "engagement," which seemed comforting but was really no less risky than what Bush had tried. If Bush had sought to impose freedom and democracy on a recalcitrant region through the power of his words and the force of U.S. arms, Obama sought to improve relations with some of America's fiercest enemies in order to ease tensions and reduce threats. The question was whether the effort to improve bilateral relations was worth the cost of downplaying human rights.

The clearest test would come in his engagement with the increasingly dangerous regime in Tehran.

TEST CASE: IRAN

Each new president takes office with a confidence that borders on cockiness. After winning the nation's highest office and assuming the world's most powerful perch, a new president can't help but think that he will succeed where others have failed. With more brains, more effort, and a better staff around the Oval Office, he will solve the problems that bedeviled his predecessors. From no region have problems bedeviled recent presidents more than the Middle East, with its combustible mix of authoritarian rule, stunted economic growth, educational backwardness, intra-Islamic hatreds, and terrorist violence. And on no challenge have presidents sought to make their mark more than Middle East peace.

But for all their differences in outlook, all their promises of new approaches, our recent presidents all have been heavily influenced by a conventional wisdom about the Middle East that is widely shared across America's foreign policy establishment and that focuses on the interrelated issues of Israeli-Palestinian conflict, Syria's role in the conflict, and U.S. relations with Iran. As Obama assumed office, this conventional wisdom posited all of the following:

- The region's central issue is the Israeli-Palestinian conflict because that conflict engenders broad sympathy for the Palestinian cause, prevents Arab states from making peace with Israel, attracts and motivates jihadists, and fuels conflict in Iraq, Afghanistan, and elsewhere.
- The right combination of concessions from Israeli and Palestinian leaders will produce peace, and the United States must pressure Israel, in particular, to make painful concessions.
- With such peace, the United States can make progress on broader Arab-Israeli peace, the wars in Iraq and Afghanistan, Iranian and Syrian sponsorship of terrorism, and Iran's pursuit of nuclear weapons.
- The United States can convince Syria to make peace with Israel, loosen its ties to Iran, and turn toward the West.
- Washington can strike a "grand bargain" with Tehran through which the two sides can build a new relationship—Washington would assure Tehran that it will not seek "regime change," and Tehran would abandon its

nuclear weapons program, dispense with state-sponsored terrorism, and cooperate with the United States to bring stability to Iraq, Afghanistan, and the region.[53]

Conventional wisdom at the ready, Obama went to work on Israeli-Palestinian peace, Syrian outreach, and Iranian engagement.

On the Israeli-Palestinian conflict, Bush had tilted toward Israel, declaring that Palestinian leaders had to abandon terrorism if they hoped to win Washington's favor. Obama tilted the other way—perhaps to show the Muslim world his even-handedness, perhaps because he viewed Israel as the biggest obstacle to peace. He pressured Israeli Prime Minister Benjamin Netanyahu to freeze Jewish settlements as a way to restart peace talks while asking nothing tangible of Palestinian leaders. He elevated an awkward Israeli announcement about a settlement expansion in a Jewish community in northern Jerusalem, which occurred while Vice President Biden was visiting Israel in early 2010, into a major controversy. After Israel apologized and Biden was already on his way back to Washington, Obama ordered Secretary of State Clinton to dress down Netanyahu by phone and refused to issue a joint statement when Netanyahu visited Washington a few weeks later. In early 2011, he called for an Israeli-Palestinian agreement based on Israel's 1967 borders—which Israel's leaders believe would threaten its security— and pressured Israel to return to negotiations even though Palestinian Authority leaders had reached an accord to bring Hamas, the terrorist group committed to Israel's destruction, into their government.

On Syria, Obama aides and key Democratic lawmakers visited Damascus repeatedly in the early months of Obama's tenure. In February 2009, Assistant Secretary of State Jeffrey D. Feltman met with Syria's foreign minister, marking the highest-level visit by a U.S. official to Damascus in more than four years. Also in February, the Commerce Department approved an export license for Boeing 747 spare parts for Syria's national airline. In April, Feltman returned to Damascus, this time with National Security Council aides, to attend Syrian National Day celebrations. In June, the White House announced that Obama would appoint the first U.S. ambassador to Syria since 2005 (when Bush recalled his ambassador amid widespread suspicions that Syrian officials were involved in the murder of Lebanon's president). In July, the administration said it would ease sanctions on Syria and Obama's Middle East envoy, George Mitchell, told Syrian leader Bashar al-Assad that Washington would process all eligible applications for export licenses as quickly as possible. In early 2010, Obama named his U.S. ambassador to Syria and the State Department lifted its travel warning to Syria.[54]

On Iran, Obama said during his presidential run that he would meet, without preconditions, with the leaders of even the most objectionable of governments—including the Holocaust-denying president of Iran, Mahmoud

Ahmadinejad. Though his pledge proved controversial, he did not abandon it. Once in office, Obama offered talks with Iranian leaders to find a way forward, promising "meaningful incentives" for doing so.[55] He wrote to Iran's Supreme Leader, Ayatollah Ali Khamenei, in early 2009, seeking "dialogue and engagement between the two nations."[56] Richard Holbrooke, Obama's envoy to Afghanistan and Pakistan, met briefly in early 2009 with Iran's deputy foreign minister, Mahdi Akhundzadeh, at an international conference about Afghanistan.

None of it worked.

With Obama pressuring Israel to make concessions, Palestinian Authority President Mahmoud Abbas sat on his hands, refusing to meet with Netanyahu. Netanyahu-Abbas talks probably would not have produced anything of note anyway. No lasting peace was in sight because Palestinian leaders had neither accepted, nor prepared their people to accept, the existence of Israel. Palestinian "rejectionism" dates back to the early twentieth century, to even before Britain's Peel Commission of 1937 recommended two states in Palestine—one for Jews, one for Palestinian Arabs. Rejectionism was the ideological fuel behind the Palestinian Liberation Organization even during the "Oslo years" of relative peace in the 1990s, and today it drives the agenda of Hamas and prevents even the "moderate" Abbas from taking concrete steps toward peace. Palestinian leaders have rejected every reasonable peace offer that Israeli leaders have offered, and they will continue to do so until they decide to move from rejectionism to acceptance of a Jewish state next door.[57]

Obama was no more successful with Syria. While al-Assad has long hinted at peace with Israel when speaking to the West, he has done no such thing in the Arab world. Syria remained among the world's main state sponsors of terrorism and, in early 2010, Damascus sent Syrian-made Fateh-110 missiles to Hezbollah, began training terrorists in using surface-to-air missiles, and began importing nuclear-related military equipment from North Korea. Syrian leaders refused to meet with the International Atomic Energy Agency to discuss the Syrian nuclear program that Israel revealed when it bombed an undeclared nuclear facility in late 2007.[58] Al-Assad mocked Obama's efforts to coax Syria away from Iran and terrorism by hosting meetings with Iran's Ahmadinejad, Hezbollah's Hassan Nasrallah, and Hamas' Khaled Meshaal in early 2010. Soon thereafter, U.S. and Israeli officials charged that Syria sent long-range Scud missiles to Hezbollah, putting Jerusalem, Tel Aviv, and Israel's nuclear installations within the group's range of fire.[59]

Nor, most ominously, did "engagement" bear fruit with Iran. Tehran brushed aside Obama's entreaties and continued to threaten Israel, arm Hezbollah and Hamas, and make progress on its nuclear program. Iran repeatedly boasted that it was enriching more uranium at higher levels of purity while opening new enrichment sites across the country. The United States pushed a fourth round of sanctions against Iran through the United Nations Security

Council, but only after weakening them enough to secure Chinese and Russian approval that they would not force Iran to change course. In Washington, determination to prevent a nuclear Iran was giving way to recognition that Iran would likely achieve a nuclear weapons capability at some point. One sign of the shift was Secretary of State Clinton's talk of creating a U.S.-directed "nuclear umbrella" to protect the Arab states. Another was a March/April 2010 piece by James M. Lindsay and Ray Takeyh in *Foreign Affairs*, house organ of America's foreign policy establishment, titled "After Iran Gets the Bomb: Containment and Its Complications,"[60] outlining a series of steps through which Washington could make the best of things.

Failure on the Israeli-Palestinian, Syrian, and Iranian fronts was all too predictable, for it emerged from the faulty premises of conventional wisdom. America's foreign policy elite had long viewed the region through the wrong end of the telescope. The experts advised policymakers first to narrow their focus to the Israeli-Palestinian conflict and then broaden it to larger Middle East peace because, they said, solving the former was the key to solving everything else. In reality, the Israeli-Palestinian conflict was demonstrably not the key to all regional things. It did not drive the terrorism of al Qaeda (including the September 11 attacks), nor did it fuel the insurgencies of the last decade in Iraq or Afghanistan. Moreover, Egypt and Jordan have made peace with Israel; Iran, Syria, Saudi Arabia, and others in the region have not—and the Israeli-Palestinian conflict did not drive any of their decisions.

In fact, the road to regional peace and progress runs through Tehran, which has fueled much of the regional unrest. Tehran has worked with Syria to arm and train the terrorists who can prevent the onset of any real Israeli-Palestinian peace by launching attacks against Israel at key moments of negotiation, forcing an Israeli military response that, in turn, will derail peace-making. It has stoked chaos in Iraq and Afghanistan and sought to destabilize Sunni regimes in the region. It has challenged the United States for regional influence. It has pursued nuclear weapons, which has so worried more than a dozen states in the region that they have vowed to start their own nuclear weapons program in response. And it has shown little interest in crafting the "grand bargain" with the United States that so many U.S. foreign policy experts have suggested is there for the taking—if only Washington would work harder to achieve it.

The tragedy of Obama's "engagement" policy with Iran extended beyond its failure, however. Reflecting his realist outlook, Obama calculated that, to improve U.S.-Iranian relations, he should largely avoid criticism of the regime in Tehran. In his Cairo speech, for instance, he covered a wide range of issues between the United States and the Muslim world, but he did not criticize the human rights record of a regime that was stoning adulterous women to death; hanging teenage homosexuals in public; arresting, torturing, and killing democracy-seeking students and labor leaders; closing independent newspapers and broadcast stations; and imposing dress and hair restrictions on men and women.

Facing prospects of a nuclear-armed, terrorist-sponsoring, anti-American regime in Tehran, the United States would like nothing more than for Iranians to topple the regime and replace it with a democratic government that, presumably, would change course. But, again reflecting his realism, Obama reacted tentatively when Iranians demonstrated the potential (albeit not the guarantee) of accomplishing that very goal in June 2009. Hundreds of thousands of Iranians stormed the streets in a "Green Revolution" to protest a crooked election that gave Ahmadinejad a second term. In brave and brazen fashion, they shouted "Death to the Dictator" in an apparent reference to the Supreme Leader, who had blessed the election results. Ahmadinejad ordered government forces to restore order, sending the Iranian Revolutionary Guard Corps and other loyalists to clear the streets. They arrested, jailed, tortured, and murdered indiscriminately, gunning down a beautiful young woman, Neda Agha-Soltan, whose gruesome death was captured on video and became a symbol of the government's brutality.

Obama did little to push a democratic revolution forward, apparently fearing that it would not succeed and that, in the meantime, overt U.S. support for it would dash his hopes of building a new relationship with Tehran's current leaders. So, Obama downplayed the differences between Ahmadinejad and opposition leader Mir-Hossein Mousavi. He refused to align himself with democracy-seeking Iranians, saying, "[I]t's not productive, given the history of the U.S.-Iranian relations, to be seen as meddling—the U.S. President meddling in Iranian elections."[61] When a State Department official asked the social networking service Twitter not to perform a planned upgrade that would have temporarily shut down the service, jeopardizing the ability of demonstrators to communicate with one another in real time, the White House almost had him fired.[62] Only after European leaders spoke forcefully and Tehran ramped up its horrific attacks did Obama adopt a more assertive tone.

The regime *did* restore order, ending hopes that the Green Revolution would bring a brighter day to Iran. To be sure, no U.S. assistance could have guaranteed a different outcome. Nevertheless, no one can know what might have happened if Obama had taken a bolder approach to the uprising by aligning the United States forcefully behind the demonstrators and offering moral, financial, logistical, and other support. The dictates of realism had trumped the possibilities of U.S. human rights promotion.

CONCLUSION

A terrorist attack; a nation transformed; two presidents with strikingly different views on how to address the challenge. The first decade after September 11 both ushered in a profoundly new phase of U.S. foreign policy and showcased the possibilities and limits of U.S. human rights promotion.

Bush reminded us that a president's words still can send shock waves across the world, shaping behavior not only by governments but also by once-powerless people who seek freedom and democracy. He also came to learn, and to remind us in the process, that the advance of human rights requires more than inspiring talk. Its success is predicated on a stick-to-it-ness, both on the ground in oppressed nations and half a world away in the comfortable confines of Washington.

Obama, the far more articulate successor to Bush, reserved his soaring rhetoric on human rights for limited occasions. A foreign policy realist, he sought to repair and improve relations with allies and adversaries alike. When traveling overseas or reacting to global events from the White House, he often sidestepped questions of human rights in particular countries rather than risk the ruffling of diplomatic feathers. But if Bush's efforts to advance freedom and democracy on the cheap backfired in key hotspots of the Middle East, Obama's reticence to forcefully support the protestors of Iran may have cost Washington a golden opportunity to transform both that nation and the region writ large.

Obama would have other chances, however. As he was finishing his second year in office, an incident in a tiny country in North Africa triggered an Arab Spring that threatened to remake the Arab world.

NOTES

1. George W. Bush, Acceptance Speech at the 2000 Republican National Convention, August 3, 2000.
2. Bush, Acceptance Speech.
3. George W. Bush, Second Presidential Debate, October 11, 2000.
4. Bush, Second Presidential Debate.
5. Donald H. Rumsfeld, Remarks at the Pentagon, September 10, 2001, www.defense.gov/speeches/speech.aspx?speechid=430.
6. As noted in chapter 2, the flow of U.S. foreign aid dollars reflected the shifting priorities of U.S. foreign policy. From the Marshall Plan of 1948 to the end of the 1980s, policymakers distributed foreign aid largely to bolster U.S. efforts to fight the Cold War. In the 1990s, they shifted it markedly to regional challenges, such as Middle East peace and the post–Cold War transition to democracy in Eastern Europe. After 9/11, they steered it significantly toward the war on terror. In 1998, the top ten recipients of U.S. foreign aid were, in order, Israel, Egypt, Ukraine, Jordan, India, Russia, Peru, Ethiopia, Haiti, and Georgia. By 2008, and reflecting major aspects of the war on terror, the top ten recipients were Afghanistan, Israel, Egypt, Iraq, Jordan, Pakistan, Kenya, South Africa, Colombia, and Nigeria. See Curt Tarnoff and Marian

Leonardo Lawson, "Foreign Aid: An Introduction to U.S. Programs and Policy," Congressional Research Service, April 9, 2009; Keith Brown and Jill Tirnauer, "Trends in U.S. Foreign Assistance over the Past Decade," United States Agency for International Development, August 17, 2009.

7. Mary Habeck, *Knowing the Enemy* (New Haven, CT: Yale University Press, 2006), 4.

8. Walid Phares, *Future Jihad: Terrorist Strategies against the West* (New York: Palgrave Macmillan, 2005), 61–67. Also useful are the other two books in Phares's trilogy about the jihadist network—*The War of Ideas: Jihadism against Democracy* (New York: Palgrave Macmillan, 2007), and *The Confrontation: Winning the War against Future Jihad* (New York: Palgrave Macmillan, 2008)—as well as Habeck, *Knowing the Enemy*, and Ilan Berman, *Winning the Long War* (Lanham, MD: Rowman & Littlefield, 2009).

9. Vali Nasr, *The Shia Revival: How Conflicts within Islam Will Shape the Future* (New York: W. W. Norton, 2006), 35–38.

10. Raymond Ibrahim, ed., *The al Qaeda Reader* (New York: Broadway Books, 2007), 13.

11. She is a Somali native who fled to the West and later served in the Dutch Parliament. At the time of this writing, she is a visiting fellow at the American Enterprise Institute, requires round-the-clock protection due to threats from radical Islamists, and is the author of several heartrending books about her life, including *The Caged Virgin: An Emancipation Proclamation for Women and Islam* (New York: Free Press, 2002); *Infidel* (New York: Free Press, 2007); and *Nomad: From Islam to America: A Personal Journey through the Clash of Civilizations* (New York: Free Press, 2010).

12. She is a Syrian-born American who lives in hiding in the United States due to threats from radical Islamists and is the author of the controversial book, *A God Who Hates: The Courageous Woman Who Inflamed the Muslim World Speaks Out against the Evils of Islam* (New York: St. Martin's Press, 2009).

13. She is a Lebanese American journalist, founder and president of the American Congress for Truth, and author of two books that urge the West to confront Islam: *Because They Hate: A Survivor of Islamic Terror Warns America* (New York: St. Martin's Press, 2006), and *They Must Be Stopped: Why We Must Defeat Radical Islam and How We Can Do It* (New York: St. Martin's Press, 2008).

14. She is a leading Muslim reformist who lives as an openly gay and feminist Muslim in Canada, lectures and writes widely, runs the Moral Courage Project at New York University, and is author of *The Trouble with Islam Today: A Muslim's Call for Reform in Her Faith* (New York: St. Martin's Griffin, 2003), and *Allah, Liberty and Love: The Courage to Reconcile Faith and Freedom* (New York: Free Press, 2011).

15. A women's rights advocate, she is cofounder and executive director of the American Islamic Congress.

16. A physician who earned his medical degree on a Navy scholarship, he is founder and executive director of the American Islamic Forum for Democracy.

17. George W. Bush, Address to a Joint Session of Congress, September 20, 2001.

18. Bush, Address to a Joint Session.

19. White House, "The National Security Strategy of the United States of America," September 2002.

20. George W. Bush, Address to the Nation, September 11, 2001.

21. Bush, Address to a Joint Session.

22. George W. Bush, Address at the United States Military Academy, West Point, June 1, 2002.

23. George W. Bush, Second Inaugural Address, January 20, 2005.

24. Condoleezza Rice, Remarks at the American University, Cairo, June 20, 2005.

25. George W. Bush, Address to the American Enterprise Institute, February 26, 2003.

26. George W. Bush, Address aboard the USS *Abraham Lincoln*, May 1, 2003.

27. George W. Bush, Address at the Twentieth Anniversary of the National Endowment for Democracy, United States Chamber of Commerce, November 6, 2003.

28. Michael McFaul, *Advancing Democracy Abroad: Why We Should and How We Can* (Lanham, MD: Rowman & Littlefield, 2010), 5–6.

29. Adrian Karatnycky and Peter Ackerman, "How Freedom Is Won: From Civic Resistance to Durable Democracy," Freedom House, 2005, http://old.freedomhouse.org/uploads/special_report/29.pdf.

30. Barack Obama, Address to the British Parliament, London, May 25, 2011.

31. Among the many writings on this subject, see "Iraq and the Future of Transformation," in Frederick W. Kagan, *Finding the Target: The Transformation of American Military Policy* (New York: Encounter Books, 2006).

32. Editorial, "A Vote to Persevere," *Washington Post*, January 31, 2005. Also reflecting the euphoria, the *New York Times* wrote in its editorial of the same day, "This page has not hesitated to criticize the Bush administration over its policies in Iraq, and we continue to have grave doubts about the overall direction of American strategy there. Yet today, along with other Americans, whether supporters or critics of the war, we rejoice in a heartening advance by the Iraqi people. For now at least, the multiple political failures that marked the run-up to the voting stand eclipsed by a remarkably successful election day."

33. Lawrence J. Haas, "Hezbollah's Seizure of Power in Lebanon Dooms Peace Talks and Puts Israel at Risk," *Sacramento Bee*, February 10, 2011; MESOP Newsletter Daily, "Hezbollah-Led Bloc Dominates Lebanon's New Government," www.mesop.de/2011/06/15/hezbollah-led-bloc-dominates-lebanons-new-government-realite-eu.

34. Freedom House, *Freedom in the World* Country Ratings, 1973–2011.

35. McFaul, *Advancing Democracy*, 3.

36. Ryan Lizza, "The Consequentialist: How the Arab Spring Remade Obama's Foreign Policy," *New Yorker*, May 2, 2011.

37. Carlos Lozado, "So Much for Idealism," *Washington Post*, May 17, 2009.

38. Barack Obama, Inaugural Address, January 20, 2009.

39. Barack Obama, Address to the Muslim World, Cairo, Egypt, June 4, 2009.

40. Barack Obama, Address at the Nobel Peace Prize Ceremony, Oslo, Norway, December 10, 2009.

41. See, for instance, Obama, Inaugural Address.

42. Joe Biden, Remarks at the Forty-Fifth Munich Conference on Security Policy, Hotel Bayerischer Hof, Munich, February 7, 2009.

43. Closing the detention center, however, proved hard to do, with states across the country refusing to house any of the prisoners who were there. As of early 2012, the center remained open.

44. Lizza, "Consequentialist."

45. Lizza, "Consequentialist."

46. Robert McMahon, "Human Rights Reporting and U.S. Foreign Policy," Council on Foreign Relations, April 9, 2009.

47. Hillary Clinton, quoted in Mark Landler, "Clinton Scores Points by Admitting Past U.S. Errors," *New York Times*, April 18, 2009.

48. Helene Cooper, Michael Wines, and David E. Sanger, "China's Role as Lender Alters Obama's Visit," *New York Times*, November 15, 2009.

49. Joshua Kurlantzick, "A Nobel Winner Who Went Wrong on Rights," *Washington Post*, December 13, 2009; David Feith and Bari Weiss, "Denying the Green Revolution: The State Department Cuts Off Funding to Support Iran's Democrats," *Wall Street Journal*, October 23, 2009.

50. Barack Obama, Remarks at Strasbourg Town Hall, Strasbourg, France, April 3, 2009, CBS News, www.cbsnews.com/stories/2009/04/03/politics/100days/worldaffairs/main4918137.shtml.

51. Obama, Address to the Muslim World.

52. Barack Obama, Press Conference, April 4, 2009, Strasbourg, France. See, for instance, Steve Benen, "Political Animal," www.washingtonmonthly.com/archives/individual/2009_04/017614.php.

53. Classic examples of this conventional wisdom include a January 24, 2011, letter to President Obama from more than a dozen Washington luminaries, including former House Foreign Affairs Committee Chairman Lee Hamilton and former National Security Advisor Zbigniew Brzezinski, which argued that U.S. failure to engineer Middle East peace "has left a

vacuum that threatens to deepen the State of Israel's isolation, undermine Palestinian moderation, and endanger American interests in the region and beyond," and stated that a clear statement of U.S. principles on the Israeli-Palestinian conflict would "help diminish Iranian influence in the region, improve Israel's security, and reduce the risk of a military conflict with Iran." Another example is the late 2006 report of the Iraq Study Group, established by Congress and co-chaired by Hamilton and former Secretary of State James Baker, that included the following language: "The United States cannot achieve its goals in the Middle East unless it deals directly with the Arab-Israeli conflict and regional instability. There must be a renewed and sustained commitment by the United States to a comprehensive Arab-Israeli peace on all fronts: Lebanon, Syria, and President Bush's June 2002 commitment to a two-state solution for Israel and Palestine. This commitment must include direct talks with, by, and between Israel, Lebanon, Palestinians (those who accept Israel's right to exist), and Syria."

54. Mathew R. J. Brodsky, "Hope over Experience with Syria," *InFocus*, vol. 4., no. 1 (Spring 2010).

55. Biden, Remarks at the Forty-Fifth Munich Conference.

56. Christiane Amanpour, "Obama Sent Letter to Iran Leader before Election, Sources Say," CNN Politics, http://articles.cnn.com/2009-06-24/politics/iran.obama.letter_1_iranian-leader-tehran-university-iranian-government?_s=PM:POLITICS.

57. Benny Morris, *One State, Two States* (New Haven, CT: Yale University Press, 2009); Allis Radosh and Ronald Radosh, *A Safe Haven: Harry S. Truman and the Founding of Israel* (New York: HarperCollins, 2009).

58. Brodsky, "Hope over Experience."

59. Charles Levinson and Jay Solomon, "Syria Gave Scuds to Hezbollah, U.S. Says," *Wall Street Journal*, April 14, 2010.

60. James M. Lindsay and Ray Takeyh, "After Iran Gets the Bomb: Containment and Its Complications," *Foreign Affairs* (March/April 2010).

61. White House, "Remarks by President Obama and President Lee Myung-Bak of the Republic of Korea in Joint Press Availability," June 16, 2009, www.whitehouse.gov/the_press_office/Remarks-by-President-Obama-and-President-Lee-of-the-Republic-of-Korea-in-Joint-Press-Availability.

62. Lizza, "Consequentialist."

Epilogue

Of Challenges and Opportunities

U.S. human rights promotion is a story of dramatic success that is somewhat offset by tragic error and missed opportunity; of idealism and its practical limits; of clashes between America's long-term goal of advancing freedom and democracy around the world and such short-term goals as protecting national security, ensuring regional stability, and guaranteeing access to natural resources. Most strikingly, it's a story that demonstrates America's unique and enduring power to shape the course of history and make the world a safer, more prosperous place.

Through the course of this story, presidents have exploited the power of their "bully pulpit" to support democratic movements and pressure authoritarian regimes, distributed foreign aid to support friends and influence adversaries, and deployed military force to halt horror and protect vulnerable populations. Among their more dramatic successes, presidents and Congresses and, through them, the nation at large rescued Europe with the Marshall Plan in the late 1940s, won the Cold War in the late 1980s, facilitated famine relief in Somalia and ended genocide in the Balkans in the 1990s, and protected vulnerable Libyans from a vengeful leader during the Arab Spring of recent years. Through these efforts and others, the United States has promoted human rights for tens of millions of people, providing a major boost for the historic advance of freedom and democracy across Europe, Asia, Africa, and Latin American since the end of World War II.

Over the last seventy-five years, however, the United States has been neither consistent in its approach nor wholly effective in its efforts. When necessary, it has sacrificed human rights at the altar of more pressing foreign policy considerations, such as when it chose not to forcefully assist popular uprisings in East Germany in 1953, Hungary in 1956, and Czechoslovakia in 1968 for fear of evoking a major military confrontation with the Soviet Union. George H. W. Bush reacted with restraint after the Tiananmen Square massacre in Beijing in 1989 for fear of upsetting U.S.-China relations, and Barack Obama did not aggressively support the democracy movement in Iran in 2009 for fear of complicating his "engagement" effort with Tehran. Meanwhile, Washington's misguided hints that it would forcefully intervene to assist anti-government forces in Hungary in 1956 and Iraq in 1991 encouraged those forces to redouble their efforts, setting them up for slaughter when the dictators took their revenge and Washington hung back.

The U.S. challenge of how to effectively promote human rights, and when to try, will not grow easier in the years ahead. Across the world, the advance of human rights has stalled. As noted earlier, Freedom House reported in early 2012 that, with regard to political rights and civil liberties, "slightly more countries registered declines than exhibited gains over the course of 2011. This marks the sixth consecutive year in which countries with declines outnumbered those with improvements"—the longest period of retrenchment since the nonprofit began publishing its annual survey in 1972.[1]

In China, the authoritarian regime cracked down more forcefully on democratic activism at home, sentencing leading dissidents to prison and censoring the Internet, while growing its economy and stepping more boldly on the world stage. In addition, elected leaders—in places like Russia, Ukraine, Kyrgyzstan, Hungary, Turkey, Venezuela, Nicaragua, and Ecuador— clamped down on democracy after taking office, expanding their powers while restricting opposition parties, the judiciary, the media, financial institutions, and nongovernmental organizations. Meanwhile, public support for freedom and democracy fell in many parts of Asia and Africa as people on the ground chose to trade political freedom for the promise of domestic tranquility and higher living standards. The global democratic retreat and disheartening public attitudes about democracy presented significant new challenges to U.S. human rights promotion efforts.[2]

Moreover, Washington faced tough questions about how to promote human rights in a region that, until recently, history seemed to forget—the Middle East and North Africa. Since late 2010, millions of people have poured into the streets, toppling dictators in Tunisia, Egypt, Libya, and Yemen and inciting protests in Syria, Jordan, Saudi Arabia, Algeria, Morocco, Bahrain, and elsewhere. Whether this Arab Spring will plant the seeds of a freer, more democratic region or merely enable a new set of autocrats to replace the old remains a very open question.

As of early 2012, the results were decidedly mixed, as religious and political splits of long vintage played out on different stages.

- In Tunisia, the nation that launched the Arab Spring was making perhaps the most inspiring transition from strongman to democratic rule, with free elections, an independent media, a thriving civil society, and elected leaders who pledge to promote tolerance and respect the rule of law.
- In Egypt, the military was spearheading the transition to a post-Mubarak future, but parliamentary elections in which the Muslim Brotherhood and the even more fundamentalist Nour Party captured two-thirds of the seats raised serious questions about whether the new government will respect human rights or replace secular authoritarianism with an Islamist version. [3]
- In Libya, post-Gaddafi society remains very much in flux, with rebel forces patrolling the streets, interim leaders still needing to write a new constitution and hold elections, and Libyans in different regions of the country worried about how they will fare in a new political structure.
- In Yemen, ex-President Ali Abdullah Saleh was wielding power behind the scenes despite his agreement to step down, military forces that remained loyal to him continued to gun down civilians, opposition forces struggled to unify into a viable alternative to the long-time strongman, secessionist forces were gathering strength in the South, and the nation seemed headed toward civil war.
- In Syria, a defiant President Bashar al-Assad left no doubt that he would do whatever it took to retain power, continuing a slaughter that had claimed more than ten thousand lives (including children), violating every one of his pledges to stop the violence and move toward reform, and provoking calls for international intervention of the kind that sped Gaddafi's fall in Libya.

For the United States, the region presents both vexing challenges and extraordinary opportunities.

For starters, it is home to much of the world's oil, on which the global economy is so dependent, as well as to terror-sponsoring states that threaten the United States and its interests. Iran is challenging U.S. influence in the region and marching toward nuclear weaponry while upgrading the reach of its ballistic missiles. Iran and Syria continue to arm, fund, and protect Hezbollah, Hamas, and other terrorist groups. Israel, a key U.S. ally, is surrounded by countries and groups that seek its destruction and, as of early 2012, it faced cooler relations with a post-Mubarak Egypt and a more Islamic Turkey.

But even if the region seems to offer only mounting dangers for the United States and its allies at this writing, the future could well be brighter. Half of the people of the Middle East and North Africa are under twenty-five, and they are increasingly repelled by autocracies that have not served them well. Unemployment among the region's "youth" (those fifteen to twenty-four) was 24 percent in 2009, more than twice the rate for adults. When the young flee the region for greener pastures, the poor quality of their education leaves them unprepared for the increasingly sophisticated jobs that the global economy offers.[4] Despite governmental efforts to control information, the young have more access to the Internet and social media through which they learn about the greater opportunities that other societies offer. They want more freedom, more democracy, and more prosperity for themselves, and they will undoubtedly be change agents in a region that has stagnated for far too long.

A freer, more democratic region would benefit the United States in myriad ways. Liberal democracies do not tend to sponsor terrorism, so a freer, more democratic Middle East would reduce threats to the United States and its allies. It also would reduce the need for a robust U.S. military presence in the region to ensure peace, especially if it brought an end to the terror-sponsoring, hegemony-seeking regime in Tehran. A future of free-market economies across the region, meanwhile, would provide greater trade and investment opportunities for U.S. businesses, generating more prosperity in the United States.

The question, as always, is how to get from here to there without compromising other U.S. foreign policy priorities. As we saw in the Palestinian territories in 2006, an all-too-speedy push for elections without a strong foundation for sustained freedom and democracy can bring to power anti-democratic forces that, in turn, then dispense with the niceties of human rights and increase the threats to U.S. interests. That could well happen again if, in Egypt and elsewhere, radical Islamist forces use the ballot box to gain power and then act accordingly. Moreover, the rise of hostile forces in Saudi Arabia and other oil-rich nations could threaten the flow of oil to the West.

Asked in May 2011 about the seeming contradiction between promoting democracy in some places while standing by authoritarian allies in others, Secretary of State Hillary Clinton said,

> I wouldn't accept the premise. I think that we believe in the same values and principles, full stop. We believe that countries should empower their people. We believe that people should have certain universal rights. We believe there are certain economic systems that work better for the vast majority of people than other subsystems. So I think we're very consistent. I think that's been a cornerstone of American foreign policy for at least the last century. At the same time, we live in the real world. And there are lots of countries that we deal with because we have interests in common. We have certain security issues that we are both looking at. Obviously, in the Middle East, Iran is an overwhelming challenge to all of us. We do business with a lot of countries whose economic systems or political systems are not ones we would design or choose to live under. And we have encouraged consistently, both publicly and privately, reform and recognition and protection of human rights.[5]

With the "real world" very much in mind, Obama has taken a country-by-country approach to the Arab Spring. He stood behind U.S. allies in Saudi Arabia, Jordan, and Bahrain but pushed aside another ally, Egypt's Mubarak, when he thought it was time for him to go. Working with his European counterparts, he deployed force to protect Libyan rebels who were under the threat of slaughter by strongman Muammar Gaddafi, helping to topple the latter. But he was slow to urge Syria's al-Assad to leave office even as al-Assad suppressed Syria's uprising in horrific fashion by killing thousands of people.

Obama's decisions about where to push and where to stand back seemed to reflect not just longstanding U.S. interests but also his particular outlook on the region. Why, for instance, did he intervene in Libya and not Syria, especially when the latter sponsors and funds terrorism while working closely with the dangerous regime in Tehran? Perhaps the decision reflected Obama's longstanding hopes of convincing al-Assad to turn away from Iran and make peace with Israel, of persuading the Syrian strongman to change his behavior rather than trying to unseat him.

Moving forward, the United States will need both a strategic vision as well as the flexibility to adapt it to such "facts on the ground" as U.S. relations with a particular nation, the nation's role in protecting U.S. interests, and the nation's political and cultural history. A comprehensive and effective strategy for the region would include at least the following elements:

- *Speak consistently, not episodically.* If the three rules of real estate are "location, location, location," then the three rules of communications are "repetition, repetition, repetition." Presidents must speak regularly and forcefully about U.S. support for human rights because the Arab people, in particular, have reason to be skeptical. They know that, in the interest of regional stability, Washington traditionally supported pro-Western autocracies in Cairo, Riyadh, and elsewhere who regularly abused human rights. The support that we provided helped the autocrats ignore the aspirations of their people. The president must make clear that, whether speaking to friendly or adversarial governments, he (or she) will push for reforms that will fully imbed democratic values and structures into the societies that these governments oversee. That will nurture support among the restive people of the Greater Middle East who are seeking freer and more prosperous lives for themselves and their families.
- *Respect the home turf.* While nurturing the values that, we believe, lie deep within the soul of every human being, the United States must not seek to impose its own formula for freedom and democracy on the region. The people of this region, with their own ethnic and religious roots, their own histories and cultures, must pursue their own paths to freer and more

tolerant societies. They may decide to build a U.S.-style federal system or a European-style parliamentary system or something else entirely. The United States should work with them to ensure that, whatever they create, their political, economic, and social structures reflect the values of freedom and tolerance, transparency and accountability.

- *Build beyond elections.* As Middle East expert Kenneth M. Pollack put it recently, "[E]lections do not equal democracy."[6] Washington and its partners in the nonprofit community must help transitioning nations to plant the values and create the institutions that ensure long-term freedom and democracy. The values include free speech and free assembly, tolerance and nonviolence, transparency and accountability, women and minority rights, and respect for the rule of law. The institutions include opposition parties, a free and independent media, and a thriving civil society that can hold government accountable. The alternative to deeply engrained democracy is one-time democracy, which could pave the way for authoritarian forces to gain control and then, as we have seen in this region and beyond, subvert the democratic process to maintain power.
- *Tie U.S. aid to human rights.* Washington should condition its economic, military, and political aid as much as possible on a nation's progress in protecting human rights. Even with its cash-strapped federal government, the United States retains enormous capacity to influence the direction of another government through economic aid, diplomatic support, military sales and cooperation, trade and investment, and leverage over the lending decisions of multilateral development banks. By linking U.S. aid to governmental practices, a president can put his rhetorical commitment to advancing human rights into tangible form, thus not only influencing foreign governments but also nourishing support among foreign peoples.
- *Focus on the long term.* For the United States, the conflict between long-term visions of more freedom and democracy and the short-term exigencies of protecting U.S. national security interests remains a fact of life. But, for Washington, it must not be a paralyzing one. Yes, Washington must set human rights considerations aside from time to time. Nevertheless, it must make clear, through word and deed, that it retains its long-term goal of advancing freedom and democracy and will pursue it whenever possible. It must avoid the trap of moving from one short-term exigency to another and losing sight of the long-term picture. It also must resist the age-old warnings of pro-American autocrats that U.S. promotion of freedom and democracy will invariably hand power to anti-American Islamic fundamentalists. Instead, it should nurture home-grown democratic forces that can become viable alternatives to authoritarianism of any kind.

In the coming years, as the region marinates in more turmoil, the United States will make its share of mistakes there and elsewhere. It will push too hard in some places, not hard enough in others. It will assist democratic forces effectively in some places, complicate matters in others. We don't know, of course, what the future will bring. We do know, however, that human rights promotion has assumed a role in U.S. foreign policy that even the most skeptical president cannot ignore.

Consider Obama. He took office in early 2009 with a distinctly different view than his predecessor about America's role in the world. Rather than boldly promote human rights through a "freedom agenda," Obama would lower the rhetoric and seek warmer relations with allies and adversaries alike. Though he spoke about human rights episodically, he largely avoided public confrontations over human rights with authoritarian regimes in Beijing, Tehran, and elsewhere. When the Arab Spring erupted in Tunisia in late 2010 and spread across the region, he was slow to react.

In May 2011, however, Obama went to the State Department to deliver a major address on U.S. policy toward the Greater Middle East. After reviewing recent events and relating them to America's revolutionary roots, he said, "[W]e face a historic opportunity. We have the chance to show that America values the dignity of the street vendor in Tunisia more than the raw power of the dictator. There must be no doubt that the United States of America welcomes change that advances self-determination and opportunity. Yes, there will be perils that accompany this moment of promise. But after decades of accepting the world as it is in the region, we have a chance to pursue the world as it should be." [7]

"The United States," he went on, "opposes the use of violence and repression against the people of the region."

> The United States supports a set of universal rights. And these rights include free speech, the freedom of peaceful assembly, the freedom of religion, equality for men and women under the rule of law, and the right to choose your own leaders—whether you live in Baghdad or Damascus, Sanaa or Tehran. And we support political and economic reform in the Middle East and North Africa that can meet the legitimate aspirations of ordinary people throughout the region. Our support for these principles is not a secondary interest. Today I want to make it clear that it is a top priority that must be translated into concrete actions, and supported by all of the diplomatic, economic and strategic tools at our disposal. Let me be specific. First, it will be the policy of the United States to promote reform across the region, and to support transitions to democracy. [8]

It is a policy with which most of our postwar presidents would have been quite comfortable.

NOTES

1. Arch Puddington, "Full Report Essay: The Arab Uprisings and Their Global Repercussions," *Freedom in the World 2012*, Freedom House, www.freedomhouse.org/report/freedom-world/freedom-world-2012.

2. Joshua Kurlantzick, "The Great Democracy Meltdown: Why the World Is Becoming Less Free," *New Republic*, June 9, 2011; John Kampfner, *Freedom for Sale: Why the World Is Trading Democracy for Security* (New York: Basic Books, 2010).

3. As the *Atlantic*'s Jeffrey Goldberg put it, "[T]he majority of voters in the Arab world's most populous country chose either a party whose motto is 'Islam is the Solution' [Muslim Brotherhood] or a party that believes that medieval Arabia is an appropriate state model [Nour Party]." Jeffrey Goldberg, "Was the Arab Spring a Victory for Extremism?" Bloomberg, December 23, 2011.

4. Farzaneh Roudi, "Youth Population and Employment in the Middle East and North Africa: Opportunity or Challenge?" United Nations Expert Group Meeting on Adolescents, Youth and Development, July 22, 2011.

5. Jeffrey Goldberg, "Hillary Clinton: Chinese System Is Doomed, Leaders on a 'Fool's Errand,'" *Atlantic Monthly*, May 10, 2011.

6. Kenneth M. Pollack, "America's Second Chance and the Arab Spring," *Foreign Policy*, December 5, 2011, www.foreignpolicy.com/articles/2011/12/05/americas_second_chance. Later in December, former Soviet dissident Natan Sharansky expanded upon the point with regard to Egypt, writing, "Nothing is instantaneous in politics. To think of elections as a panacea, let alone a sure road to real democracy, is to evince a failure of historical imagination. The proper role of the free world is not to encourage or to stop elections. Its role should be to formulate, and to stick by, a policy of incremental change based on creating the institutions that will lead ineluctably to pressure for more and more representative forms of government. The free world should place its bet on freedom—the hope and demand of Tahrir Square—and work toward a civil society defined by that value." Natan Sharansky, "The West Should Bet on Freedom in Egypt," *Washington Post*, December 16, 2011.

7. Barack Obama, Address on the Middle East and North Africa, State Department, May 19, 2011.

8. Obama, Address.

Bibliography

Ali, Ayaan Hirsi. *Infidel*. New York: Free Press, 2007.

———. *Nomad: From Islam to America: A Personal Journey through the Clash of Civilizations*. New York: Free Press, 2010.

———. *The Caged Virgin: An Emancipation Proclamation for Women and Islam*. New York: Free Press, 2002.

Allen, Richard V. "Richard Nixon, LBJ, and the Invasion of Czechoslovakia." *Hoover Digest*, January 30, 1999, www.hoover.org/publications/hoover-digest/article/6425.

———. "The Man Who Won the Cold War." *Hoover Digest*, January 30, 2000, www.hoover.org/publications/hoover-digest/article/7398.

Apodaca, Clair. *Understanding U.S. Human Rights Policy*. New York: Routledge, 2006.

Ayittey, George B. N. "The Somali Crisis: Time for an African Solution." Cato Institute, Policy Analysis No. 205, March 28, 1994.

Beckerman, Gal. *When They Come for Us, We'll Be Gone: The Epic Struggle to Save Soviet Jewry*. New York: Houghton Mifflin Harcourt, 2010.

Behrman, Greg. *The Most Noble Adventure: The Marshall Plan and the Time When America Helped Save Europe*. New York: Free Press, 2007.

Beinart, Peter. *The Good Fight: Why Liberals—and Only Liberals—Can Win the War on Terror and Make America Great Again*. New York: HarperCollins, 2006.

Berman, Ilan. *Winning the Long War*. Lanham, MD: Rowman & Littlefield, 2009.

Bloomfield, Lincoln. "From Ideology to Program to Policy: Tracking the Carter Human Rights Policy." *Journal of Policy Analysis and Management*, vol. 2, no. 1 (Autumn 1982).

Brinkley, Douglas. "Democratic Enlargement: The Clinton Doctrine." *Foreign Policy* (Spring 1997).

Brodsky, Mathew R. J. "Hope over Experience with Syria." *InFocus*, vol. 4, no. 1 (Spring 2010).

Brown, Keith, and Jill Tirnauer. "Trends in U.S. Foreign Assistance over the Past Decade." United States Agency for International Development, August 17, 2009.

Buchan, Alastair. "A World Restored?" *Foreign Affairs*, July 1972.

Burr, William, ed. *The Kissinger Transcripts: The Top Secret Talks with Beijing and Moscow*. New York: New Press, 1999.

Cherny, Andrei. *The Candy Bombers: The Untold Story of the Berlin Airlift and America's Finest Hour*. New York: P. G. Putnam's Sons, 2008.

Cmiel, Kenneth. "The Emergence of Human Rights Politics in the United States." *Journal of American History*, vol. 86, no. 3 (December 1999).

Cohen, Roberta. "Integrating Human Rights in U.S. Foreign Policy." Brookings Institution, April 2008.

Cohen, Stephen. "Conditioning U.S. Security Assistance on Human Rights Practices." *American Journal of International Law*, vol. 76, no. 2 (April 1982).

Dallek, Robert. *Harry S. Truman*. New York: Henry Holt, 2008.

De Crevecoeur, J. Hector St. John. *Letters from an American Farmer*. Philadelphia: Matthew Carey, 1793.

Donovan, Robert J. *Conflict and Crisis: The Presidency of Harry S. Truman*. New York: W. W. Norton, 1977.

Dudziak, Mary L. "Birmingham, Addis Ababa, and the Image of America: International Influence on U.S. Civil Rights Politics in the Kennedy Administration." In *Window on Freedom: Race, Civil Rights, and Foreign Affairs 1945–1988*, edited by Brenda Gayle Plummer. Chapel Hill: University of North Carolina Press, 2003.

———. "Desegregation as a Cold War Imperative." *Stanford Law Review*, vol. 41 (1988).

———. "The Little Rock Crisis and Foreign Affairs: Race, Resistance, and the Image of American Democracy." *Southern California Law Review*, vol. 70, no. 6 (September 1997).

Elshtain, Jean Bethke. *Just War against Terror: The Burden of American Power in a Violent World*. New York: Basic Books, 2003.

Finer, S. E. *The Man on Horseback: The Role of the Military in Politics*. 2nd edition. Harmondsworth: Penguin Books, 1976.

Fraser, Donald M. "Human Rights and U.S. Foreign Policy." *International Studies Quarterly*, vol. 23, no. 2 (June 1979).

Freedom House. *Freedom in the World* Country Ratings, 1973–2011, www.freedomhouse.org/report-types/freedom-world.

Friedman, Thomas L. *The Lexus and the Olive Tree*. New York: Farrar, Straus and Giroux, 1999.

———. *The World Is Flat*. New York: Farrar, Straus and Giroux, 2005.

Fukuyama, Francis. "The End of History?" *The National Interest*, Summer 1989.

Gabriel, Brigitte. *Because They Hate: A Survivor of Islamic Terror Warns America*. New York: St. Martin's Press, 2006.

———. *They Must Be Stopped: Why We Must Defeat Radical Islam and How We Can Do It*. New York: St. Martin's Press, 2008.

Gaddis, John Lewis. *Surprise, Security, and the American Experience*. Cambridge, MA: Harvard University Press, 2004.

———. *The Cold War: A New History*. New York: Penguin Press, 2005.

Gates, Robert. *From the Shadows*. New York: Simon & Schuster, 2006.

Gauthier-Villars, David. "How 'The Family' Controlled Tunisia." *Wall Street Journal*, June 20, 2011.

Glendon, Mary Ann. *A World Made New: Eleanor Roosevelt and the Universal Declaration of Human Rights*. New York: Random House, 2001.

Goldberg, Jeffrey. "Danger: Falling Tyrants." *Atlantic Monthly*, June 2011.

———. "Hillary Clinton: Chinese System Is Doomed, Leaders on a 'Fool's Errand.'" *Atlantic Monthly*, May, 2011.

Goldhagen, Daniel Jonah. "The Sudan Crisis: Obama's Hypocrisy and Culpability." *New Republic*, June 22, 2011.

Gurr, Ted Robert, Keith Jaggers, and Will H. Moore. "The Transformation of the Western State: The Growth of Democracy, Autocracy, and State Power since 1800." *Studies in Comparative International Development*, vol. 25, no. 1 (Spring 1990).

Habeck, Mary. *Knowing the Enemy*. New Haven, CT: Yale University Press, 2006.

Howard, Michael. "The Prudence Thing: George Bush's Class Act." *Foreign Affairs* November/December, 1998.

Huntington, Samuel P. *The Third Wave: Democratization in the Late Twentieth Century*. Norman: University of Oklahoma Press, 1991.

Ibrahim, Raymond, ed. *The al Qaeda Reader*. New York: Broadway Books, 2007.

Ishay, Micheline R., ed. *The Human Rights Reader*. New York: Routledge, 2007.

Just, Richard. "Yet Another Disgrace." *New Republic*, November 28, 2010.

Kagan, Frederick W. *Finding the Target: The Transformation of American Military Policy*. New York: Encounter Books, 2006.

Kagan, Robert. *The Return of History and the End of Dreams*. New York: Alfred A. Knopf, 2008.

Kampfner, John. *Freedom for Sale: Why the World Is Trading Democracy for Security*. New York: Basic Books, 2010.

Kaplan, Robert D. "Kissinger, Metternich, and Realism." *Atlantic Monthly*, June 1999.

Karatnycky, Adrian, and Peter Ackerman. "How Freedom Is Won: From Civic Resistance to Durable Democracy." Freedom House, 2005, http://old.freedomhouse.org/uploads/special_report/29.pdf.

Kempe, Frederick. *Berlin 1961: Kennedy, Khrushchev, and the Most Dangerous Place on Earth*. New York: G. P. Putnam's Sons, 2011.

Kengor, Paul. "Summer of Appeasement: When Ford Snubbed Solzhenitsyn." *American Spectator*, October 8, 2010.

Kennan, George F. *American Diplomacy: 1900–1950*. Chicago: University of Chicago Press, 1951.

———. Kennan (signed as "X"). "The Sources of Soviet Conduct." *Foreign Affairs*, July 1947.

Keys, Barbara. "Kissinger, Congress, and the Origins of Human Rights Diplomacy." *Diplomatic History*, vol. 34, no. 5 (November 2010).

Kirkpatrick, Jeane J. "Dictatorships and Double Standards." *Commentary*, November 1979.

Kissinger, Henry. *Years of Upheaval*. Boston: Little, Brown, 1982.

Korey, William. "Jackson-Vanik: Its Origin and Impact as Russia Nears 'Graduation.'" *Harriman Review*, vol. 14, nos. 1–2 (November 2002).

Kurlantzick, Joshua. "The Great Democracy Meltdown: Why the World Is Becoming Less Free." *New Republic*, June 9, 2011.

Levy, Jack. "Domestic Politics and War." In *The Origin and Prevention of Major Wars*, edited by Robert Rotberg and Theodore Rabb. New York: Cambridge University Press, 1989.

Lindsay, James M., and Ray Takeyh. "After Iran Gets the Bomb: Containment and Its Complications." *Foreign Affairs*, March/April 2010.

Lizza, Ryan. "The Consequentialist: How the Arab Spring Remade Obama's Foreign Policy." *New Yorker*, May 2, 2011.

Lynn-Jones, Sean M. "Why the United States Should Spread Democracy." Discussion Paper 98-07, Center for Science and International Affairs, Harvard University, March 1998.

MacEachin, Doug, and Janne E. Nolan, co-chairs, Discourse, Dissent, and Strategic Surprise: Formulating American Security in an Age of Uncertainty, Institute for the Study of Diplomacy, Edmund A. Walsh School of Foreign Service, Georgetown University. "The Soviet Invasion of Afghanistan in 1979: Failure of Intelligence or of the Policy Process?" Working Group Report No. 111, September 26, 2005.

Magstadt, Thomas M. "Emigration and Citizenship: Implications for Soviet-American Relations." Cato Institute, Policy Analysis No. 70, May 2, 1986.

Mandelbaum, Michael. *The Case for Goliath: How America Acts as the World's Government in the 21st Century*. New York: PublicAffairs, 2005.

———. *The Ideas That Conquered the World: Peace, Democracy, and Free Markets in the Twenty-First Century*. New York: Public Affairs, 2002.

Manji, Irshad. *Allah, Liberty and Love: The Courage to Reconcile Faith and Freedom*. New York: Free Press, 2011.

———. *The Trouble with Islam Today: A Muslim's Call for Reform in Her Faith*. New York: St. Martin's Griffin, 2003.

McFaul, Michael. *Advancing Democracy Abroad: Why We Should and How We Can*. Lanham, MD: Rowman & Littlefield, 2010.

McMahon, Robert. "Human Rights Reporting and U.S. Foreign Policy." Council on Foreign Relations, April 9, 2009.

McManus, John F. "A Republic, If You Can Keep It." *New American*, November 6, 2000.

Mead, Walter Russell. *Special Providence: American Foreign Policy and How It Changed the World*. New York: Routledge, 2002.

———. "The Tea Party and American Foreign Policy." *Foreign Affairs*, March/April 2011.

Mearsheimer, John J. "Why We Will Soon Miss the Cold War." *Atlantic Monthly*, August 1990.

Mihajlov, Mihajlo. "Notes of a Survivor." *New Leader*, July 31, 1978.
Morgenthau, Hans J. *In Defense of the National Interest: A Critical Examination of American Foreign Policy.* New York: Alfred A. Knopf, 1951.
———. "To Intervene or Not to Intervene." *Foreign Affairs*, vol. 45, no. 3 (April 1967).
Morris, Benny. *One State, Two States.* New Haven, CT: Yale University Press, 2009.
Moynihan, Daniel Patrick. "The Politics of Human Rights." *Commentary*, August 1977.
Nasr, Vali. *The Shia Revival: How Conflicts within Islam Will Shape the Future.* New York: W. W. Norton, 2006.
Paine, Thomas. *Common Sense.* New York: Fall River Press, 1995.
Pfluger, Friedbert. "Human Rights Unbound: Carter's Human Rights Policy Reassessed." *Presidential Studies Quarterly*, vol. 19, no. 4 (Fall 1989).
Pham, J. Peter. "What Is in the National Interest? Hans Morgenthau's Realist Vision and American Foreign Policy." *American Foreign Policy Interests*, vol. 30 (2008): 256–65.
Phares, Walid. *The Confrontation: Winning the War against Future Jihad. New York: Palgrave Macmillan*, 2008.
———. *Future Jihad: Terrorist Strategies against the West.* New York: Palgrave Macmillan, 2005.
———. *The War of Ideas: Jihadism against Democracy.* New York: Palgrave Macmillan, 2007.
Power, Samantha. "Bystanders to Genocide: Why the United States Let the Rwandan Tragedy Happen." *Atlantic Monthly*, September 2001.
Puddington, Arch. "Democracy under Duress." *Journal of Democracy*, vol. 22, no. 2 (April 2011).
Radosh, Allis, and Ronald Radosh. *A Safe Haven: Harry S. Truman and the Founding of Israel.* New York: HarperCollins, 2009.
Rieffer, Barbara Ann J., and Kristan Mercer. "U.S. Democracy Promotion: The Clinton and Bush Administrations." *Global Society*, vol. 19, no. 4 (October 2005).
Rosati, Jerl A. "Jimmy Carter, a Man before His Time? The Emergence and Collapse of the First Post–Cold War Presidency." *Presidential Studies Quarterly*, vol. 23, no. 3 (Summer 1993).
Rubin, Michael. "Is American Support for Middle Eastern Dissidents the Kiss of Death?" *AEI Middle Eastern Outlook*, December 2006.
Russett, Bruce. *Grasping the Democratic Peace: Principles of a Post–Cold War World.* Princeton, NJ: Princeton University Press, 1993.
Schlesinger, Arthur M., Jr. "Human Rights and the American Tradition." *Foreign Affairs*, vol. 57, no. 3 (1978).
———. *The Imperial Presidency.* New York: Popular Library, 1973.
Schneider, Mark L. "Human Rights Policy under the Carter Administration." *Law and Contemporary Problems*, vol. 43, no. 2 (Spring 1979).
Schweizer, Peter. *Reagan's War: The Epic Story of His Forty-Year Struggle and Final Triumph over Communism.* New York: Anchor Books, 2003.
Sharansky, Natan. *The Case for Democracy.* New York: PublicAffairs, 2004.
Shestack, Jerome J. "Human Rights, the National Interest, and U.S. Foreign Policy." *Annals of the American Academy of Political and Social Sciences*, vol. 506 (November 1989).
Soares, Joan A. "Strategy, Ideology, and Human Rights: Jimmy Carter Confronts the Left in Central America, 1979–1981." *Journal of Cold War Studies*, vol. 8, no. 4 (Fall 2006).
Stohl, Michael, David Carleton, and Steven E. Johnson. "Human Rights and U.S. Foreign Assistance from Nixon to Carter." *Journal of Peace Research*, vol. 21, no. 3 (1984).
Sultan, Wafa. *A God Who Hates: The Courageous Woman Who Inflamed the Muslim World Speaks Out against the Evils of Islam.* New York: St. Martin's Press, 2009.
Tarnoff, Curt, and Marian Leonardo Lawson. "Foreign Aid: An Introduction to U.S. Programs and Policy." Congressional Research Service, April 9, 2009.
Thompson, Nicholas. *The Hawk and the Dove: Paul Nitze, George Kennan, and the History of the Cold War.* New York: Henry Holt, 2009.
United States House Foreign Affairs Subcommittee on International Organizations and Movements. *Human Rights in the World Community: A Call for U.S. Leadership*, March 27, 1974.

Vogelgesang, Sandy. *American Dream, Global Nightmare: The Dilemma of U.S. Human Rights Policy*. New York: W. W. Norton, 1980.

———. "Diplomacy of Human Rights." *International Studies Quarterly*, vol. 23, no. 2 (June 1979).

Walzer, Michael. *Arguing about War*. New Haven, CT: Yale University Press, 2004.

Weekly Standard. "The View from the Gulag: An Interview with Natan Sharansky." June 21, 2004.

Weisman, Steven R., ed. *Daniel Patrick Moynihan: A Portrait in Letters of an American Visionary*. New York: PublicAffairs, 2010.

Western, Jon. "Sources of Humanitarian Intervention: Beliefs, Information, and Advocacy in the U.S. Decisions on Somalia and Bosnia." *International Security*, vol. 27, no. 1 (July/August 1999).

White House. "A National Security Strategy of Engagement and Enlargement." February 1995.

———. "The National Security Strategy of the United States of America." September 2002.

Widmer, Ted. *Ark of the Liberties: America and the World*. New York: Hill and Wang, 2008.

Wood, Gordon. *The Idea of America: Reflections on the Birth of the United States*. New York: Penguin Press, 2011.

———. *The Radicalism of the American Revolution*. New York: Vintage Books, 1991.

Wright, Robin. *Rock the Casbah: Rage and Rebellion across the Islamic World*. New York: Simon & Schuster, 2011.

Zelizer, Julian E. *Arsenal of Democracy: The Politics of National Security—From World War II to the War on Terrorism*. New York: Basic Books, 2010.

Index

Abbas, Mahmoud, 149
Abourezk, James, 85
abuse intervention, 11
Acheson, Dean, 51, 67
Adams, Abigail, 7
Adams, John, 25
Afghanistan, 108–109
Afshari, Ali, 45n64
Agha-Soltan, Neda, 151
Ahmadinejad, Mahmoud, 148, 149, 151
AI. *See* Amnesty International
Aidid, Mohammad Farrah, 123
Aiken, George, 48
Akhundzadeh, Mahdi, 148
Albright, Madeleine, 3, 44n30
Allen, Richard V., 63, 113
American exceptionalism, 25, 146
American Experiment, 23, 98n6
American Revolution, 6
Amnesty International (AI), 93
Andropov, Yuri, 96
Angell, Norman, 31
anti-Western ideology, 133–134
Arabella (ship), 14, 23
Arab-Israeli conflict, 154n53
Arab Spring: human rights issues of, 2;
    individuals and groups driving, 42;
    iron-fisted strongmen toppled during,
    10, 38; Obama's approach to, 161;
    rights-abusing regimes and, 41
Aristides, Jean-Bertrand, 131

The Arthashastra (Kautilya), 5
Aspin, Les, 123
al-Assad, Bashar, 2, 34, 135, 148, 149, 159
authoritarian regime, 39, 40

Baker, James, 120–121
Bandar, Prince, 120
Barre, Mohamed Siad, 123

Al Bashir, Omar, 19n19

Beirut bombings, 135
Ben Ali, Zine, 1–2
Berlin Wall speech (Kennedy), 12, 26,
    56–58
Bernstein, Carl, 113
Biden, Joe, 145
bin Laden, Osama, 132
Bonner, Elena, 95
Bosnia, 36, 123, 124

Al Bouazizi, Muhammad, 1–2

Brezhnev, Leonid, 34, 88; diplomatic coup
    of, 94; Reagan attacking doctrine of,
    111
Brezhnev Doctrine, 111
Brown, Sam, 104
Brownell, Herbert, 65
Brown v. Board of Education, 68

Brzezinski, Zbigniew, 126n12, 154n53, 143

Buddhism, 5

Bukovsky, Vladimir, 34, 105

Bullock, Bob, 130

bully pulpit, 14, 21, 33, 70, 157

Burke, Edmund, 25

Bush, George H. W.: global stability focus of, 103; New World Order vision of, 16; Poland's economic aid from, 115; realism period launched by, 116; Somalia and troops sent by, 123; world changes during tenure of, 116

Bush, George W., 13, 34, 37; freedom and democracy calls from, 139–140; Hussein toppled by, 139; Iraq policies of, 154n32; Iraq's liberation statement of, 32; Middle East's lack of freedom and, 29; U.S. citizens grew weary of, 143; war on terror of, 17, 136–137

Bush, Laura, 130

Bush Doctrine, 129, 137; freedom and democracy advancement in, 138; preemptive action in, 137–138; state sponsored terrorism in, 137; three elements of, 137–138

Byrne, Malcolm, 62

Cambodia, 9, 77

capitalism, 6, 133

Carleton, David, 106

Carter, Jimmy: foreign policy crisis of, 106–107; foreign policy failure of, 107–108; human rights abuse ignored by, 108; human rights focus of, 103, 104–105; human rights policy of, 16; hypocrisy charges vulnerability of, 106; inconsistency of, 126n7

The Case for Democracy (Sharansky), 89

Ceausescu, Nicolai, 10

Cedar Revolution, 33, 140

Charter 77, 40, 95

Chavez, Hugo, 145

checks and balances, 23

Cheney, Dick, 92

China, 118, 158

Chinese students, 3

Churchill, Winston, 28

citizenship, 88

civil rights: Kennedy, J. F., issues of, 68–69; Truman's struggles of, 67; U.S. hurt by, 68

Civil Rights era, 66

Clemenceau, Georges, 27

Clinton, Bill: democratic enlargement doctrine of, 16, 30, 122; economic optimism under, 122; economy interest of, 121; free and democratic nations expansion of, 103; national security dollars and, 31; national security strategy of, 122; Somalia mission continued by, 123

Clinton, Hillary, 145, 148, 149, 160

Cmiel, Kenneth, 92

Code of Hammurabi, 5

Cold War: nuclear weapons testing and, 38–39; Reagan's view of, 111; Truman's containment strategy during, 60; U.S. foreign policy shaped by, 82; U.S. human rights promotion during, 47–48; U.S. victory in, 125

commencement address (Solzhenitsyn), 90

Common Sense (Paine), 23, 25

communism: countries falling into, 110; Gorbachev reforming, 10, 39, 97; Soviet-style, 63. *See also* totalitarian regimes

Conference on Security and Cooperation, 94

Confucius, 5

Congress: foreign aid tightening by, 87; human rights hearings of, 76; human rights promotion role of, 85–87; Truman addressing, 50–53

Connor, Bull, 69

containment strategy, 60

country-by-country approach, 41

Cranston, Alan, 85

cultural practices, 11, 161

Cuomo, Mario, 121

Czechoslovakia, 62, 63

Dalai Lama, 34, 145

A Day in the Life of Ivan Denisovich (Solzhenitsyn), 90

Dayton Accords, 124

Dean, Andrea M., 45n50

Declaration of Independence, 19n8

"Declaration of War against Americans", 135

declinism, 98n6

de Crevecoeur, J. Hector St. John, 22, 23, 25

democracy: building, 140–141; Bush, G. W. calling for, 139–140; Bush Doctrine advancing, 138; global retreat of, 158; Helsinki Accords producing fervor for, 96; human rights and, 19n15; in Middle East, 160; terrorism not sponsored by, 160; U.S. benefiting from advancement of, 30; U.S. inconsistencies in, 19n19; U.S. needing long-term planning for, 162; U.S. promoting, 54. *See also* freedom

democratic enlargement doctrine, 16, 30, 122

democratic transition: Iraq and planning of, 141; of Russia, 30

democratization, second wave of, 77

Department of Defense (DoD), 131

Derian, Patricia M., 105

de-Stalinization policy, 61

Dewey, Thomas E., 65

diplomatic coup, 94

DoD. *See* Department of Defense

domino theory, 31–32, 45n50

Dubcek, Alexander, 62

Dudziak, Mary L., 66

Dulles, Allen, 61

Dulles, John Foster, 65, 68, 117

Durban II conference, 146

Early, Steve, 48

Eastern Europe: Charter 77 from, 40, 95; Soviet-style communism in, 63

East Germany, 60–61

economy: aid for, 115; Clinton, B., interest in, 121; Clinton, B., investment in, 31; Clinton, B., surge in, 122; geo-economics and, 128n61; reform of, 163

education reimbursement fee, 87–88

Egypt, 164n3; free world and, 164n6; parliamentary elections in, 159; protests in, 2

Eisenhower, Dwight D.: domino theory of, 31–32; Supreme Court decision capitalized on by, 68

embassy, U.S., 107, 135

emigration, 88

"The End of History?" (Fukuyama), 122

English Bill of Rights, 6

enlightened self-interest, 28

Enlightenment period, 6

Epictectus, 5

ethnic cleansing, 124

Europe, 53–54. *See also* Eastern Europe

evil empire, 33, 91, 110

al-Faisal, Saud, 120

Fascell, Dante, 127n30

Fathy, Bashem, 41

Faubus, Orval, 65

FDR. *See* Roosevelt, Franklin

Feltman, Jeffrey D., 148

Fenwick, Millicent, 94

Ford, Gerald: private diplomacy approach of, 81; realism approach of, 15, 75; Solzhenitsyn meeting refused by, 92

Ford, Robert, 34

Ford Foundation, 93

foreign aid, 55; Congress tightening, 87; national security element of, 58; regimes practicing torture receiving, 99n23

Foreign Assistance Act of 1961, 35, 58

foreign dignitaries, 66–67, 69

Foreign Operations Administration, 55

foreign policy: Carter, J., crisis of, 106–107; Carter, J., failure of, 107–108; Cold War shaping, 82; Congress influencing, 85–87; enlightened self-interest of, 28; human rights element in, 76; human rights promotion in, 12, 16, 125; human rights promotion task of, 27, 145; Jackson-Vanik amendment and goals of, 87; in Middle East, 150; Morgenthau's vision of, 80; presidents' doctrines on, 59; realism approach in, 15; September 11, 2001, changing, 133; shifting priorities in, 152n6; strategic goals and challenges in, 11

"four freedoms", 19n14, 28, 50

Fox, Vincente, 130

Franklin, Benjamin, 24

Fraser, Donald, 99n23, 85, 127n30
fraudulent elections, 42
free countries, 128n62
freedom: Bush, G. W., calling for,
    139–140; Bush Doctrine advancing,
    138; Helsinki Accords producing fervor
    for, 96; Middle East lacking, 29; moral
    responsibility of, 91; movement, 88;
    Negroes and, 69; prosperity from, 26;
    security goes with, 29; U.S.
    inconsistencies in, 19n19; U.S. needing
    long-term planning for, 162; U.S.
    promoting, 54
Freedom House,: free countries listed by,
    128n62; human rights expansion found
    by, 8; people power movements and,
    140; stalled human rights findings of, 9
Freedom in the World, 8, 9
free peoples, 47
free world, 164n6
Friedman, Thomas, 30–31
Fukuyama, Francis, 122

Gabriel, Brigitte, 153n13
Gaddafi, Muammar, 2, 32, 36, 42, 159
Gaddis, John Lewis, 79
Gates, Robert, 97
Gedmin, Jeff, 45n64
geo-economics, 128n61
Gephardt, Richard, 117
Ginzburg, Alexander, 96
glasnost, 89
Glassboro, spirit of, 63
global community, 70
global stability, 103
Goldberg, Jeffrey, 164n3
Golden Arches theory, 31
Goldhagen, Daniel Jonah, 19n19
Gorbachev, Mikhail, 114, 117; communist
    system reform by, 10, 39, 97; reforms
    promoted by, 89
Gore, Al, 130
grant-making institutions, 36
The Great Illusion (Angell), 31
Greece, 31, 35, 51, 53
Green Revolution, 151
Griffith, William, 64
Gromyko, Andrei, 82

The Gulag Archipelago (Solzhenitsyn), 15,
    75, 90

Haass, Richard, 79, 143
Habeck, Mary, 134
Haig, Alexander, 127n21
Hamas, 13, 141
Hamilton, Lee, 154n53
Hamiltonians, 79
Hammurabi (king), 5
Hariri, Rafik, 140
Hariri, Saad, 142
Harkin, Tom, 85
Harriman, Averill, 51
Harvard University, 90–91
Havel, Vaclav, 42, 95, 116
Helmy, Abdallah, 42
Helsinki Accords, 76, 115; freedom and
    democracy fervor from, 96; Reagan
    thinking U.S sellout with, 94; Soviet
    Union influenced by, 97; Soviet Union
    monitored by, 94
Hertzberg, Rick, 110
Hezbollah: in Lebanon, 142; suicide
    bombings by, 135
Hobbes, Thomas, 6
Ho Chi Minh, 3
Holbrooke, Richard, 123, 148
Honecker, Erich, 116
hostage crisis, 107
Hu Jintao, 41
human rights: abuse intervention and, 11;
    American Revolution advancing, 6;
    annual reports required on, 86; Arab
    Spring issues of, 2; behind-the-scenes
    promotion of, 34–35; Carter, J., focus
    on, 103, 104–105; Carter, J., foreign
    policy of, 16; Carter, J., ignoring abuses
    of, 108; Congressional hearings on, 76;
    in Declaration of Independence, 19n8;
    defining, 5; democracy and, 19n15;
    Freedom House finding expansion of,
    8; Freedom House finding stalling of, 9;
    Haig's speech on, 127n21; Kennedy, J.
    F., call for, 56; Kissinger's
    pronouncements on, 83; Kissinger's
    realism influencing, 84; monotheistic
    religions' guides to, 5; Mubarak's
    abuses of, 41; NGOs monitoring of,

92–94; origin and nature of, 19n14; presidents promoting, 34; Somalia abusing, 123; Soviet Union abusing, 103; U.S. challenges of, 158, 162; U.S. foreign policy element of, 76; U.S. one-sided policy in, 126n12; U.S. over-promising, 15; Western concept of, 5, 6. *See also* Arab Spring; civil rights
Human Rights Council, 146
human rights promotion: challenges to, 18; Congress' role in, 85–87; country-by-country approach in, 41; difficult issues in, 10–11; events and activities in, 14; main points of, 37–42; in Middle East and North Africa, 158–159; moral responsibilities in, 14; new architecture of, 97; operational goal of, 15; organized labor's role in, 90; political activism in, 41; post-World War II period of, 15; risks inherent in, 13; tarnishing idea of, 12–13; Truman's bold leadership in, 52; U.S. Cold War, 47–48; U.S. foreign policy task of, 27, 145; U.S. priorities in, 38; U.S. sense of specialness in, 22–26; U.S. short and long term goals and, 157; in U.S. foreign policy, 12, 16, 125; of U.S., 2–4, 21, 27, 48; words one element in, 58
Human Rights Watch, 93
Humphrey, Hubert, 78, 85
Hungary, 15; de-Stalinization policy and, 61; Soviet Union troops sent to, 61; U.S. disappointing protestors of, 63–64
Huntington, Samuel P., 8, 8–9, 77
Hussein, Saddam, 103; Bush, G. W., topples, 139; Kuwait invaded by, 118–119; uprisings suppressed by, 119
Hyland, William G., 97
hypocrisy, 106

Ibrahim, Anwar, 41
idealism, 27; realism's dispute with, 81, 104; of Wilson, W., 27
ideals, 66–67
IFOR. *See* International Implementation Force
inaugural address (Obama), 144

In Defense of the National Interest (Morgenthau), 80
industrialization, 7
Ingersoll, Robert, 86
Institute of International Affairs, 127n30
International Implementation Force (IFOR), 124
international peace, 28, 52
international relations, 50
Iran: fraudulent elections in, 42; help from West tainting, 45n64; Iraq and maintaining balance with, 120; nuclear weapons in, 149; Obama, B., seeking dialogue with, 148, 149; Obama, B., engagement policy for, 150–151; U.S. complicated relationship with, 106–107
Iran-Contra affair, 127n27
Iranian Revolution, 107, 134
Iraq: Bush, G. W., policies in, 154n32; Bush, G. W., statement of liberation of, 32; democratic transformation planning in, 141; Iran and maintaining balance with, 120; Muslim sects battling for control of, 141; U.S.-led invasion of, 13. *See also* Hussein, Saddam
iron-fisted strongmen, 10, 38
Ishay, Micheline R., 6
Islam, 134, 136
Israel, 131, 134, 136, 149
Israeli-Palestinian conflict, 154n53, 147–148

Jackson, Andrew, 25
Jackson, Henry "Scoop", 85, 87, 94, 104
Jacksonians, 79
Jackson-Vanik amendment, 38, 115; foreign policy goals and, 87; Nixon and Kissinger opposing, 88–89; Sakharov proponent of, 89; Soviet Union's demise role of, 35, 89–90
Jasser, Zuhdi, 153n16
Javitz, Jacob, 78
Jefferson, Thomas, 6, 24
Jeffersonians, 79
Jews, 87–88
jihadism, 134
Jim Crow laws, 65
John Paul II, 113
Johnson, Lyndon, 15

Johnson, Steven E., 106
Jones, John, 67

Kant, Immanuel, 29
Kaplan, Robert D., 84
Kasparov, Garry, 41
Kautilya, 5
Kennan, George, 60, 79
Kennedy, Edward, 85
Kennedy, John F., 15, 24; Berlin Wall
    speech of, 12, 26, 56–58; civil rights
    issues and, 68–69; human rights call of,
    56
Khamenei, Ayatollah Ali, 148
Khmer Rouge, 9, 36, 77
Khrushchev, Nikita, 26, 61
Kirkland, Lane, 90
Kirkpatrick, Jeane J., 107
Kissinger, Henry: human rights and
    realism of, 84; human rights
    pronouncement of, 83; Jackson-Vanik
    opposed by, 88–89; realism dictates
    adhered to by, 83–84; Soviet Union
    criticism lacking from, 100n64
Knowing the Enemy (Habeck), 134
Kosovo, 36, 124
Kosygin, Alexei, 63
Krauthammer, Charles, 111
Kristoff, Nicholas D., 42
Kuchma, Leonid, 140
Kurds, 119
Kuwait, 118–119

labor unions, 7, 113
Landa, Malva, 96
Lansing, Robert, 65
Latin America, 82
Lawyers Committee for Human Rights, 93
Lebanon, 135, 142
Leeson, Peter T., 45n50
Leviathan (Hobbes), 6
Lewis, Anthony, 105, 108
liberal democracies, 160
Libya, 159
Lincoln, Abraham, 14, 26
Lindsay, James M., 149
Liu Xiaobo, 41
Lizza, Ryan, 145
Locke, John, 6

Lodge, Henry Cabot, 68

Magstadt, Thomas, 88
Manhattan Project, 49
Manji, Irshad, 153n14
Mao Zedong, 9, 82
Marcos, Ferdinand, 10
Marshall, George C., 44n30, 53
Marshall Plan, 11, 15, 35, 53–55
martial law, 114
Mattar, Ghayath, 34
McFaul, Michael, 29, 33
McGrory, Mary, 98n1
Mead, Walter Russell, 50, 79
Meany, George, 90
Mearsheimer, John J., 117
melting pot, 23
Meredith, James, 69
Meshaal, Khaled, 149
Metternich, Prince, 79
MHG. *See* Moscow Helsinki Group
Middle East: democracy in, 160; freedom
    lacking in, 29; human rights promotion
    in, 158–159; political and economic
    reform in, 163; presidents bedeviled by,
    147; regional stability sought in, 138;
    U.S. foreign policy in, 150; U.S. future
    relations with, 159–160; U.S. peace
    failures in, 154n53
Mikati, Najib, 142
military force: Obama using, 42; presidents
    threatening, 36; Soviet Union's use of,
    108–109
military regimes, 77
Millennium Challenge Account, 35
Milosevic, Slobodan, 9, 124
Milton, John, 6
Mitchell, George, 117, 148
Mohammed, prophet, 134
Molotov, Vyacheslav, 49
monotheistic religions, 5
moral responsibilities, 14, 91
Morgenthau, Hans J., 80
Mosaddeq, Mohammad, 107, 146
Moscow Helsinki Group (MHG): Soviet
    leaders going after, 96; Soviet Union
    monitored by, 95
Moscow Protocols, 63
Mousavi, Mir-Hossein, 151

Moynihan, Daniel Patrick, 98n1, 84
Mubarak, Hosni, 19n19, 2; downfall of, 18n7, 32; human rights abuses of, 41; Nour running for president and, 33, 140, 142
Muslims, 134, 141
Mutual Security Act of 1951, 35, 55
My Lai Massacre, 77

Nagy, Imre, 61
Nasrallah, Hassan, 149
National Economic Council, 121
National Endowment for Democracy (NED), 112
National Interest, 80
national interest, 82
national security: Clinton, B., economic investment and, 31; Clinton, B., strategy for, 122; foreign aid element in, 58; presidents' approaches to, 81; U.S. short-term goal of, 11–12
Nazism, 84
NED. *See* National Endowment for Democracy
Netanyahu, Benjamin, 148
New World Order, 16
NGOs. *See* nongovernmental organizations
Niebuhr, Reinhold, 79
Nixon, Richard, 68; Jackson-Vanik opposed by, 88–89; national interest remarks of, 82; private diplomacy approach of, 81; realism approach of, 15, 75; U.S. cynical and embittered with, 78; U.S. predominance over according to, 78
Nobel Peace Prize speech, 144
nongovernmental organizations (NGOs), 92–94
North Africa: human rights promotion in, 158–159; political and economic reform in, 163; United States' future relations with, 159–160
Nour, Ayman, 33, 140, 142
Novotny, Antonin, 62
nuclear weapons, 38–39, 149

Obama, Barack: American exceptionalism and, 25; Arab Spring approach of, 161; bilateral relations improvement sought

by, 146; Gaddafi and military power used by, 42; Human Rights Council joined by, 146; inaugural address of, 144; Iranian dialogue sought by, 148, 149; Iranian engagement policy of, 150–151; Israeli-Palestinian conflict approach of, 148; Nobel Peace Prize speech of, 144; public confrontations avoided by, 163; as self-described realist, 129; Syria and failed dialogue attempts of, 149; U.S. relations nurtured by, 17, 129; U.S. support of universal rights stated by, 163
Office of Special Protocol, 69
Operation Restore Hope, 123
Orange Revolution, 33, 140
organized labor, 90

Paine, Thomas, 23, 25
Palestine: Hamas controlling parliament of, 13, 141; Israeli conflict with, 154n53, 147–148; Israel rejectionism by, 149
Palestinian Liberation Organization, 149
Palmer, Ronald, 93
Passos, John Dos, 98n6
Patriot missile defense system, 119
Pentagon bureaucracy, 131
people power movements, 140
perestroika, 89
Perle, Richard, 89
Poland: Bush, G. H. W., providing economic aid to, 115; martial law imposed in, 114; Solidarity and unrest in, 112–113; Solidarity legalized again in, 114; Solidarity member prime minister of, 115
Pollack, Kenneth M., 162
Pol Pot, 9, 36, 77
Popper, David, 83
post–World War II period, 15
Powell, Colin, 123, 146
Prague Spring, 47, 62
preemptive actions, 137–138
presidents (U.S.): behind-the-scenes human rights promotion by, 34–35; consistency from, 161; foreign policy doctrines of, 59; human rights promoted by, 34; individuals and groups

178 *Index*

supported by, 36–37; Middle East bedeviling, 147; military force threatened by, 36; national security interests of, 81; power of words of, 33, 58; rights-abusing regimes pressured by, 35–36. *See also specific presidents*
private diplomacy, 81
prosperity, 26, 91
protests: in East Germany, 60; in Egypt, 2; U.S. government sending signals and, 63–64
public cynicism, 76
Puddington, Arch, 9

Qadhi, Entsar, 41

al Qaeda, 132, 135

race issues, 65–70
Radio Free Europe, 47, 63–64, 95, 119

al-Rantawi, Oraib, 41

Rayburn, Sam, 48
Reagan, Ronald, 16; Brezhnev Doctrine attacked by, 111; Cold War view of, 111; freedom leads to prosperity noted by, 26; Helsinki Accords a U.S sellout and, 94; Iran-Contra affair of, 127n27; shining city upon hill description of, 24; Soviet Union as evil empire statement of, 33, 91, 110; Soviet Union's human rights abuse and, 103; Soviet Union's totalitarian darkness and, 109
Reagan Doctrine, 111
realism: Bush, G. H. W., launching new period of, 116; Ford, G., and Nixon's approach of, 15, 75; idealism's dispute with, 81, 104; Kissinger adhering to dictates of, 83–84; Metternich practitioner of, 79; Obama and, 129; U.S. foreign policy approach of, 15
rejectionism, 149
repression, 96
Revolutionary War, 26
Rhodes, Benjamin, 145
Rice, Condoleezza, 138, 139
Richards, Ann, 130
rights-abusing regimes, 35–36, 41

Rockefeller Foundation, 93
Rogers, William D., 85
Roosevelt, Eleanor, 7, 48
Roosevelt, Franklin (FDR), 7, 79; death of, 48, 50; four freedoms of, 19n14, 28, 50; moral and material betterment words of, 99n13
Rose Revolution, 33, 140
Rostow, Walt, 56
Rousseau, Jean-Jacques, 6
Rumsfeld, Donald H., 131–132
Russett, Bruce, 29
Russia, 30

. *See also* Soviet Union

Rwanda, 123

Safire, William, 118
Sakharov, Andrei, 34, 89, 95
Saleh, Ali Abdullah, 159
Samir, Bassem, 41
satellite countries, 60, 61
Schlesinger, Arthur, Jr., 19n8, 126n7
Scowcroft, Brent, 118, 120, 121
second wave of democratization, 77
self-interest, U.S., 27
September 11, 2001, 37; anti-Western ideology and, 133–134; al Qaeda warnings prior to, 135; terrorist attacks of, 132; typical preoccupations before, 130–132; U.S. foreign policy changed on, 133; U.S. shocked by, 134–135; war on terror after, 152n6, 129
Serbian forces, 124
Shah of Iran, 107
Sharansky, Anatoly, 95, 96
Sharansky, Natan, 44n30, 89, 164n6; in prison, 109; Soviet Union's real nature and, 110
Shevardnadze, Eduard, 140
Shia Muslims, 134, 135
Shi'ites, 119
Smith, Gordon, 89
Snyder, John W., 48
Solidarity, 112–113; outlawing, 114; Poland legalizing, 114; Poland's prime minister member of, 115; Poland's unrest and, 112–113

Solzhenitsyn, Aleksandr, 15, 34, 75, 145; *A Day in the Life of Ivan Denisovich* by, 90; Ford, G., refusing meeting with, 92; freedom's moral responsibilities speech of, 91; *The Gulag Archipelago* by, 15, 75, 90; Harvard commencement address of, 90–91

Somalia, 36; Bush, G. H. W., sending troops to, 123; Clinton, B., continuing mission in, 123; human rights abuses in, 123

Somoza, Anastasio, 111

South Vietnam, 31

Soviet-style communism, 63

Soviet Union: Afghanistan military operation of, 108–109; communism and, 63; Czechoslovakia and troops of, 63; education reimbursement fee required by, 87–88; as evil empire, 33, 91, 110; Helsinki Accords influencing, 97; Helsinki Commission monitoring, 94; as human rights abuser, 103; Hungary and troops sent by, 61; Jackson-Vanik amendment role in demise of, 35, 89–90; Jews treatment by, 87–88; Kissinger's lack of criticism of, 100n64; MHG disbanded by, 96; MHG organized to monitor, 95; satellite countries weakening grip of, 60, 61; Sharansky and real nature of, 110; totalitarian darkness of, 109; U.S. relationship with, 38–39, 49; U.S. role in collapse of, 115. *See also* Cold War; communism

Stalin, Joseph, 9, 49, 61

Stassen, Harold, 55

State Department: Carter administration changes to strengthen the human rights focus of, 105; Congressional changes to strengthen human rights focus of, 76, 86; Democracy building programs of, 37, 41, 76, 83; Human rights reports of, 34, 83, 86; U.S. civil rights struggle with, 67, 69; Work with Amnesty International, 93

state sponsored terrorism, 137

Stiles, Ezra, 26

Stohl, Michael, 106

strategic goals, 11

Sudan, 19n19

suffragette movement, 7

suicide bombings, 135

Sultan, Wafa, 153n12

Sunni Muslims, 134, 135

Supreme Court decision, 68

Al-Suwaij, Zainab, 153n15

Syria, 148, 149, 159

Takeyh, Ray, 149

Ten Commandments, 5

terrorism: acts of, 67; global network in, 132, 137; liberal democracies not sponsoring, 160; September 11, 2001, attacks of, 132; state sponsored, 137. *See also* September 11, 2001; war on terror

Tiananmen Square, 3, 118

Tito, Josip Broz, 124

top-down transitions, 140

torture, 99n23

totalitarian regimes, 19n19; domestic and international behavior of, 44n30; international peace undermined by, 28, 52; Soviet Union and darkness of, 109

Treaty of Paris, 26

Treaty of Westphalia, 6

Truman, Harry, 13, 15; civil rights struggles of, 67; Cold War containment strategy of, 60; Congress addressed by, 50–53; free peoples supported by, 47; Greece and Turkey funds request of, 31, 35, 51, 53; human rights promotion leadership of, 52; as ill prepared, 49

Truman Doctrine, 15, 52

Tunisia, 2, 159

Turkey, 31, 35, 51, 53

UDHR. *See* Universal Declaration of Human Rights

unilateralism, 17

UNITAF. *See* United Nations international task force

United Nations international task force (UNITAF), 123

United States (U.S.): Bush, G. W. and citizens of, 143; civil rights hurting, 68;

Cold War human rights promotion of, 47–48; Cold War shaping foreign policy of, 82; Cold War victory of, 125; cultural practices respect by, 11, 161; decline predictions of, 98n6; democratic advancement benefiting, 30; East Germany covert aid provided by, 61; embassy of, 107, 135; essential role of, 14; events influence of, 10; foreign dignitaries facing racial discrimination in, 66–67, 69; freedom and democracy inconsistencies of, 19n19; freedom and democracy promoted by, 54; future strategies of, 17; global community ideals promoted by, 70; Helsinki Accords a sellout of, 94; human rights challenges facing, 158, 162; human rights foreign policy element of, 76; human rights one-sided policy of, 126n12; human rights over-promised by, 15; human rights promotion and goals of, 157; human rights promotion of, 2–4, 21, 27, 48; human rights promotion priorities of, 38; human rights promotion task of, 27, 145; Hungary protestors disappointed by, 63–64; ideals and actions mismatch of, 66–67; Iran's complicated relationship with, 106–107; Iraq invasion led by, 13; Jefferson declaring staying power of, 24; larger global role of, 51; long-term freedom and democracy planning of, 162; melting pot of, 23; Middle East and North Africa future relations with, 159–160; Middle East foreign policy of, 150; Middle East peace failures of, 154n53; Nixon's view of predominance of, 78; Nixon symbolic of cynical and embittered, 78; Obama nurturing relations of, 17, 129; Obama's statement of universal rights support by, 163; public cynicism in, 76; race issues in, 65–70; realism foreign policy approach of, 15; sense of specialness of, 22–26; September 11, 2001, changing foreign policy of, 133; September 11, 2001, shocking, 134–135; short-term national security goal of, 11–12; Soviet Union relationship with, 38–39, 49; Soviet Union's collapse and role of, 115; strategic vision for, 161–163; Vietnam War involvement of, 77. *See also* Cold War; Congress; democracy; the West

United States Agency for International Development (USAID), 58; universal brotherhood, 5

Universal Declaration of Human Rights (UDHR), 19n14, 7

universal rights, 163

U.S. *See* United States

USAID. *See* United States Agency for International Development

USS Abraham Lincoln, 139

USS Cole, 135

Vance, Cyrus, 19n14

Vandenberg, Arthur, 51, 65

Vanik, Charles A., 87, 104

Vietnam War, 75, 77

Vogelgesang, Sandy, 12

Voice of America, 63–64, 95

Voltaire, 6

Walesa, Lech, 42, 113, 116

Walker, Martin, 128n61

Wallace, George, 69

Wallace, Henry, 90

war on terror: of Bush, G. W., 17, 136–137; after September 11, 2001, 152n6, 129

War or Peace (Dulles, JF), 65

Warsaw Pact troops, 63

waves of democratization, 8–9

the West, 45n64; human rights concept of, 5, 6; ideology against, 133–134

Wilson, Woodrow, 25, 27, 65

Wilsonians, 79

Winthrop, John, 14, 23

Wojtyla, Karol Jozef, 113

Wolfowitz, Paul, 120–121

Wood, Gordon, 6, 23

words, power of, 33, 58

world changes, 116

Yang Jianli, 41

Yanukovych, Viktor, 140

Yellow Revolution, 10

Yeltsin, Boris, 30
Yemen, 159

Zatopek, Emil, 62
Zhou En Lai, 65

About the Author

Lawrence J. Haas, a former senior White House official and award-winning journalist, is senior fellow for U.S. foreign policy at the American Foreign Policy Council. He writes widely on foreign and domestic affairs, is often quoted in newspapers and magazines, and appears frequently on TV and radio. At the White House, he was communications director for Vice President Gore and, before that, for the White House Office of Management and Budget.

Haas writes columns for the McClatchy-Tribune News Service and blogs for the *Commentator*. His op-eds have appeared in the *New York Times*, *USA Today*, the *Los Angeles Times*, the *Washington Examiner*, the *Baltimore Sun*, the *Miami Herald*, the *Houston Chronicle*, the *Sacramento Bee*, and scores of other newspapers. He also has written articles for the *Journal of International Security Affairs*, *Democratiya*, *InFocus*, and other journals. The author of four books and a contributor to others, Haas has appeared on CNN, FOX, CNBC, C-SPAN, Voice of America, Al Hurra, NPR, the BBC, and many local TV and radio shows, and he has spoken before scores of groups across the country and beyond.